Transformative Practice in Higher Education

This insightful book transforms crisis reflections into longer term guidance for a responsive, engaged pedagogy within contemporary higher education (HE).

In recent years, HE institutions worldwide have seen a seismic shift that has compelled them to rapidly transition to online and blended learning models. This book captures the ingenuity and resilience of educators who not only weathered the storm but emerged from it with innovative practices that have permanently transformed the landscape of teaching and learning in universities.

Through interdisciplinary accounts and scholarly perspectives across diverse disciplines and geographies, it highlights care, creativity, and resilience in practices that build community, support learners, and foster engaged learning. Each chapter offers enduring lessons for learner-centred, responsive pedagogy, detailing innovations that practitioners permanently integrated across delivery formats.

This key title is written for HE practitioners across the globe, whether they are teaching in the context of a subject discipline or identify themselves as blended or integrated professionals. Its insights will provide inspiration, guidance, and points for reflection for all those who wish to engage with critical pedagogies and long-term transformation in contemporary HE.

Alicja Syska is a Learning Developer and lecturer in education and history at the University of Plymouth, UK. She is a researcher, podcaster, editor-in-chief of the *Journal of Learning Development in Higher Education* (*JLDHE*), and a Senior Fellow of AdvanceHE.

Carina Buckley leads the Learning Design team at Solent University, UK. She is a Principal Fellow of AdvanceHE, a member of the *JLDHE* editorial board, and co-host of the *Learning Development Project* podcast.

Gita Sedghi is a professor of chemistry education at the University of Liverpool, UK. She has received the National Teaching Fellowship, Principal Fellowship of AdvanceHE, and RSC Excellence in Higher Education Award for creating high-quality inclusive resources for a diverse community of students.

Nicola Grayson is a senior lecturer in academic development in the Centre for Learning Enhancement and Educational Development at Manchester Metropolitan University, UK. She is a Senior Fellow of AdvanceHE.

Transformative Practice in Higher Education

Innovative Approaches to Teaching and Learning

Edited by Alicja Syska, Carina Buckley, Gita Sedghi, and Nicola Grayson

LONDON AND NEW YORK

Designed Cover Image: Getty Images

First published 2025
by Routledge
4 Park Square, Milton Park, Abingdon, Oxon OX14 4RN

and by Routledge
605 Third Avenue, New York, NY 10158

Routledge is an imprint of the Taylor & Francis Group, an informa business

© 2025 selection and editorial matter, Alicja Syska, Carina Buckley, Gita Sedghi, and Nicola Grayson; individual chapters, the contributors

The right of Alicja Syska, Carina Buckley, Gita Sedghi, and Nicola Grayson to be identified as the authors of the editorial material, and of the authors for their individual chapters, has been asserted in accordance with sections 77 and 78 of the Copyright, Designs and Patents Act 1988.

All rights reserved. No part of this book may be reprinted or reproduced or utilised in any form or by any electronic, mechanical, or other means, now known or hereafter invented, including photocopying and recording, or in any information storage or retrieval system, without permission in writing from the publishers.

Trademark notice: Product or corporate names may be trademarks or registered trademarks, and are used only for identification and explanation without intent to infringe.

British Library Cataloguing-in-Publication Data
A catalogue record for this book is available from the British Library

ISBN: 978-1-032-82142-9 (hbk)
ISBN: 978-1-032-82140-5 (pbk)
ISBN: 978-1-003-50314-9 (ebk)

DOI: 10.4324/9781003503149

Typeset in Galliard
by SPi Technologies India Pvt Ltd (Straive)

Contents

List of Contributors	ix
Acknowledgements	xv
Foreword	xvi
Introduction	1

SECTION 1
Curating Time and Reflective Space to Transform Practice — 7
NICOLA GRAYSON

1 What Providing Time and Space Taught Us About Fostering Students' Learning — 13
   CHAD MCDONALD AND REBECCA PARRY

2 What the Medium of 'Focusing' Taught Me About Mattering, Wellbeing, and Belonging for Students — 20
   FARRUKH AKHTAR

3 What Pivoting Academic Skills Support Online Has Taught Us About the Importance of a Robust Learning Culture — 29
   HELEN JAMIESON AND JULIE NOLAN

4 What the CHAMELEON Framework Taught Us About Equitable and Adaptable Pedagogy — 39
   LAURA DAVIES AND JOSEPH DAVIES

5 What Designing Accessible Academic Development Provision Taught Me About Compassionate Education — 47
   SEAN AFNÁN MORRISSEY

6 What a Compassionate Approach to Transforming
  Practice Taught Me About Driving Institutional Change   55
  MARTIN COMPTON

SECTION 2
Building Connections to Transform Practice in Higher Education   65
ALICJA SYSKA

7 What an Online Tea Break Taught Us About Collaboration   71
  CARINA BUCKLEY AND REBECCA COHEN

8 What Active Engagement with My Community Taught
  Me About Driving Professional Scholarship   79
  LEE FALLIN

9 What Personalisation at Scale Taught Us About Student
  Belonging   87
  LYNN GRIBBLE AND JANIS WARDROP

10 What Shared Learning Spaces Taught Me About
   Student Belonging   94
   LUCINDA BECKER

11 What Podcasting Taught Us About Innovative
   Pedagogy as Disruption in Higher Education   102
   JULIA BOHLMANN AND MICKY ROSS

12 What Podcasting Taught Me About Writing:
   Revelations from Behind the Mic   110
   ALICJA SYSKA

SECTION 3
Crossing Boundaries: Individual and Institutional Impact in Higher Education   119
GITA SEDGHI

13 What Advocating for My Expertise Taught Me About
   Authentic Leadership   125
   NICOLA GRAYSON

14 What Floating in Pandemic Hyper Space Taught Us About Grounding Creative Academic Practice in the Here and Now — 133
SANDRA ABEGGLEN, TOM BURNS, JOHN DESIRE, JANET GORDON, FABIAN NEUHAUS, AND SANDRA SINFIELD

15 What a New LMS Adoption Taught Us About the Nature and Range of Supports Needed for Academic Stakeholders — 139
DARINA M. SLATTERY

16 What Blended Learning Taught Me About the Strengths of Collaboration for Interdisciplinarity — 147
ZOË ENSTONE

17 What Co-Design Has Taught Us About Transformative Practice and Academic Development — 155
SANDRIS ZEIVOTS, DEWA WARDAK, ANDREW CRAM, AND JOANNE NASH

18 What Democracy in Action Taught Me About Student Empowerment — 164
ANDREA TODD

SECTION 4
Homo ex Machina: Transforming Practice to Keep Sight of Our Humanity — 173
CARINA BUCKLEY

19 What Digital Confidence Practice and Research Has Taught Us About Supporting Digital Change — 177
RACHEL BANCROFT, RACHEL CHALLEN, AMANDA NEYLON, AND BETHANY WITHAM

20 What a Person-Centred, Values-Based, and Blended Approach Taught Us About Transformative Online Pedagogies in Healthcare Disciplines — 186
DEBBIE HOLLEY, ANNE QUINNEY, AND JOHN MORAN

21 What Blended Learning Taught Us About Supporting the Teaching of an Applied, Practical-Based Degree Course   193
DANIEL JAMES TINNION, THOMAS RYAN SIMPSON, AND MITCHELL JAMES FINLAY

22 What Educational Participatory Archiving Taught Us About Online Altruism and Collective Knowledge   203
NICHOLAS BOWSKILL, MELODY HARROGATE, AND DAVID HALL

23 Painting by Numbers? What My Lockdown Teaching Experiments, Followed by Encounters with a New Kind of Unit Design, Taught Me About Fine Art and Its Special Approach to Higher Education Teaching and Learning   211
PAUL O'KANE

Afterword   219

Index   *222*

Contributors

Sandra Abegglen is a researcher in the School of Architecture, Planning and Landscape at the University of Calgary, Canada. Her research focuses on digital education, hybrid pedagogy, academic literacies, creative learning and teaching methods, collaboration, inclusion, identity, and visual narratives. She is the principal investigator for playful hybrid higher education and TALON, the Teaching and Learning Online Network.

Farrukh Akhtar is an associate professor at Kingston University, UK, and a National Teaching Fellow. Renowned for her innovative and creative curricula, she delivers transformative learning experiences that encompass social care and creative life writing genres. Her current research focuses on student wellbeing, inclusivity, and community. Farrukh is a Focusing practitioner and craniosacral therapist.

Rachel Bancroft is head of the Learning and Teaching Support Unit at Nottingham Trent University, UK. She leads a multidisciplinary team of digital learning specialists who support digital learning in the School of Arts and Humanities and is a Senior Fellow of AdvanceHE. Rachel is currently writing about digital confidence alongside her other interests around ethical, inclusive, and accessible approaches for digital learning and teaching.

Lucinda Becker is professor of pedagogy in the Department of English Literature at the University of Reading, UK. She has a keen interest in student partnership and online learning. Lucinda is director of the Literature and Languages Foundation Year. She is also the author of many study skills books.

Julia Bohlmann is an academic development adviser at the University of Glasgow, UK. Her research interests are intercultural learning and teaching, decolonising the curriculum, antiracist education, and internationalisation of higher education.

Nicholas Bowskill is currently a senior lecturer at University of Derby, UK, specialising in online learning and digital education. He has more than 30 years' experience of teaching, learning, and research in different universities including new, old, and ancient institutions. During this time, he has worked on national and international research projects in digital education.

Carina Buckley is the instructional design manager at Southampton Solent University, UK, where she leads on the enhancement of learning and teaching. She has a PhD in archaeology and is a Principal Fellow of AdvanceHE. A co-host of the *Learning Development Project* podcast, Carina is also an editor of the *Journal of Learning Development in Higher Education*.

Tom Burns was an associate teaching professor in the Centre for Teaching Enhancement at London Metropolitan University, UK, with a special focus on praxes that ignite student curiosity and develop power and voice. Tom set up adventure playgrounds, community events, and festivals for his local community and fed arts-based practice into his learning, teaching, and assessment practices. He sadly passed away before the book was published, leaving an inspiring legacy behind.

Rebecca Cohen is a learning designer with extensive experience in further education, higher education, and industry. She is interested in the interplay between technology and learning and innovative digital learning strategies. She has recently completed a PhD in film and holds a PGCE along with Fellowship of AdvanceHE (FHEA).

Rachel Challen is an associate professor in educational development; interim head of learning, teaching, and student experience for the School of Arts and Humanities at Nottingham Trent University, UK; and a principal fellow of AdvanceHE. Rachel's work is focused on all aspects of enhancing the student experience through the thoughtful development of colleagues and curriculum, including digital pedagogies.

Martin Compton (PFHEA, SCMALT) is the AI and innovation in education lead working out of the King's Academy at King's College London, UK. His research focuses on AI literacy, teaching modalities, lecturer observation, and transnational education.

Andrew Cram is a lecturer in educational development and evaluation with the Business Co-Design unit at the University of Sydney Business School, Australia. He is a digital education generalist with over 20 years of experience in learning design, academic development, leadership, and learning technologies management.

Joseph Davies is senior lecturer and assistant director for graduate EAP at Duke Kunshan University, China. He holds an MA in TESOL with applied linguistics, a DELTA, and Senior Fellowship of AdvanceHE (SFHEA). His current research focuses on feedback literacy and EAP pedagogy within Sino–foreign higher education contexts.

Laura Davies is senior lecturer and assistant director of EAP at Duke Kunshan University, China. She holds an MA in TESOL with applied linguistics, a DELTA specializing in HE ELT management, and Senior Fellowship of AdvanceHE (SFHEA). Her current research focuses on equitable HE course and assessment design.

John Desire is senior lecturer in the Centre for Teaching Enhancement at London Metropolitan University, UK, with a special focus on teaching, learning, and assessment practices – both face-to-face and online – that ignite student curiosity and harness their creativity.

Zoë Enstone is an associate professor and associate head of the School of Humanities: English Literature at York St John University, UK. She was previously subject director for the Liberal Arts Programme and has ongoing research interests in the transition to university, academic skills development, and interdisciplinary pedagogies.

Lee Fallin is a lecturer in education at the University of Hull, UK. Following a decade of work in an academic advising role, he holds Certified Leading Practitioner in Learning Development status. Lee is an editor of the *Journal for Learning Development in Higher Education* and a member of the LearnHigher Working Group.

Mitchell James Finlay is senior lecturer in sport and exercise science (biomechanics and strength and conditioning) at UA92, UK. Alongside his PhD, 'The efficacy of acute preconditioning strategies on sport performance' and applied practice, Mitch formed PRISES with co-contributors. In 2023, the group received an award for outstanding collaboration.

Janet Gordon is a senior lecturer in technology enhanced learning in the Centre for Teaching Enhancement at London Metropolitan University, UK. Janet is interested in the facilitation of learning and of communities of learners, appreciative inquiry, service design, and governance.

Nicola Grayson is a senior lecturer in academic development in the University Teaching Academy at Manchester Metropolitan University, UK. She is a Senior Fellow of AdvanceHE. Nicola supports her peers to publish their educational research and works to enhance opportunities for career progression for HE educators in the widest sense.

Lynn Gribble is an associate professor internationally and nationally and a UNSW awarded education focused academic. Using her keen interest in transformative learning through engagement, belonging, and personalization of each student's learning experience, and this has evolved further to focus on ethical use of AI in the workplace.

David Hall is a senior lecturer in education with the University of Derby, UK. With a focus on improving the way we learn and teach, he is enthusiastic about exploring the transformative potential of technology in education.

Melody Harrogate is programme leader for the MA Education and Senior Lecturer in Education at University of Derby, UK. With 30 years of leading teaching and learning in further and higher education, Melody continues to explore technology and its potential role in ethically enhancing teaching and learning.

Debbie Holley is professor of learning innovation at Bournemouth University, UK. A National Teaching Fellow and a passionate educator, she blends learning to motivate and engage a diverse student body. Her research interests in digital, augmented, and immersive worlds influence national policy through her published work, keynote addresses, and policy articles.

Helen Jamieson is the head of student engagement at Edge Hill University, UK. She is the strategic lead for the delivery of academic skills support at the university and manages the Student Engagement team. Helen has a keen interest in learning cultures, evaluation, and performance measurement.

Chad McDonald is a senior academic and study skills tutor at Manchester Metropolitan University, UK. Much of his work has focused on students who are at transition points in higher education, especially in arts and humanities disciplines. Chad is an editor of the *Journal of Learning Development in Higher Education*.

John Moran is the healthcare skills and technology team leader in the Faculty of Health and Social Sciences at Bournemouth University, UK. He has extensive experience in a wide range of digital health simulations and works across the disciplines to support virtual reality innovation in the curricula.

Sean Afnán Morrissey is the academic development lead for learning and teaching at the University of Strathclyde, UK. His research interests include staff peer-support networks, inclusive approaches to curriculum development, leadership in learning and teaching, and compassionate pedagogies. He is a programme director and leads collaboratives projects and staff development projects in China and the Middle East.

Joanne Nash is an educational developer and lecturer at the University of Sydney Business School, Australia, who specialises in co-designing subjects to improve both the student and teacher experience. Her research focuses on learning spaces, team teaching, and strategic curriculum transformation.

Fabian Neuhaus, PhD, is an associate professor at the University of Calgary, Canada, School of Architecture, Planning and Landscape. His research in the urban environment focuses on the topics of habitus, type, and ornament. He has worked in Switzerland, Germany, Canada, and the UK. He is passionate about the scholarship of learning, teaching, and design pedagogy.

Amanda Neylon is the director of digital technologies at Nottingham Trent University, UK, where she leads on the strategic direction and operational running of the university's technology to drive its digital sophistication.

Julie Nolan (MA, PGCTHE, FHEA, BA) is student engagement and communications manager at Edge Hill University, UK. She operationally manages the UniSkills team and strategically leads student communications across library and learning services, student services, and careers. Julie oversees student engagement activities, events, campaigns, and communications, including welcome, induction, and transitional support.

Rebecca Parry is an associate lecturer in the Faculty of Arts and Social Sciences at the Open University, UK. Prior to teaching in higher education, Rebecca taught English language in further education. She has been involved in widening participation in education for over 20 years.

Anne Quinney has written extensively about the scholarship of teaching and learning. Recently retired, she was principal lecturer in the Centre for Excellence in Learning at Bournemouth University. Anne's recent successes included introducing student-centred university-wide assessment and feedback policies and the design and delivery of the fully online PGCert.

Micky Ross is a lecturer at English for academic study within the School of Modern Languages and Cultures at the University of Glasgow, UK. His research interests include autoethnographic and reflective academic writing, the queering of academic literacies, and teaching English as an international language.

Sandra Sinfield is an associate teaching professor in the Centre for Teaching Enhancement at London Metropolitan University, UK. Sandra is interested in creativity as liberatory and holistic practice in higher education; she has developed theatre and film in unusual places and inhabited SecondLife as a learning space.

Darina M. Slattery is associate professor at the University of Limerick (UL), Ireland, where she specializes in e-learning and instructional design. Since early 2021, Darina has served in leadership roles for the UL learning management system (LMS) implementation project. From 2021 to 2022, she served as president of the IEEE Professional Communication Society.

Thomas Ryan Simpson is a ecturer in motor learning and skill acquisition at Edge Hill University. Alongside his PhD, 'How motor learning and motor skill acquisition in children can be optimised through attentional and motivational factors', Tom achieved fellowship with the Higher Education Academy, beginning pedagogical research with co-contributors.

Alicja Syska, PhD, SFHEA, is a learning developer and lecturer in education and history at the University of Plymouth, UK. She is a researcher, podcaster, and editor-in-chief of the *Journal of Learning Development in Higher Education*, with much of her work focusing on facilitating writing and publication.

Andrea Todd is an associate professor of active citizenship at the University of Chester, UK. She is passionate about student agency and empowerment.

Daniel James Tinnion is a tutor in physiology at Manchester Metropolitan University, UK. Alongside his PhD, 'Sodium citrate: refining ingestion protocols to better understand its ergogenic potential', Dan attained the status of Fellow of AdvanceHE (FHEA), forming the Pedagogical Research in Sport and Exercise Sciences (PRISES) group alongside co-contributors.

Dewa Wardak is a lecturer at the University of Sydney Business School, Australia. She is a learning scientist who co-designs engaging and authentic learning experiences for students in higher education. Her research spans broad areas including networked learning, pattern languages, object-based learning, and postdigital approaches to co-designing educational futures.

Janis Wardrop is associate professor at University of New South Wales, Australia, currently the director of education at the Centre for Social Impact. She is an academic leader and educational champion of innovation in curriculum and course design, and a recipient of the Vice Chancellor's Award for Teaching Excellence.

Bethany Witham is a learning technologist with the Learning and Teaching Support Unit at Nottingham Trent University, UK, supporting staff in the School of Arts and Humanities with digital learning and teaching. She is particularly interested in accessibility and support for neurodivergence in digital learning and teaching, and how generative AI is impacting higher education.

Sandris Zeivots is a senior lecturer at the University of Sydney Business School, Australia, who specialises in transformative educational development that is designed to be purposeful, engaging and meaningful. Sandris leverages his expertise to explore the role of co-design practice, learning spaces, and emotional engagement in higher education.

Acknowledgements

This volume originated in a special edition of the *Journal of Learning Development in Higher Education*, 'Compendium of Innovative Practice: Learning Development in a Time of Disruption', published in Autumn 2021. We are grateful to the nearly 400 contributors to this collection, and the superb editors who shaped it, for sharing their creative ideas. They inspired us to revisit some of the pandemic-era innovations with the authors who felt they have transformed their higher education practice. It has been a pleasure to work with them and open up their ideas to new audiences. To our authors: Thank you for the enthusiasm and commitment you brought to this project.

We are also grateful to everyone who supported us in this endeavour, including our fantastic editors at Routledge – Sarah Hyde, Lauren Redhead, and Maddie Gray; our institutions and colleagues – University of Plymouth, Solent University, University of Liverpool, University of Salford, and Manchester Metropolitan University; and our great champion, Dr Virna Rossi, who has offered unfailing encouragement and energy.

Finally, deep gratitude to our kind and big-hearted partners, families, and friends who have cheered us along the way.

Foreword

'In a gentle way, you can shake the world'.
— *Mahatma Gandhi (Indian leader and thinker)*

It is a privilege to write the foreword for *Transformative Practice in Higher Education: Innovative Approaches to Teaching and Learning*, a timely and groundbreaking work edited by four colleagues with considerable expertise in distinct pedagogical areas.

As a fellow educator who has navigated the turbulent waters of higher education (HE) during the COVID-19 pandemic, I have witnessed firsthand the profound shifts and adaptations that institutions and individuals have had to make during that unprecedented time. Due to its global nature and its duration (around two years in most countries), the sudden pandemic-induced digital shift became a catalyst for widespread innovation and creativity amongst educators. In the face of significant challenges, instructors developed new strategies and methodologies to ensure that effective learning continued, highlighting their resilience and dedication to their students' success. The original Compendium of Transformative Practice (*Journal of Learning Development in Higher Education*, 2021) on which this work is based is a very valuable collection of such effective, if improvised, practices, and I had the privilege to contribute a short narrative to it. Through this book, I am very pleased to see its value extended to our current post-pandemic practices.

Transformative Practice in Higher Education beautifully and skilfully captures the learning from this remarkable period of transition and transformation through four curated sections that offer a comprehensive exploration of how these pedagogical innovations have left a lasting impact on contemporary teaching practices. The book blends practical experiences with scholarly insights, making it a valuable resource for educators seeking to navigate and thrive in the ever-evolving contemporary landscape of HE.

The four sections of the book collectively support more inclusive learning design and practices by addressing the multifaceted challenges *and opportunities* that emerged during the pandemic, focusing on the silver lining, namely the professional learning that we can *currently* benefit from. As I reviewed the content of the sections with my inclusivity goggles on, I noticed that the various contributed chapters highlight inclusive learning design and practices in various ways. I saw evidence of many of the nine subsets of values that I created as an acronym of the word 'Inclusive': Intentionally equitable, Nurturing, Co-created, Liberated, User-friendly, Socially responsible, Integrative, Values-based, and Ecological (Rossi, 2023).

Many of the chapters are about being intentionally equitable and nurturing students' holistic growth through a focus less on content and more on the human (affective) aspect of teaching and learning. During the pandemic, educators became allies of their students, more compassionate and empathetic to their struggles during that time of crisis, showing 'intentionally equitable hospitality' (Rossi, 2023) in small and big ways from virtual tea breaks to substantial curriculum redesign. It strikes me to read how this has provoked a needed and welcome shift towards trauma-informed teaching approaches beyond the pandemic.

Many authors also discuss the importance of a values-based approach to teaching, learning, and assessment, for example through podcasting seen as a liberatory practice. Personalised and playful learning are highlighted as being more responsive to students' needs and a way for educators to show that students' inherent diversity is an added value rather than an issue to fix. Equally, co-creation (for instance co-design with students) and the benefits of universal design for learning (UDL) approaches come to the fore together with an emphasis on cross-pollination practices. Interdisciplinarity, a form of cross-pollination, has close ties with inclusivity as they both aim to honour multiple perspectives and interweave diverse knowledges (Rossi, 2023).

Importantly, this book is not just a reflection on the exceptional work done during the pandemic; it is a forward-looking guide that leverages the legacy of that transformative period to support and enhance current and future educational practices. The innovations and insights documented here serve as a foundation for ongoing improvements in teaching and learning, ensuring that the creative responses to a crisis continue to inform and enrich higher education well into the future. It strikes me that the chapters' titles highlight not only how many pandemic interventions were beneficial for students but also how they became a catalyst for rich personal learning for *educators* stretching past the pandemic crisis into contemporary practices.

The editors of this collection, Dr Alicja Syska, Dr Carina Buckley, Prof. Gita Sedghi, and Dr Nicola Grayson, who I know through various shared professional activities, bring a wealth of experience and expertise to this work. Their dedication to advancing HE is evident in their extensive contributions to the field, both as scholars and practitioners. Their collaborative effort in compiling this book reflects their commitment to fostering innovation, equity, and resilience in teaching and learning.

Transformative Practice in Higher Education is a must-read for HE practitioners across the UK and global HE institutions. Whether you are teaching in a specific discipline or working in the interdisciplinary 'third space', this book offers inspiration, guidance, and points for reflection. May this book inspire and empower you to continue innovating and transforming your teaching practices for the benefit of your students and the wider educational community.

Virna Rossi
Associate Professor and PGCert Course Leader

References

Journal of Learning Development in Higher Education. (2021). 'Special edition, compendium of innovative practice: Learning Development in a time of disruption', *Journal of Learning Development in Higher Education*, 22. Available at https://journal.aldinhe.ac.uk/index.php/jldhe/issue/view/36

Rossi, V. (2023). *Inclusive learning design in higher education: a practical guide to creating equitable learning experiences*. London: Routledge.

Introduction

It was the worst of times: times of incredulity, despair, and darkness. Yet we emerged from that darkness into a season of light, the spring of hope, a new epoch of belief. While ours may not be 'the best of times' yet, the years during and following the COVID-19 pandemic sparked opportunities for new ways of thinking, doing, and being in higher education (HE).

Much of this sense of hope was inspired by the sheer ingenuity and creativity with which we collectively met the urgent challenge at universities across the globe. HE educators quickly adapted to emergency online teaching and learning, working tirelessly and often in difficult conditions to pioneer strategies that supported student learning, salvaged feelings of belonging, and built spaces that allowed universities to remain at the forefront of innovation and collective resilience. When the initial crisis passed and the dark clouds cleared, the collective sigh of relief was followed by a deep conviction that returning to 'normality' was not a viable option. Indeed, what we did then has transformed how we think now.

The idea of transformation in HE covers a wide range of facets, including teaching practices, learning strategies, institutional cultures, and the physical and digital environments, to the extent that there is no consensus on what counts as transformation and what transformative practice is. Here, we recognise transformative practice in HE as an irreversible response to an extraordinary event that leads to a cultural change, one that opens new possibilities for mutual learning, collaboration, and inclusivity while reducing barriers to access and engagement. Transformative practices call into question the traditional or dominant ways of teaching and learning, in the service of supporting meaningful adaptations to shifting contexts and learner needs (in the spirit of Freire [1970] and hooks [2014]). They can be transferred and adapted to different settings while retaining the value of the learning. In each case, the classroom, the social structures and activities, and the entire HE landscape are configured and reconfigured as person-centred and inclusive, based on relationships that are more equitable and liberatory rather than hierarchical and power-based.

Transformation is not a process that can happen overnight; nor can it occur without a stimulus. For HE, which has heard its own death knell sounded multiple times (e.g., Readings, 1996; Hall, 2020), the 2020 pandemic was a particularly traumatic and all-encompassing crisis that threw into sharp relief the urgent need for change. What began as an emergency response to this crisis turned into a full-blown transformation in how we teach, how we learn, how we relate to each other, and what we value, and these transformations have permanently changed what we believe to be the possibilities for inhabiting higher education today. The pandemic served as a catalyst for a paradigm shift regarding how we conceptualise the university as a place, as a space, and as a set of relations. Like a prism bending light into different shapes and colours, the transformations we experienced have revealed the different qualities, patterns, and tensions that underpin all areas of our activity, forcing us to deeply reconsider the ways forward. More than that, however, they revealed our deepest values, including the need to connect with those around us, be it students or colleagues; the desire to create more space for creative approaches to teaching and learning; the longing to cross boundaries and practise inclusively; and the wish to use technology in ways that not only inform and facilitate learning but also allow for more ways of expressing ourselves and help to bring us together. What largely began as a focus on emergency remote teaching (ERT) due to the restrictions imposed by the pandemic has turned into an emphasis on digitally enhanced relational pedagogies and learning designs that allow both students and educators to thrive as creative agents of their own learning and teaching.

This book is an attempt to capture this paradigm shift, not through theoretical orientations but empirical applications that explore teaching that makes a tangible difference. It documents, reflects on, and disseminates the pedagogical insights and innovations that began as temporary fixes in response to the global online pivot of 2020, only to evolve into meaningful and sustainable solutions that have transformed our world of work. These solutions are now even more relevant and vital to encourage productive orientation to the future, given the persistence of issues such as student isolation, disengagement, and the still elusive sense of belonging, in addition to the new challenges facing global HE institutions (HEIs), including generative AI, worsening conditions at universities, and political and environmental uncertainty across the globe.

The roots of the book go back to the spectacularly successful special issue of the *Journal of Learning Development in Higher Education*, the Compendium of Innovative Practice, published in October 2021. As editors of the journal, we had invited practitioners in global HE to record and share their experience of responding to the emergency move to online teaching in the form of three-part articles that explored a specific challenge the authors faced, the solutions they devised, and the recommendations they could make for others in a related context. Written by nearly 400 international authors, the 102 short pieces published in this special edition explored different aspects of teaching and learning including balancing technology with pedagogy, rethinking assessment design, fostering student engagement and belonging, as well as implementing compassionate pedagogy and other innovative approaches that promote care and wellbeing in HE. Two years later, we followed up with the authors to see which of these innovative practices endured and transformed the ways the authors work and relate to others in their post-pandemic practice. While many of the interventions shared in the original Compendium proved appropriate mainly in the context of the emergency shift to online teaching and learning, a quarter of them transpired as genuinely transformative to the practitioners and can be seen as transferable across multiple contexts. These are the stories we share in this book collection.

In reading this book, we invite our readers to revisit the past as they would settle down with a photo album, flipping through pages that bring to mind memories of past events, people, and places and that inevitably draw comparisons with how those people and places have now changed. Returning to the dark corners of the past is not always easy or desired; although photo albums can generate a comforting nostalgia we are happy to sit with, often they can also evoke less comfortable memories and feelings we would rather forget. There is value, however, in revisiting the uncertain times of the pandemic, which forced us to reconsider everything we knew about teaching, learning, and operating within the landscape of HE, so we can see more clearly how it has changed or perhaps even transformed us as educators. Each chapter in this collection is written by an educator who went through the same challenge. Their actions, solutions, attitudes, and trajectories are documented in the pages of this book, bringing together perspectives from across the UK and global HEIs, including those practitioners who teach in the context of a subject discipline or identify themselves as blended or integrated professionals working in the so-called Third Space (Whitchurch, 2012). The diversity of contexts and approaches shared by them reflects the deep need for change and the potential of transformation in HE practice.

Given the creative nature of the solutions the authors in this volume devised to respond to the needs of their students, teams, and work spaces, we have organised the book around four key themes that mark distinctive zones of transformation.

We open the book with a collection of chapters investigating the ways their authors reconsidered how we create, use, and nurture time and space in higher education. Thus, the first section explores the value of returning to what is fundamentally necessary to begin to make sense of our current context. Curating time and space to scaffold students' learning, to connect with oneself and with each other, to develop robust services and responsive practices, to manage institutional change in an equitable and adaptable way, and to treat ourselves and each other with compassion in respect to continuous professional development become transposed into rebellious acts in the face of mounting pressures to respond in a quantifiable way. The opening chapters return us to the fundamental requirements of the people behind the practice, tracing the reflective origins of our transformative thoughts and actions to a momentary stillness that holds ground in the face of a relentless tide.

The section that follows brings together examples of innovative educational practices that focus on creating new ways to build connections. From reimagining team dynamics to exploring new technologies for student engagement, the second set of chapters invites us to reconsider not just how we teach and learn but how we forge the human connections that lie at the heart of transformative education. In an era where digital interfaces often replace face-to-face interactions, the art of building meaningful connections in HE has never been more crucial or more challenging. The insights shared in these stories promise to spark reflection and inspire new approaches to creating a more connected, authentic, and inclusive educational experience.

In the third section, the conversations move on to the impact of crossing boundaries within the dynamic landscape of HE. The discussions showcase transformative practices that drive positive change and foster creativity, collaboration, and adaptability in individuals and institutions. This section provides inspiring examples of creating opportunities to work and collaborate across academic and professional domains to open up new ways of thinking about and experiencing HE for both staff and students. These include a leadership journey within the Third Space without formal authority, creation of an international interdisciplinary online network, a shift in organisational digital culture, co-designing curricula, and empowering students through democracy in action.

Finally, the last section concentrates on human relationality in the digital environment. With the proliferation of new technologies and the increasing use of generative AI, it can be easy to focus on the tools and their affordances at the expense of the people who use them. This section prioritises the human in the machine and the possibilities for liberatory thinking that technology can offer, beginning with confidence in the use of these tools. This sense of digital confidence opens up access to connecting in online spaces and engaging in sensemaking and knowledge-building activities with others. Technology can structure, sustain, and situate knowledge, but it can also disrupt. We close the section with a call to trouble technology, to be the source of the disruption rather than the reaction to it. As technology evolves, it is our responsibility and our privilege to evolve with it and to keep sight of each other within the machine.

Altogether, what the chapters across these four sections reveal is that while the success of the emergency online pivot in 2020 often depended, as these case studies illustrate, on the creativity, digital competency, and learning design skills of individual practitioners, with good models of practice everyone in HE is poised to benefit from an increased quality of learning and teaching. It has been largely confirmed in post-pandemic scholarship that 'online and face-to-face teaching share the same values and require the same quality of teacher presence and support' (Rapanta *et al.*, 2021) and that teaching not only has to be carefully designed but also requires constant pedagogic innovation from dedicated educators (Horváth *et al.*, 2022). While we develop a more inclusive and responsive HE, however, we must also be mindful of the new crises faced by post-pandemic HE, related to the growing digitalisation of education (including the ubiquity of generative AI), rising inequalities, challenges to internationalisation, concerns about the climate crisis, and the growing geopolitical tensions that impact global collaborations in HE (de Wit and Altbach, 2023). The post-pandemic changes and trends within HE will continue to benefit from the creativity, innovation, and dedication of its members.

We hope that the lessons, innovations, and transformations shared in this collection will support educators in meeting these challenges with confidence. The album of memories and reflections the reader is about to open reveals practical models to emulate alongside inspiring stories that connect our teaching and learning community. It aims to meet pressing needs to improve blended instruction, support learners, foster resilience and community, and contribute fresh ideas to pedagogical knowledge. It is a testament to the proposition that together we can transform the post-pandemic university.

References

de Wit, H. and Altbach, P. G. (2023). International higher education for the future: major crises and post-pandemic challenges. *Change: The Magazine of Higher Learning*, 55(1), pp. 17–23. https://doi.org/10.1080/00091383.2023.2151799

Freire, P. (1970). *Pedagogy of the oppressed*. Seabury.

Hall, R. (2020). The hopeless university: intellectual work at the end of the end of history. *Postdigital Science and Education*, 2(3), pp. 830–848.

hooks, b. (2014). *Teaching to transgress: Education as the practice of freedom*. Routledge.

Horváth, D., Ásványi, K., Cosovan, A., Csordás, T., Faludi, J., Galla, D., Komár, Z., Markos-Kujbus, É. and Simay, A. E. (2022). Online only: future outlooks of post-pandemic education based on student experiences of the virtual university. *Society and Economy*, 44(1), pp. 2–21. https://doi.org/10.1556/204.2021.00026

Rapanta, C., Botturi, L., Goodyear, P., Guàrdia, L. and Koole, M. (2021). Balancing technology, pedagogy and the new normal: post-pandemic challenges for higher education. *Postdigital Science and Education*, 3(3), pp. 715–742. https://doi.org/10.1007/s42438-021-00249-1

Readings, B. (1996). *The university in ruins*. Harvard University Press.

Whitchurch, C. (2012). *Reconstructing identities in higher education: the rise of 'third space' professionals*. Abingdon: Routledge.

Section 1

Curating Time and Reflective Space to Transform Practice

Nicola Grayson

The curation of time and reflective space to process changes, communicate, compare, and problem solve cannot be calculated and subjected to metrics in the same way other features of higher education (HE) learning and teaching often are in the neoliberal massification and economic quantification of our practices (Ashwin, 2020). However, this does not mean this curation is without value or necessity. Just as Copernicus discovered that, contrary to contemporary understanding, it is not the sun that revolves around the earth but the earth that revolves around the sun in community with other planets in the solar system, so Immanual Kant reasoned that time and space do not exist within the world itself; they are *a priori* intuitions (independent of experience) that we bring to the world in order to perceive it (Kant, 2003). Kant held that space and time provide us with conditions for the possibility of knowledge and that they exist within us. Without them we cannot make sense of our perceptions, we cannot make knowledge judgements based on these perceptions, and we cannot generate rational ideas that bring totality to our experiences and our judgements. If we cannot generate ideas, we cannot move forward armed with knowledge of our current environment, nor can we consider potential appropriate problem-solving responses to it. In this vein, in order to transform practice in response to the challenges of the pandemic and the changing face of HE learning and teaching, in a manner akin to Derrida's conception of *the revenant* (Derrida, 1994), we must *begin by coming back* to these fundamental *a priori* intuitions that enable the possibility of knowledge and perception.

Ineffably haunted by the conditions required to formulate an informed response, and in a personal and political moment of reflective connection with what was lost, individually and in community we must cut through the noise of the pandemic and its challenges. Returning again to our familiar ability to solve problems, to work together, to support and inform, to research, and to connect, we are prompted kindly, but profoundly, to remember we are human, and an indefinable feature of human perception that forms the basis for the possibility of any and all knowledge is the *a priori* intuitions of space and time. We bring these to the world in order to perceive it, and in doing so, we can

DOI: 10.4324/9781003503149-2

begin the process of familiarising the unfamiliar and begin to feel at home once more in the unhomely, or *unheimlich* (Freud, 1971).

As educators, curating time and space, which cannot be quantified, measured, and reported on to influence metrics in a competitive way, becomes a political act of rebellion that is fundamentally tied to the requirements and basis of all human knowledge. We need time to reflect on our concerns and reattune our minds in order to process and make sense of our experiences and context – time to commune with one another and grieve for the loss of our familiar ways of living, working, learning, and connecting, and time to transpose our enduring needs in line with our new possibilities so that we may once again begin to feel at home and belong. We must curate space for learning and facilitate the conditions under which knowledge may be gained and acted upon by educators and learners alike – space to ask for help, space to fail, try again, and fail better, and space to share what is and isn't working and to ask each other why. Regardless of our individual experiences, or maybe in light of the collective weight and value of these, we need space and time to make valid knowledge judgements about the things we perceive. It is armed with insight into their role and necessity that we seek to create support, manage change, and curate services and development opportunities that reinforce the value and inclusion of these fundamental features.

The chapters in this section draw out the importance of granting and utilising critically reflective space: for students and their learning, to surface grief and attend to emotional wellbeing, to innovate in the practice of service delivery, and to manage large-scale institutional change. As the world kept turning, HE educators faced unprecedented precarity in terms of their jobs, future, and continued pressures with respect to their own professional development, so those providing academic development needed to proceed with compassion and insight in a way that showed empathy for their peers (and themselves) to support them behind, beyond, and within their HE roles.

In the opening chapter, Chad Macdonald and Rebecca Parry outline the importance of embedding time and space in the structure of support designed for students transitioning into higher education in relation to writing, one-off sessions, and student-led online learning. They present space and time as 'socially constructed concepts' (Foucault, 1986) and outline the powerful role these can play in foregrounding learning. In curating space for students to explore and shape their identities as writers, providing opportunities to nurture organic discussions, and centring students' voices as key catalysts to drive transformative meaning making, they demonstrate how these techniques enable students to reimagine themselves as 'insiders' who are not only 'at home' in HE but play an active role in shaping their experiences.

Chapter 2 builds on the exploration of the value of granting time and space for the development of reciprocal peer support by examining its key role in shaping and strengthening students' autonomy. Farrukh Akhtar contemplates how the technique of 'focusing' might be used in a pedagogical setting as students turn to HE institutions to meet their emotional needs. Akhtar explains how focusing gives students time to connect with one another and space to surface specific emotions, allowing them to acknowledge and express their emotional wellbeing in a way that positively promotes feelings of belonging and mattering in the social domain. In connecting to the wisdom held in the body, Akhtar argues, students develop autonomy and ownership; they cultivate listening skills and develop rapport, opening up experiential learning opportunities with positive effects that extend far beyond the bounds of the academy.

Akhtar's exploration of the role of autonomy in driving social confidence connects to the theme of cultivating space to drive ideas and innovation beyond traditional approaches in Chapter 3. Helen Jamieson and Julie Nolan outline how, when faced with a lack of physical university space, curating blended spaces for community, innovation, and ideation enabled the cultivation of a sense of belonging and the development of community and a robust learning culture. Viewed through Brookfield's critical lenses, they explore how Learning Development at Edge Hill University became pedagogically transformed in response to the 'online pivot' (Brookfield, 2017). Jamieson and Nolan acknowledge the importance of time in respect to communications and ongoing dialogue, and the value of informal 'safe' spaces in respect to facilitating connection, strengthening structure workstreams, and developing confidence. In evaluating the impact of the transformation, Jamieson and Nolan are clear that space, time, and permission to innovate presented a valuable opportunity to be 'untethered by the boundaries of normality', which consequently played a key role in the realisation and cultivation of professional identity for staff.

The two key features Jamieson and Nolan emphasise as crucial for establishing conditions that positively enhance the student experience – creating space for authentic critical reflection and actively listening – are incorporated by Laura Davies and Joseph Davies into their compassionate and empathetic framework for managing institutional change. In Chapter 4, Davies and Davies reflect on how the humanistic features of the CHAMELEON framework facilitate an equitable and adaptable approach to managing and navigating institutional change with compassion and empathy. The framework appeals to both senior leaders and those subject to leadership and policy decisions. It utilises principles such as openness, negotiation, and attention to localising approaches that are effectively tailored to the appropriate context. The framework opens up space for cross team communication, enables facilitation of a timely response to challenges such as generative AI for English for academic purposes (EAP) students and staff, and promotes cross team collaborative development by utilising and harnessing synergy.

In Chapter 5, Sean Morrisey acknowledges the impact of current pressures in HE on staff wellbeing and also, thereby, on their ability to engage with continuous professional development. Addressing a decline in engagement due to the many barriers staff face in relation to accessing this type of support, Morrisey advocates an approach that has transformed academic development at the University of Strathclyde. Driven by equitable access and concerns for wellbeing, his approach is characterised by compassionate pedagogy to the benefit of both educators and their learners. Working with recognition of the barriers instead of denying or negating them, Morrisey creatively acknowledges the challenges of the current HE context through approaches that utilise informal learning spaces alongside formal development opportunities and offer micro-continuous professional development (CPD) in the face of time pressures to carve out personal and professional development in a way that is responsive and authentic.

Martin Compton also takes a responsive and compassionate approach to academic development, showing the transferability of this approach and how it might be employed at scale. In Chapter 6, he outlines how the privileged centrality of academic development necessitates traversing a political tension as support, and those delivering it, risks being viewed as interventionist. He advocates an approach that gives primacy to values and the principles of empathy, inclusion, and learner centredness. In doing so, Compton holds, we must grant time and space for staff to surface deeper issues in alignment with their personal and professional development and encourage open engagement that allows people to process and work through their feelings. Compton's use of HyFlex modelling and his curation of space for staff to experiment with approaches to generative AI thereby challenge the dominant narrative, which pressures us to value only that which can be measured and quantified as impactful. In ascribing value to the time we must take to surface the affective and emotional elements of our roles as educators, compassionate pedagogy is transposed into an act of rebellion that refocuses our attention on the people behind the pedagogy, enabling a more authentic dialogic relationship between educators and learners, and among educators and their peers.

Space and time form the conditions for the possibility of knowledge, and along these lines, the chapters in this section show space and time as conditions of the possibility of transforming practice in our response to the pandemic. So we begin by coming back to ourselves and the things we need in order to practise as ourselves and ascertain what will work for us within this context, and what will need to be adapted, adjusted, or lost. We begin the process of solving problems and seeking informed solutions by familiarising the unfamiliar by subjecting it to our processes, our connections, and our contemplative examination. We try to become at home in the unhomely, but to do this, we need to curate time and reflective space, whether this is recognised in interventionist policies designed to guide and steer us or not.

References

Ashwin, P. (2020) *Transforming university education: a manifesto*. London: Bloomsbury Publishing.

Brookfield, S. (2017) *Becoming a critically reflective teacher* (2nd ed.). San Francisco: Jossey-Bass.

Derrida, J. (1994) *Specters of Marx: the state of the debt, the work of mourning, and the New International*. New York: Routledge.

Foucault, M. (1986) 'Of other spaces', *Diacritics*, 16(1), pp. 22–27. https://doi.org/10.2307/464648

Freud, S. (1971) *The standard edition of the complete psychological works of Sigmund Freud*. United Kingdom: Hogarth Press.

Kant, I. (2003) *Critique of pure reason*, ed. H. Caygill. Basingstoke, Hampshire: Palgrave Macmillan.

Chapter 1

What Providing Time and Space Taught Us About Fostering Students' Learning

Chad McDonald and Rebecca Parry

Higher education (HE) appears to be in a constant state of flux with new solutions continually suggested to transform practice. Yet, in isolation, these ideas do not necessarily support students' learning; indeed, the opposite can happen given the competing priorities that squeeze the time and space available in contemporary HE. This chapter foregrounds why we must protect the time and space available to foster students' learning. In doing so, we recognise that time and space are socially constructed concepts, drawing on Foucault's (1986, p. 23) emphasis that 'we live inside a set of relations'. We focus on the importance of providing time and space for students who are transitioning into university-level study as starting university can lead to a specific form of culture shock (Askham, 2008). As Bartholomae (1986) has argued, every time students sit down to write, they must invent the university anew. They must learn to speak the language of their discipline – or languages, for there is never one monolithic discourse. In doing so successfully, students must imagine themselves as 'insiders' who have the authority to speak their disciplines. This requirement presents a challenge for new students as they attempt to locate themselves in spaces that are not immediately nor naturally theirs – navigating such spaces risks alienating or, at the very least, stifling their voices. As educators, we must work to create learning environments that offer students the time and space to speak. Sustaining meaningful relationships underpins this approach.

Making Time and Space to Foster Learning

The onset of the COVID-19 pandemic required everyone in HE to adapt overnight to the creation of emergency online classrooms. Reflex decisions had to be made to keep universities open. As 2020 and 2021 unfolded, there was a gradual—if bumpy—move towards a 'new normal' and increased opportunities to make the time and space to reflect on the lessons we had learnt. In McDonald and Parry (2021, p. 4), we argued that the key learning point from the pandemic should be the 'reaffirmation of dialogue and collaboration' at the core of teaching and learning in HE. In arguing this point, we recognised the need for time and space to make sure the focus remained on students' learning.

Our specific context was as Learning Developers supporting first-year undergraduate students who were embarking on a social work apprenticeship programme. This degree course had a block style of delivery, meaning the students studied one module at a time, with the rest of their week devoted to on-the-job learning. Time and space were needed to nurture relationships among the subject academics, Learning Developers, and the students to create meaningful learning opportunities for the latter.

Although the initial involvement of two Learning Developers with this course was due to prosaic reasons connected to working hours, the impact on our subsequent approach was significant. Through our involvement in the course over two academic years, we held regular planning meetings with our academic colleagues. These meetings were shaped by COVID-19: In 2020 by its onset and in 2021 by reflecting on the lessons we had learnt across the year. In these meetings, we constructively challenged each other to refine our approaches to facilitating students' learning. Our questioning was supported—rather than restricted—by the pandemic. At that time, none of us were familiar with teaching online. This situation had an unexpected bonus, as it meant the potential expectations and baggage that could have shaped on-campus sessions were removed. Being forced to teach in a different type of space liberated our collective approach.

Our questioning and discussion of alternative perspectives influenced the subsequent sessions, which were all co-taught by a Learning Developer and a subject lecturer. The collaborative approach meant the distinction between Learning Developer and academic became blurred, mirroring Skillen's (2006) suggestion that effective co-teaching leads to permeable boundaries between roles. Such blurring allowed for 'disciplinary meta-knowledge' to be 'surfaced' to support the students in developing their awareness of their discipline (Johnson and Bishopp-Martin, 2024, p. 19). Co-teaching meant that, at times, both the academic and Learning Developer took on roles that Gravett and Winstone (2019, p. 727) have ascribed to Learning Developers, including 'interpreter', 'coach', 'dialogue partner', 'listener', and 'intermediary' for the students.

In Lillis's (2001, p. 158) terms, we worked together to 'make language visible'. But, of course, this is only one side of the coin. For the approach to be meaningful in practice, students must feel they are 'essential to the conversation' (Werder *et al.*, 2010, p. 30). Creating such dialogue required inductive classroom strategies that emphasised 'a genuine quest for something undetermined at the beginning' (Noddings, 1992, p. 23). The dialogic approach encouraged the students to reflect on and share their study strategies with the whole group so that, in turn, their differing perspectives and experiences shaped how our sessions unfolded. In this way, the module was not driven by a 'pedagogy of what' but rather by a 'pedagogy of how' (Canton, 2023, p. 76), with the Learning Developers, academics, and students inventing the university together online—at a time when the physical campus was inaccessible.

Lessons from Lockdown: Adventures in Time and Space

Since our earlier reflections, Chad's teaching has returned to take place primarily in physical classrooms on campus, while Rebecca now teaches courses specifically designed for correspondence learning. Chad's role remains in a centrally located Learning Development team, while Rebecca is a lecturer in an academic faculty. In the following vignettes, we switch to the first-person singular, with Chad writing the first two case studies and Rebecca the final one. We believe these vignettes typify how our work together during the pandemic has continued to underpin and shape our practice, especially the importance of making time and space to enhance our students' learning.

Creating Time and Space for Diverse Writers

In 2021, I was invited by two academic colleagues to work with them to co-construct the structure and delivery of an academic study skills module for digital arts students studying a foundation year programme. I have now worked with three cohorts of students studying this module. There have been about 100 students taking the compulsory module each academic year. The cohorts are always diverse: Most of the learners have been first-generation students, having previously completed vocational qualifications; a large portion have had disabilities; and a significant minority have been mature learners. In developing the module, my conversations with my colleagues focused on how we wanted the students to recognise and explore their unique voices as writers through creating outputs across multiple genres. The module's assessment asks the students to create three texts: an autobiography, an essay on the evolution of digital storytelling, and a reimagining of a traditional tale for a contemporary audience. By doing so, students must navigate 'their knowledge of textual possibilities and their knowledge of relevant content in order to create a structure that achieves their communicative goals in a manner that is appropriate for their intended audience' (Canton, 2023, p. 73). Each genre requires them to use their voice in a different way.

In emphasising students' voices, we have framed each of the module's 11 weeks around an open question, such as 'How can I structure my work?' and 'How can I express myself confidently in my academic writing?'. The questions are intended to reinforce how the students will need to approach their entire course by drawing on the information they have to hand alongside their prior knowledge and experiences. In the module's opening lecture, for instance, I start by asking the students the question, 'What kind of writer are you?' The students are asked to share a one-word response that is captured in a 'word cloud', a visual collage that provides greater prominence to any words that have been suggested by more than one person. The students work in groups to talk through the collated responses. They can focus on the word they initially input or different ones that have piqued their interest. The words used have varied over the years, including pithy reflections ('blurter', 'orator', 'honest'), metaphors ('snail', 'Lightning McQueen', 'tree'), and emojis ('😵'). The teaching team also share their words, offering glimpses into our own struggles with getting words onto the page. This activity emphasises that we are all writers, and there are different ways to be a writer. It highlights that writing skills are not tricks to be mastered; rather, they are cultivated through a life-long journey of trial and error (Barnett, 2018). We can explore and question the effectiveness of different writing strategies, but, ultimately, time and space are needed to shape our identities as writers.

Creating Time and Space for Students in 'One-Off' Sessions

Through centring students' learning, we are forced to shift our attention in sessions away from what we are doing to what our students are learning. Students need time and space to grapple with key concepts. So far in this chapter we have considered the value of collaboration between academics and Learning Developers in modules where the learning outcomes have specifically foregrounded the development of academic skills or literacy development. Teaching a series of sessions naturally offers more time and space to explore key concepts and different strategies. Yet, as Learning Developers working within the parameters of another's curriculum, there is not always the luxury of such an approach (Canton, 2023). Our contention, however, is that time and space can still be made in discrete or 'one-off' sessions to enhance students' learning.

I recently taught a group of first-year Art History students who were studying a core module focused on the theoretical foundations of their discipline. Some of these texts were dense and complicated. The module leader emphasised the value of these texts as part of the students' immersion into their discipline, alongside the practical need to use the texts to write an annotated bibliography as part of the module's assessment. In a one-off, two-hour session, the students were guided to work in small groups to use textmapping to develop their understanding of each text (see Middlebrook, 2007). Every group wrestled with a different text. Participants from each group then contributed to a jigsaw activity, where new groups were created comprising participants who had each read a different text. The students were asked to share their texts with their new group to consider possible connections across the material.

Throughout the session, the subject lecturer and I supported the students by asking them questions exploring both the process of textmapping and the contents of the texts. At the same time, there were long periods in the session when we took a step back and left the students to read and engage with their texts without interruption. This approach meant the onus was on the students to work together to make meaning from the texts, foregrounding the centrality of working with their peers to enhance their learning (Barnett, 2018). It emphasised that learning is more than a product; it involves the processes required to develop knowledge and understanding.

The session provided time and space for us to adapt to the group's needs rather than focusing on prescribed content. In reflecting on the approach, several students stated that the session gave them the time to practise their skills and to seek feedback from their peers and tutors. The positive feedback—from the students and lecturer—emphasises that the key to session design is considering what will have the most impact on students' learning. There are always lots of strategies that could be used, so it is vital to identify what is most important for our students at a given time. This approach avoids overloading sessions, instead providing opportunities to nurture organic discussions. It empowers students to explore and own their learning, whether that is through engaging with challenging texts or other elements of their degree.

Creating time and Space for Student-Led Online Learning

I found online 'classrooms' a rather stilted space during the early months of the pandemic. The videotelephony software we were using at the time had been designed for business meetings rather than for teaching students. This situation meant the technology appeared to promote the transmission of knowledge rather than stimulate dialogue and debate. We therefore had to redouble our efforts during the pandemic to engage our students actively in our sessions. In doing so, we sought to centre their voices by making sure they had the time to speak and through encouraging them to take the lead in developing their learning. We identified the importance of giving students time and space before, during, and after each session. Our sessions during COVID-19 also reminded us of what students bring to their current learning and how their knowledge and understanding develop over time. I now regularly teach online, but I keep these lessons of the pandemic in mind.

I currently teach an introductory module for first-year undergraduate students studying across a wide range of social sciences disciplines (including criminology, economics, human geography, and politics). The module is taught entirely online. Drawing on our experiences from teaching during the pandemic, I encourage my students to use their knowledge and prior experiences as a gateway that scaffolds their learning on the module. This approach gives the students the time and space to reflect on their understanding both as a starting point and as they progress throughout their course, recognising how these experiences will shape their engagement with their studies more broadly (Brodie, 2013).

The students undertake module tasks before meeting me and their peers in an online classroom. These activities include audio and video resources designed to promote students' engagement and understanding of the module's material and core concepts. In a session towards the start of the module, we explore the meaning of 'difference', 'inequality', and 'pattern'. Rather than offering set definitions of these terms, I ask the students to write short autobiographical texts, like those found on social media sites. The students then answer a series of 'true' or 'false' polls about the contents of what they have written, such as whether they included their gender, age, social class, job, hobbies, and so on in their biographies. They discuss the results of these polls with other students in virtual breakout rooms. Through the aid of some prompts, the students identify patterns, which categories may refer to 'difference', and which could lead to 'inequalities'. Finally, the breakout groups come back together to share and discuss the concepts as a whole class in order to write agreed definitions of 'difference', 'inequality', and 'pattern'. This approach avoids students being given predetermined definitions that they may not fully understand. Instead, through pre-session work, alongside discussion, sharing, listening, reflecting, and individual work during the session, the students make meaning for themselves. This approach validates the students' ideas, giving them opportunities to consolidate their learning. In other words, it shows them the significance of their voices.

Reclaiming Time and Space

In this chapter, we have emphasised that time and space are required to foster students' learning. Our approach may feel like going 'back to basics'. In some ways, it is. Yet if we are to transform practice in meaningful ways, we must get the basics right. Time and space are scarce commodities in contemporary HE, which leads to 'squabbling over the same limited resources in territorial spaces' (White and Webster, 2023, p. 3). It is in this climate that a recent polemic argued that 'study skills' was a 'Tinkerbell' that should be scrapped and replaced with 'specialised subject support delivered by Academics' (Richards and Pilcher, 2023, p. 592). Reductive binaries are not the answer. Instead, we hope that we have shown how making time and space to work with our colleagues can create environments of mutual trust, where opportunities for constructive challenge can enhance students' learning. Our experiences suggest that this approach can be transformative when colleagues from noncontingent disciplines and professions work together. These differing perspectives not only enhance each other's approaches but also foster an environment where students have the confidence to participate, as there is no singular voice of authority gatekeeping knowledge.

Time and space must also be protected in our direct work with students. Guiding students in their use of time and space before, during, and after sessions helps to emphasise that learning is an active and continual process. In making time and space, we must switch from focusing on ourselves as educators to foregrounding what our students are learning. We must encourage our students to use their knowledge and experiences to shape their engagement with their studies. It is important that we adapt this approach while our students are transitioning into HE. By doing so, we can help to temper the loss of their unique voices as they navigate a series of new challenges and experiences. If we get this right, we can help our students invent a university where their voices are not just heard but where they truly matter. In this way, we can see the metaphor of Tinkerbell differently. We suggest that through providing time and space—and with a little bit of 'fairy dust'—we can give our students the opportunity and room needed to fly.

References

Askham, P. (2008) 'Context and identity: exploring adult learners' experiences of higher education', *Journal of Further and Higher Education*, 32(1), pp. 85–97. https://doi.org/10.1080/03098770701781481

Barnett, L. (2018) 'Learning Development', in I. M. Kinchin and N. E. Winstone (eds.), *Exploring pedagogic fragility and resilience: case studies of academic narrative*. Leiden: Brill, pp. 187–204.

Bartholomae, D. (1986) 'Inventing the university', *Journal of Basic Writing*, 5(1), pp. 4–23. https://doi.org/10.37514/JBW-J.1986.5.1.02

Brodie, L. (2013) 'Problem-based learning', in L. Hunt and D. Chalmers (eds.), *University teaching in focus: a learning-centred approach*. Abingdon: Routledge, pp. 145–163.

Canton, U. (2023) 'Teaching writing in Learning Development', in A. Syska and C. Buckley (eds.), *How to be a Learning Developer in higher education: critical perspectives, community and practice*. Abingdon: Routledge, pp. 71–79.

Foucault, M. (1986) 'Of other spaces', *Diacritics*, 16(1), pp. 22–27. https://doi.org/10.2307/464648

Gravett, K. and Winstone, N. E. (2019) '"Feedback interpreters": the role of Learning Development professionals in facilitating university students' engagement with feedback', *Teaching in Higher Education*, 24(6), pp. 723–738. https://doi.org/10.1080/13562517.2018.1498076

Johnson, I. and Bishopp-Martin, S. (2024) 'Conceptual foundations in Learning Development', in A. Syska and C. Buckley (eds.), *How to be a Learning Developer in higher education: critical perspectives, community and practice*. Abingdon: Routledge, pp. 15–24.

Lillis, T. B. (2001) *Student writing: access, regulation, desire*. London: Routledge.

McDonald, C. and Parry, R. (2021) 'Working in partnership to deliver a skills course to social work apprentices: avoiding technological determinism', *Journal of Learning Development in Higher Education*, 22, pp. 1–6. https://doi.org/10.47408/jldhe.vi22.772

Middlebrook, R. D. (2007) 'Overview of textmapping.' Available at: http://www.textmapping.org/overview.html (Accessed 15 May 2024).

Noddings, N. (1992) *The challenge to care in schools: an alternative approach to education*. New York: Teachers College Press.

Richards, K. and Pilcher, N. (2023) 'Study skills: neoliberalism's perfect Tinkerbell', *Teaching in Higher Education*, 28(3), pp. 580–596. https://doi.org/10.1080/13562517.2020.1839745

Skillen, J. (2006) 'Teaching academic writing from the "centre" in Australian universities', in L. Ganobcsik-Williams (ed.), *Teaching academic writing in UK higher education: theories, practice and models*. London: Palgrave Macmillan, pp. 140–153.

Werder, C., Ware L., Thomas, C. and Skogsburg, E. (2010) 'Students in parlor talk on teaching and learning', in C. Werder and M. Otis (eds.), *Engaging student voices in the study of teaching and learning*. Sterling, VA: Stylus.

White, S. and Webster, H. (2023) 'Hey you! They're calling you Tinkerbell! What are you going to do about it?', *Journal of Learning Development in Higher Education*, 29, pp. 1–10. https://journal.aldinhe.ac.uk/index.php/jldhe/article/view/1120/865

Chapter 2

What the Medium of 'Focusing' Taught Me About Mattering, Wellbeing, and Belonging for Students

Farrukh Akhtar

Introduction

In this chapter, I build on the emotional insights gained from working with students and their grief during the pandemic. Taking time and space to acknowledge students' emotional wellbeing was profoundly appreciated by them and contributed to the development of a sense of belonging in relation both to their course and to the wider university. In this chapter I explore my work in developing peer support networks for students in higher education (HE) using a medium called Focusing (Gendlin, 1981) to draw out its impact on students' sense of mattering, belonging, and wellbeing.

Enabling students to feel they are part of a collegial community has always been an important priority in my practice, but my approach to this changed significantly during the COVID-19 pandemic. As a course leader of an undergraduate programme, I was faced with 160 students who all experienced some form of emotional turmoil; about 30 students were directly affected by the loss of loved ones, and the remainder were vicariously affected by the grief of their peers.

Students turned to the university to meet their emotional needs at this critical time, even though the cause of their distress lay outside the bounds of HE's immediate responsibilities. The knowledge of students' emotional needs led me to reevaluate the boundaries of the usual pedagogical frameworks that educators adhere to, and to reconsider my understanding of belonging, which aligned with Strayhorn's (2019, p. 4) definition that 'sense of belonging refers to students' perceived social support on campus, a feeling or sensation of connectedness, and the experience of mattering or feeling cared about, accepted, respected, valued by, and important to the campus community.'

Just as a young person might take for granted the emotional support provided by loved ones at home, students expected the university to offer them strategies and methods for managing their precarious lives and the unprecedented challenges they were facing in community with their peers (and with staff). It seemed that feeling that one *mattered* and having a sense of *belonging* for students translated as an expectation that one would be emotionally supported when at their most vulnerable.

DOI: 10.4324/9781003503149-4

My focus in this chapter is on the social aspect of belonging and the extent to which students feel connected to their peers and lecturers. In addition, I concentrate on the psychological aspects, which involve the sense of who students' are and how they feel about themselves and their lives. The concept of 'mattering' is also a helpful here, as it relates to students' sense of the extent to which they experience themselves as mattering to others. Whilst a sense of belonging relates more to one's sense of connection to a group, mattering refers to the quality of an individual's connections to others (Dixon and Tucker, 2008).

All of these concepts relate significantly to students' sense of emotional wellbeing.

The Connection Between Wellbeing and Sense of Belonging and Mattering

Research into students' sense of belonging and mattering in HE has proliferated in recent years, largely because it seems to be a good indicator of wellbeing (Hartley, 2020) and is integrally connected to academic attainment (Keyes et al., 2012).

The ground has shifted from Baumeister and Leary's original belonging hypothesis, where sense of belonging was defined as 'a need to form and maintain at least a minimum quantity of interpersonal relationships' (Baumeister and Leary, 1995, p. 499) to a much more nuanced understanding of four domains of belonging: academic spaces, social spaces, internal spaces (relating to one's personal internal or psychological space), and external spaces (relating to one's external surroundings, including the campus environment) (Ahn and Davis, 2020). Students are actively looking for inclusivity and connection in all four of these domains and value the social domain, with its sense of connection with other students, over and above the need to do well academically (Blake et al., 2022).

The relationships among student mattering, a sense of belonging, and wellbeing are closely intertwined. Mattering refers to students' perception that they are important and valued members of the academic community. When students feel that they matter, they are more likely to experience a strong sense of belonging, which is the feeling of being an integral part of the academic community. This sense of belonging is crucial for their wellbeing, as it provides emotional support, enhances self-esteem, and reduces feelings of isolation. Research has shown that when students feel they belong and matter, their overall wellbeing improves, leading to better mental health and academic success. For instance, Freeman, Anderman, and Jensen (2007) found that students' sense of belonging in school was positively correlated with their emotional and psychological well-being, which in turn influenced their academic performance and persistence in education.

HE students' mental health tends to be poorer than that of the general nonstudent adult population; this has been attributed to the specific stresses that students often face (Campbell et al., 2022). For example, 40% of students score their mental health as below average (Blake et al., 2022), with anxiety and depression reported as common conditions. States of mental and emotional wellbeing can impact on students' whole experience of being at university, affecting their ability to socially engage with their peers, the wider university. Having a sense of belonging and feeling that one matters can also act as a buffer against poor mental health. Choi et al. (2021), for example, found that having a strong sense of belonging moderated the relations between racial microaggressions and depressive symptoms in Black and minority ethnic students.

As I reflected on the expectations of my students, I wondered if these arose from a place where they felt that they mattered and belonged, and so felt able to reach out when they were at their most vulnerable. If this was the case, then it seemed that the usual pedagogical boundaries that educators adhered to might need reviewing. There was, rightfully, attention being paid to the curricula, and to preparing students for employability and graduate skills (Pereira et al., 2019); these included the attainment of 'soft skills' such as teamwork (Devedzic et al., 2018), but there needed to be space in the pedagogical frame for students to learn to relate to themselves and others at a more emotional level.

It was at this time that I stumbled upon the medium of 'Focusing': a way of connecting to the wisdom held in the body. I was immediately alerted by its potential to equip students to manage their emotional wellbeing as well as providing a structured way of forming positive relationships with their peers.

What Is Focusing?

Focusing is a way of *tuning in* to what is held in the body and also to what may be emotionally most alive for us at any given time. It is a method created by Eugene Gendlin (1981) as a result of his involvement in Carl Rogers's (1961) seminal research on the effectiveness of psychotherapy. Rogers concluded that it was the nature of the client–therapist relationship that determined the effectiveness of treatment. Gendlin, however, noticed that people who achieved successful outcomes in psychotherapy did so because they tended to *relate to themselves* in a specific way whilst undergoing psychotherapy. Further study of this enabled Gendlin (1981) to distil this way of relating to oneself and to also devise a method that enabled it to be taught to others.

In this way, Focusing oriented psychotherapy was developed (Gendlin, 1996). However, Gendlin then went on to devise a technique called 'Focusing partnerships' in which two people alternate between Focusing and listening. One person Focuses while the other acts as a 'companion' or listener, with the latter trained to actively listen and offer specific responses. The two then switch roles. Gendlin (2003) found that Focusing partnerships could achieve better outcomes than Focusing within a client–therapist mode due to the sense of equality and reciprocity that lies at the heart of this technique and the autonomy it gives to Focusers, enabling them to manage and 'own' the process. Moreover, he found that both roles (Focuser and companion) were equally vital: Focusers benefit from the experience of being fully heard by another, and companions value the gift of learning when they actively listen to another; each role benefits without getting in the way of the other one's process.

How Focusing Can Be Used in a Pedagogical Context

Focusing offers a number of pedagogical opportunities. First, it offers a framework students can use to connect to their emotional worlds. Once students grasp the basic steps involved, they find that simply *giving space* to specific emotions somehow makes those feelings more manageable. Taking the time to connect with these emotions means people may gain insights that lead to gentle but deep changes.

To be in the presence of someone who provides a safe and nonjudgemental listening space as a companion in the process can be a new experience for some students. When students experience being fully heard, they are more likely to feel connected to other students, to feel they matter and are accepted just as they are.

Similarly, the Focuser then switches place to offer the gift of listening fully to the other person. Students learn to be in a mutually respectful and supportive relationship both with themselves and another; this facilitates their participation in being part of a wider peer support network. It can take time to master Focusing skills. They are usually taught over five blocks or modules. However, I have also seen students develop positive relationships in the two-day introductory training I offer (which aligns to the first module). Students go on to take the connections they have forged with others with them into the rest of the course, and it is my hope that these cultivated relationships will contribute to a wider peer support network that will support them beyond the academy into their personal and working lives.

Preparing for Focusing

To help students make an informed decision about attending the two-day introductory workshop to Focusing, I offer an initial one-to-one taster session in which we discuss their interest in the medium and what they hope to gain from the main workshop. The taster session provides a space in which they can share any personal issues or worries—for example, if they are managing high levels of anxiety or worrying about a previous history of depression that they fear is preventing them from building effective relationships with their peers. We then decide together whether the workshop may be the right space for them.

Students tend to be open in discussing these issues and their stories, highlighting how important personal and social connections are to them. If they wish to engage with this, I facilitate a brief exercise in which they connect to the 'felt sense' in their bodies. The exercise involves the person connecting with whatever comes into their awareness; a felt sense can be a feeling or a sensation (Purton, 2021). I offer gentle suggestions, enabling them to 'stay with' whatever shows up. Often something shifts, either in the physical sensation itself or in their awareness or understanding of it. For example, a student might connect with a sense of anxiety in their chest. As they stay with this sensation, they might realise the anxiousness is not about failing an assignment; it is about getting it in on time so they can attend to their sick child.

Altogether, the taster session supports students in making an informed decision about the helpfulness of attending the two-day introductory workshop. If they feel the workshop is not appropriate, I make sure to signpost them to other resources in the university so they feel listened and responded to.

Focusing Workshops

Focusing workshops are conducted by trained Focusing practitioners (approved by the British Focusing Association or the International Focusing Institute) and are best carried out in small groups to ensure there is time and space for each person's voice to be heard and to maximise opportunities for students to work with different peers over the span of the course.

From the outset, care is taken to set out 'ground rules' to create a sense of safety with a prompt to be mindful of what one shares and *how* one shares it, and an emphasis on authenticity without oversharing. The approach is discussed but also modelled to students in demonstrations by the educators.

Gendlin's (1981) six steps of Focusing involve initially 'clearing a Space': setting aside distractions to create mental space, then tuning into the 'felt sense' – that vague, nonverbal sense of an issue as it is being experienced in the body at that time. The Focuser than tries to find the 'handle', the words or images that capture this felt sense. They then take some time to ensure that the words or images being verbalised accurately resonate with the body's sensation. They might ask open-ended questions to the body to understand the felt sense's meaning. Finally, they accept whatever insights they might receive without judgment and take a moment to be with how this new understanding feels in their body.

Each workshop consists of four to five smaller sessions that break down the basic steps involved in Focusing into smaller digestible ones. For example, it takes time for students to feel confident that they are connecting with their 'felt sense'. Each session builds on the one before, beginning with some preliminary exercises introducing specific concepts, usually around an explicit aspect of connecting with one's emotions. Participants work in pairs, taking turns to practise the steps involved in that aspect. It is essential that each session assigns specific small, attainable steps for both the Focuser and the listening companion to practice, and that these build on the ones they covered in the previous workshop (Cornell, 2008).

By the end of the two days, students have worked through all the necessary steps involved, practicing Focusing to a basic level, and have developed significant skills as a companion, building on their ability to listen deeply to one another. They are then able to move forward to set up Focusing partnerships amongst themselves so that they can have swaps on a regular basis, if they wish.

It is striking how quickly students can learn to connect to their emotions with compassion and without judgement, and how powerful it is for them to then speak about what they are sensing, in the supportive space of being listened to without words of advice or rescue. Similarly, it can also be freeing to know that as a companion, your sole responsibility is to offer the gift of listening as fully as possible. Companions don't have to take on board any of the Focuser's emotions or offer solutions; they simply listen. For some, this can sow the seeds of establishing healthier boundaries in other personal relationships.

Reflecting on Focusing

The students I have worked with report positive changes in the way they relate to themselves and in the quality of the relationships they build with others as a result of their engagement with the medium of Focusing. For some, the workshops have been transformative in enabling them to manage their emotions generally and have been especially helpful in supporting them in managing anxiety. I have seen students move from being wary onlookers to telling the group that they feel accepted and feel like they belong.

However, as with all interventions, it is important to be aware of some caveats. Focusing is not for everyone. Some students will have well-defined patterns of self-care that work for them, and they may not be interested in learning alternative strategies if these are not specifically needed. Also, the idea of relating to one's body will not appeal to all students, and this preference and insight need to be respected.

Focusing workshops can be conducted on campus or online but need to be conducted by a trained professional who is a qualified Focusing practitioner. The need for specialist training will have resource implications for those considering the introduction of Focusing to their students. However, once staff are trained in relation to the medium, students who attend Focusing workshops develop lifelong skills and can join a global Focusing peer support network, as part of either the British Focusing Association or the International Focusing Institute.

If financial resources preclude Focusing workshops from being carried out, there are still a number of transferable aspects of learning that can be taken away from the technique, which have wide applicability. Educators can use their creativity in setting up sessions that may use creative writing, arts, and crafts, to enable students to connect to their emotional worlds. Aspin and Moore (2023) offer several structured creative arts–based exercises that facilitate this type of access.

In planning such activities, it is crucial to create time and space within and also beyond the formal curriculum where students can connect with each other emotionally in a safe environment. The importance of clear boundaries cannot be overemphasised. For many, especially vulnerable students, showing distress or getting upset is understood as a sign of inadequacy. Reframing this to create spaces where emotions are acknowledged and accepted can be a game changer: Students are supported and enabled to own their emotions, although some may need to be supported to access wider resources around their emotional wellbeing in the academy and beyond.

The students I have worked with have a longing to be seen and accepted within the academy and to feel *at home* there. Students in emotional distress value a structured environment where the rules of managing their own emotions and being with others are clearly set out for them, including an invitation to remain appropriately careful about not oversharing. In my experience, students value the participation of educators in such sessions beyond the confines of the formal curriculum and enjoy connecting to them within different types of boundaries.

The scope for creativity and ingenuity in devising such spaces and in carving out specific time to engage in these types of activity is limited by educators' other necessary commitments and by a lack of specialist knowledge. However, Focusing has many parallels with mindfulness practices, which may be useful and valuable to consider bringing into pedagogical spaces. Xiong et al. (2022) found that of students attending a 14-week mindfulness course, many reported this having a positive impact on their learning experience. Whatever time is given and whatever spaces are created, it is important to ensure that they align with students' timetables and assessment commitments in order to be equitable and to maximise attendance.

Conclusion

The post-pandemic landscape places an imperative on educators to consider active approaches to address student wellbeing, mattering, and the development of a sense of belonging. In order to address these important features, which directly impact on the student experience within HE, we should consider expanding the pedagogical frame to grant time and space for focused attention on the positive development of emotional wellbeing to be embedded within the curriculum.

Activities such as the two-day Introduction to Focusing workshop offer a safe, structured framework that students can use to relate to themselves and to their peers—a framework that could have a positive impact beyond those relationships relevant to HE, extending into the sphere of students' personal lives. Offering such workshops as part of students' ongoing induction activities may provide a powerful way for students to arrive, settle, and begin participating in a supportive peer community, thereby demonstrating not only that they matter to one another, but also that they belong and can feel at home both within the academy and beyond.

Those wishing to explore the significance and implications of Focusing further can do so by visiting the British Focusing Association website at https://www.focusing.org.uk/ and the International Focusing Institute at https://focusing.org/

References

Ahn, M. Y. and Davis, H. H. (2020) 'Students' sense of belonging and their socio-economic status in higher education: a quantitative approach'. *Teaching in Higher Education* (Online ahead of print), 1–14.

Aspin, S. and Moore, J. (2023) 'Focusing with images'. *Person-centered & Experiential Psychotherapies*, 22(2), 171–190. https://doi.org/10.1080/14779757.2022.2110147

Baumeister, R. F. and Leary, M. R. (1995) 'The need to belong: desire for interpersonal attachments as a fundamental human motivation'. *Psychological Bulletin*, 117(3), 497–529. https://doi.org/10.1037/0033-2909.117.3.497

Blake, S., Capper, G., and Jackson, A. (2022, October) 'Building belonging in higher education: Recommendations for developing an integrated institutional approach'. WONKHE and Pearson. Available at https://wonkhe.com/wp-content/wonkhe-uploads/2022/10/Building-Belonging-October-2022.pdf (Accessed 27 January, 2024).

Campbell, F., Blank, L. and Cantrell, A. (2022) 'Factors that influence mental health of university and college students in the UK: a systematic review'. *BMC Public Health*, 22, 1778. https://doi.org/10.1186/s12889-022-13943-x

Choi, S., Weng, S., Park, H., Lewis, J., Harwood, S. A., Mendenhall, R. and Huntt, M. B. (2021) 'Sense of belonging, racial microaggressions, and depressive symptoms among students of Asian descent in the United States'. *Smith College Studies in Social Work*, 91(2), 115–141. https://doi.org/10.1080/00377317.2021.1882922

Cornell, A. W. (2008) *The power of focusing: a practical guide to emotional self-healing*. New Harbinger Publications.

Devedzic, V., Tomic, B., Jovanovic, J., Kelly, M., Milikic, N., Dimitrijevic, S., Djuric, D. and Sevarac, Z. (2018) 'Metrics for students' soft skills'. *Applied Measurement in Education*, 31 (4), 283–296. https://doi.org/10.1080/08957347.2018.1495212

Dixon, A. and Tucker, C. (2008) 'Every student matters: enhancing strengths-based school counseling through the application of mattering', *Professional School Counseling*, 12(2), 123–126.

Freeman, T. M., Anderman, L. H. and Jensen, J. M. (2007) 'Sense of belonging in college freshmen at the classroom and campus levels'. *The Journal of Experimental Education*, 75(3), 203–220.

Gendlin, E. (1981) *Focusing*. New York: Bantam Books.

Gendlin, E. T. (1996) *Focusing-oriented psychotherapy*. New York: Guilford Press.

Gendlin, E. T. (2003) *Focusing: How to gain direct access to your body's knowledge*. London: Rider.

Hartley, M. (2020) 'The role of higher education in supporting student wellbeing: A review of the literature'. *Higher Education Quarterly*, 74(2), 188–206.

Keyes, C. L., Eisenberg, D., Perry, G. S., Dube, S. R., Kroenke, K. and Dhingra, S. S. (2012) 'The relationship of level of positive mental health with current mental disorders in predicting suicidal behavior and academic impairment in college students'. *Journal of American College Health*, 60(2), 126–133.

Pereira, E.T., Vilas-Boas, M. and Rebelo, C. C. (2019) Graduates' skills and employability: the view of students from different European countries. *Higher Education, Skills and Work-based Learning*, 9(4), 758–774. https://doi.org/10.1108/HESWBL-10-2018-0098

Purton, C. (2021) *The focusing oriented counselling primer: a concise introduction*. Monmouth: PCCS Books.

Rogers, C. R. (1961) *On becoming a person*. Boston: Houghton Mifflin.

Strayhorn, T. L. (2019) *College students' sense of belonging: a key to educational success for all students*. Abingdon, Oxon: Routledge.

Xiong, Y., Prasath, P. R., Zhang, Q. and Jeon, L. (2022) 'A mindfulness-based well-being group for international students in higher education: a pilot study'. *Journal of Counseling and Development*, 100(4), 374–385. https://doi.org/10.1002/jcad.12432

Chapter 3

What Pivoting Academic Skills Support Online Has Taught Us About the Importance of a Robust Learning Culture

Helen Jamieson and Julie Nolan

Introduction

In this chapter, the Student Engagement Team (SET), a student-facing support team based at Edge Hill University (EHU) in the northwest of England, critically reflects on its learning development practice through a post-pandemic lens.

In 2021 we critically reflected on our pivot to delivering fully online academic skills support (UniSkills) during COVID-19, and we recognise how our robust learning culture has enabled us to reflect, review, rethink, and recalibrate our practices. In the following exploration we have surfaced where we have adjusted and, more radically, changed our approach and pedagogy, linking each aspect to the importance of cultivating a robust learning culture allowing a safe and supportive space for innovation and ideation.

Having received a significant amount of interest across the sector, our approach has wide applicability across higher education (HE), and in this chapter we explore how practitioners across the sector can emulate and cultivate a learning culture to inform their own practice and service offer.

Critical Reflection

Our critical evaluation utilised Brookfield's (1995) model as a vehicle to inform, innovate, and transform.

Although evaluation has always been an integral part of our practice, we recognised the importance of harnessing a robust critical reflection model as we pivoted delivery of academic skills support online. We instinctively knew this would be a transformative time for teaching and learning and it would be essential to capture lessons learned to future-proof our practice.

We identified that Brookfield's (1995) model would ensure that our reflection encouraged:

- Multiperspectivity
- Comprehensive and holistic perspectives
- Exploration of experiences from different vantage points
- Opportunities to expose assumptions and practices

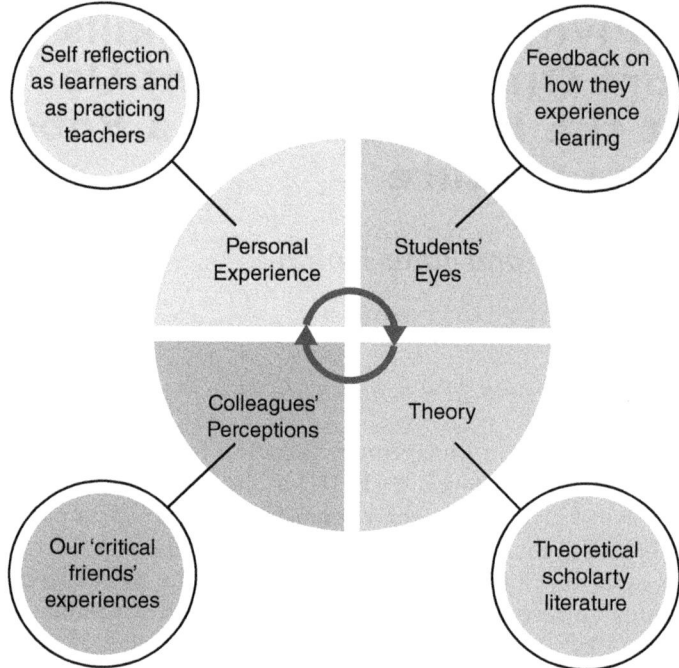

Figure 3.1 Brookfield's Four Lenses Model (1995).

Brookfield's model allowed us to reflect via four lenses, and our approach used to gather this data differed for each lens.

Lens 1: Self-Reflection

Our team of academic skills advisors (ASAs) reflected on their personal experience of the pivot online, enabling them to recognise the impact to their pedagogical practice and capture any learnings.

Five key themes emerged:

1 Challenges measuring student engagement
2 Balancing activities and interaction
3 Importance of communities of practice and colleagues' support
4 Upskilling (digital and learning technologies)
5 Resources

The granular detail within each theme contained essential insights, which we were able to integrate into our practice to help adjust our approach. The ASAs also produced a series of SWOT analyses (for strengths, weaknesses, opportunities, and threats), using these as a framework for discussion in a focus group to further reflect on their experiences.

Lens 2: Student Experience

Feedback was gathered following one-to-one appointments, webinars, and embedded delivery via a student experience survey and from comments captured via email and social media:

- 94% of students were 'satisfied' or 'very satisfied' with appointments online.
- 85% (appointments) and 92% (webinars) reported no technical issues.
- Interactive elements of webinars (polls and chat) were well received.
- Over half of students indicated a preference for synchronous (online and/or in-person) delivery.
- Students appreciated flexibility and availability of online support options.
- Students appreciated the ability to review recorded content after delivery.
- There was strong indication for preference of choice (online and/or in person options).

Lens 3: Colleagues' Perceptions

Academic colleagues were invited to provide feedback about their perceptions of our online embedded delivery, and findings mirrored several of the students' experiences, including appreciation of choice, flexibility, and accessibility of our UniSkills online offer.

Our pivot online provided opportunity to further facilitate a flipped approach to our embedded delivery. This approach was well received by both academics and their students. In addition to positive feedback, we also received useful developmental responses around the potential to expand interactive or practical elements in some of our online sessions.

Lens 4: Theoretical Literature

A comprehensive literature review was undertaken, resulting in five key themes:

1. Digital inequality
2. Digital skills
3. Student voice/students as partners
4. Inclusive learning design
5. Sense of belonging/learning communities

The pivot online highlighted that digital inequality resulted in significant barriers for students (JISC, 2020a; Lambie and Law, 2020; Nordmaan et al., 2020; Raaper and Brown, 2020). Assumptions were made that students (and staff) were both familiar and equipped with necessary skills and competencies for learning online (JISC, 2020b; Lambie and Law, 2020). But learning to navigate different technologies and platforms, alongside the wide range of new terminology, was confusing for students without support (Adedoyin and Soykan, 2020; JISC, 2020b).

There was a recognised opportunity to involve students in decision-making processes, providing a platform to voice their needs and to help shape the digital landscape for future students (Jackson, 2020; JISC, 2020a, 2020b; Whelehan, 2020).

The literature acknowledged the impact on the quality and accessibility of teaching and learning materials. The usual focus on planning, design and development was often overlooked (Adedoyin and Soykan, 2020; JISC, 2020a; Nordmaan *et al.*, 2020; Watermeyer *et al.*, 2021) and translating existing content onto new digital platforms, without reviewing design and delivery, was problematic (CAST, 2018; JISC, 2020b).

Scholars additionally advised that the lack of a physical 'university space' could impact on students' self-discipline, wellbeing and sense of belonging (Raaper and Brown, 2020) and focus should be on creating learning communities that could thrive in an online/blended environment (Elmer *et al.*, 2020; Hodges *et al.*, 2020; Lederer *et al.*, 2020, cited in Pownall *et al.*, 2022; Nordmaan *et al.*, 2020; Stadtfeld *et al.*, 2019, cited in Pownall *et al.*, 2022).

Pedagogical Transformation

Collectively the benefits from critically reflecting using Brookfield's (1995) four lenses model allowed us to identify the following key areas of pedagogical transformation.

Innovation

Pivoting UniSkills online during COVID-19 was a catalyst for change for SET. One of the key outcomes from this destabilising period was the importance of giving the team permission to cultivate and develop innovative practices, creating space for idea generation and experimentation. As a result, fledgling ideas that were speculative and embryonic were encouraged and supported, reflecting the learning culture of our team and wider service.

An example of an innovative idea in practice was a project to pilot the delivery of academic skills support in a true HyFlex approach (delivering online and in person simultaneously). ASAs worked collaboratively to manage this project, which consisted of several elements – from a consideration and rethinking of the pedagogical approach to an assessment of the information technology and audiovisual capabilities of both physical and virtual spaces. There was no predicted outcome or output expected, which gave the project leads licence to experiment and take risks in a way we would not have explored previously, pre COVID-19, when we were more risk averse and traditional in our approach.

This transformation could be emulated by giving staff space and permission to innovate and ideate. Our ASAs have since experimented with a range of innovative ideas including developing asynchronous toolkits, delivering synchronous transition support for pre-entry students, and developing a new support offer for postgraduate taught (PGT) students. Whilst not all ideas are piloted and/or successfully implemented, through critical reflection on practice there is always opportunity for whole team learning where we identify what works and learn lessons about how to improve services and support for students.

Strengthening Structure Workstreams

The introduction of workstreams has been one of the most transformative areas of our practice. The workstreams are areas of strategic importance to the wider department/Service and the University.

ASAs have an area of responsibility for a key workstream based on several factors, including their own personal interests and areas of expertise. The opportunity to lead on a workstream gives the ASAs autonomy over an area of development and allows them to drive innovation, often working collaboratively with colleagues across the wider university.

As an example, the ASA leading the Inclusive Practice workstream is actively involved in several pan-institution working groups including the University Accessibility Network and University Academic Integrity working group. They were also instrumental in the team's successful bid for an equality, diversity, and inclusion (EDI) funding award, which went towards funding a training session from UK charity AbilityNet. This training allowed for the creation of an EDI toolkit, which distilled all the learning from this training into bite-sized content.

Our workstream model means that in addition to ASAs providing academic skills support and developing skills and knowledge around pedagogy, teaching, and learning, they are also encouraged to deepen their workstream expertise. We would encourage exploration of a similar model across different settings, allowing staff to develop and share their knowledge with the wider team, which can help continually develop the service offer and ensure alignment to university priorities and the students who study within it.

Transformed Communications

Although we had a well-established internal communications framework in place for several years, which outlined channels and expectations, it became even more important during COVID-19 to ensure clear and transparent communication

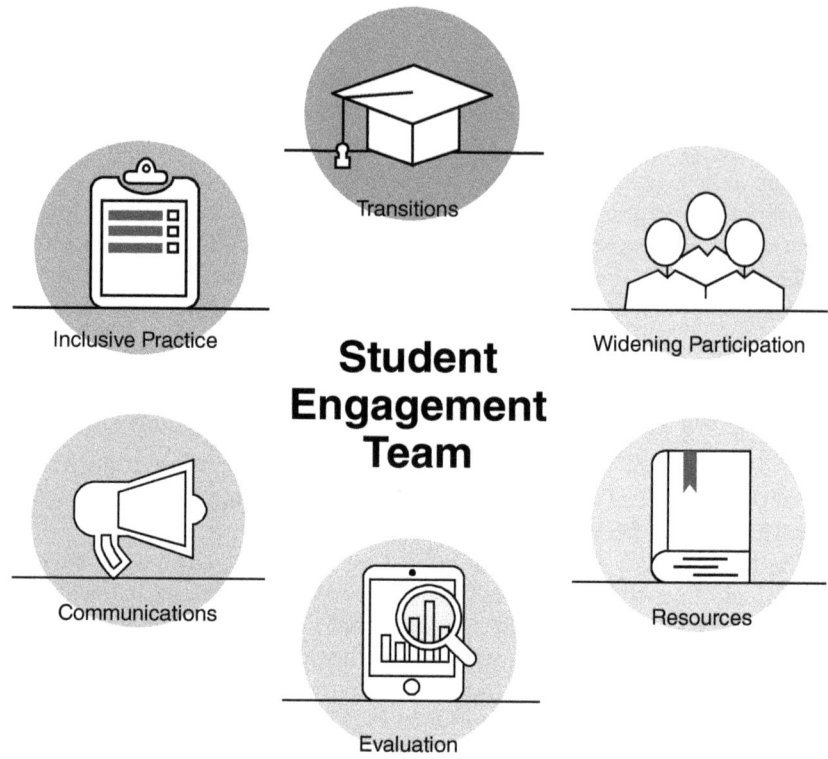

Figure 3.2 SET Workstreams: Transitions Widening Participation, Resources, Evaluation, Communications and Inclusive Practice.

across the team. A formal team meeting (every 4–6 weeks) needed to be supplemented with additional communications and more informal channels.

A new SET Microsoft (MS) Teams channel was created, and a weekly news email was quickly established to collate and share valuable information and updates across the week to help manage information overload. In addition, a weekly 30-minute virtual collective break was established so, during periods of lockdown, the team could unite and check in with each other more informally. The SET Community of Practice (CoP) also pivoted online, and this forum became even more important as a way for ASAs to share their thoughts, concerns, and ideas during this challenging period.

We have retained the weekly news email as a way of collating key information into one easy-to-digest format, and this initiative could easily be transferred into your own practice. Our more structured and integrated approach to team communications has led to increased engagement and more discursive interactions; our meetings are less didactic and more dialogic, leading to more productive outputs.

Community of Practice

Our internal CoP was established in 2019 and underwent its first annual review shortly after the initial lockdown in April 2020. SET CoP provides a dedicated space for ASAs, a combination of librarians and Learning Developers, to lead on and cultivate a unified professional identity.

As managers, one of the key transformations we have observed from SET CoP is the impact to the teams' resilience. The pandemic pivot was undoubtedly a challenging period for all, but having a protected space for ASAs to share ideas, collaborate on initiatives, discuss concerns, and reflect on practice has ultimately enhanced their confidence and capability to thrive through adversity.

Feedback from the most recent annual review revealed that ASAs found SET CoP:

- Is a valuable safe space to be open and honest
- Can adapt and implement changes quickly
- Is a place to share, feel listened to, be heard and validated
- Is supportive and provides reassurance
- Has a culture of collaboration, trust, and respect
- Provides opportunity to celebrate successes

This initiative could be easily transferred into other settings through development of local CoPs, providing autonomy and dedicated time and space for teams to share and collaborate. Although ASAs regularly share ideas freely with SET managers, one of the key elements of SET CoP's success has been providing ASAs the opportunity to meet and discuss practice *separately* from their line managers. SET CoP allows space to share any issues, updates, and successes and to collaborate on ideas and resolutions *before* feeding them into more formal routes as a full, or even resolved, picture.

Confidence Spectrum

The idea of an academic skills confidence spectrum may be considered controversial to many in the Learning Development community, but this was never an attempt to develop a homogenous group of ASAs able to deliver the same content, in the same way, using the same style and approach. On the contrary, the aim of our confidence spectrum is to ensure transparency across our academic skills and support offer, including all disciplines and modes of delivery: information skills and academic writing, in-person and online support.

The confidence spectrum was co-designed with the ASAs and discussed as part of the SET CoP agenda. It allows ASAs to self-assess the topics they feel confident to deliver, those they feel confident to support other ASAs to develop their skills in, and those they feel least confident in delivering. Most importantly it also provides a safe space for ASAs to critically reflect honestly and make a choice, without risk of expectation, to either access further support or to opt out of delivery on topics outside their comfort zone.

A peer review scheme is available for staff to shadow each other's delivery and share constructive feedback as a critical friend. Both the confidence spectrum and peer review schemes are supportive initiatives, which could be transferred into other practices through discussion, agreement, and reassurance of a safe space within teams.

Cultivated Critical Friends

One of the exponential impacts that arose from the online pivot was development of our digital learning materials. Although this was always on our agenda, the need and speed to provide accessible and engaging online learning opportunities became a key priority during the pandemic for remote students. In the following years we have continually developed and refined our digital skills, knowledge, and experience, and this progression was aided greatly through the development of a rigorous quality assurance (QA) process and cultivation of our critical friendships.

Depending on the service model followed, other teams may already have good connections with the wider learning community, and we highly recommend developing relationships with both professional and academic colleagues. Involving them in learning design and QA processes not only enriches the resources but can additionally increase their engagement and support when it comes time to promote.

We also advise working closely with the target audiences. SET employ a team of student advisors (SAs) whose core role is to provide peer-to-peer support for their fellow students through delivery of introductory academic skills, supporting ASAs as workshop chat buddies, designing and delivering targeted campaigns, and supporting the whole team as critical friends. Engaging students as partners has been integral to our development processes and ensures materials are optimally meeting the needs of our learners and reducing the risk of needing to refine content after publication.

Although additional time will need to be factored in within projects to allow for critical collaborations, we have recognised a rewarding balance between producing quick versus high-quality materials. Our critical friendships have also generated opportunities to expand our support to other collaborative projects, developed our professional networks, showcased our expertise, and enhanced our credibility.

Evaluation Matrix Development

We introduced an evaluation matrix in 2018, and this was further developed through reflection of our online pivot (Nolan and Jamieson, 2021). The matrix is an evidence-based approach that allows us to map out our key support touchpoints to ensure we are evaluating student satisfaction and impact at key opportunities. These insights help to shape and develop our support offer, providing a complementary narrative to our quantitative data and a more comprehensive understanding of student behaviours, experiences, and expectations.

To transfer this initiative into other teams and practices, we would advise first to reflect upon *what* it is that is to be evaluated, taking into consideration any gaps in current evaluation activities. Next it is necessary to identify what will be *done* with the information, what opportunities there are to transform and impact practice, and what are the potential obstructions. Finally, remember that evaluation is an iterative process and can often yield opportunities for further exploration and continuous improvement.

Conclusion

We hope you have enjoyed exploring what pivoting our academic skills support online has taught us about the importance of cultivating a robust learning culture. Whether you seek to explore transferring one or all of our practices into your own, we hope to have inspired you to approach this with an open mind and without the fear of failure as a negative concept. Encouraging mistakes and managing risks has allowed the transformations we have celebrated to happen. And the opportunity to be untethered by the boundaries of normality during the pandemic undoubtedly provided more freedom for us to be risk takers.

We value and prioritise critical reflection as much as forward planning, and it has proved enormously insightful to our practice. It has told us so much about where we want to be, recognising any gaps and providing evidence to continually support and develop individually, as a team and as a service. Our pandemic pivot provided an enhanced opportunity for us to further integrate critical reflection within our culture and appreciate the opportunity to further transform our practice.

The principle that guides our transformative practice is the importance of prioritising critical reflection alongside the delivery of a support service to students. Without creating the space and resource for robust, authentic, and honest critical reflection, which includes actively and nonjudgmentally listening to all stakeholders, we cannot create the right conditions for purposeful and meaningful changes that can ultimately enhance the student experience.

References

Adedoyin, O. B. and Soykan, E. (2020) 'Covid-19 pandemic and online learning: the challenges and opportunities', *Interactive Learning Environments*, 31(2), pp. 863–875. https://doi-org.edgehill.idm.oclc.org/10.1080/10494820.2020.1813180

Brookfield, S. (1995) 'Chapter 4: The four lenses of critical reflection', pp. 61–77, in S. Brookfield (ed.), *Becoming a critically reflective teacher*, 2nd edn. San Francisco: Jossey-Bass.

CAST. (2018) 'The UDL Guidelines', *CAST*. https://udlguidelines.cast.org/

Elmer, T., Mepham K. and Stadfeld, C. (2020) 'Students under lockdown: comparisons of students' social networks and mental health before and during the COVID-19 crisis in Switzerland', *PLoS ONE*, 15(7). https://doi.org/10.1371/journal.pone.0236337

Hodges, C., Moore, S., Lockee, B., Trust, T. and Bond, A. (2020) 'The difference between emergency remote teaching and online learning', *Educause Review*. https://er.educause.edu/articles/2020/3/the-difference-between-emer.ency-remote-teaching-and-online-learning

Jackson, A. (2020) 'The expectation gap: students' experience of learning during Covid-19 and their expectations for next year', *WONKHE*. https://wonkhe.com/blogs/the-expectation-gap-students-experience-of-learning-during-covid-19-and-their-expectations-for-next-year/

JISC. (2020a) 'Student digital experience insights survey 2020: UK higher education (HE) survey findings', *JISC*. https://www.jisc.ac.uk/reports/student-digital-experience-insights-survey-2020-uk-higher-education-findings

JISC. (2020b) 'Learning and teaching reimagined: change and challenge for students, staff and leaders', *JISC*. https://www.jisc.ac.uk/reports/learning-and-teaching-reimagined (Accessed 12 January 2021).

Lambie, I. and Law, B. (2020) 'Teaching online during a pandemic: pedagogical skills transfer from face to face support to online synchronous support provision' in '*Proceedings of the 19th European Conference on e-Learning*' 28–30 October, Glasgow: Glasgow Caledonian University, pp. 270–277. https://researchonline.gcu.ac.uk/ws/portalfiles/portal/42976118/Lambie_I._Law_B._2020_Teaching_online_during_a_pandemic_Pedagogical_skills_transfer_from_face_to_face_support_to_online_synchronous_support_provision.pdf

Nolan, J. and Jamieson, H. (2021) 'Pivoting academic skills support online: a critical reflection on practice', *Journal of Learning Development in Higher Education* 22(22). https://journal.aldinhe.ac.uk/index.php/jldhe/article/view/729/539

Nordmaan, E., Horlin, C., Hutchinson, J., Murray, J., Robson, L., Seery, M. K. and Mackay, J. R. D. (2020) 'Ten simple rules for supporting a temporary online pivot in higher education', *PLoS ONE*, 16(10). https://doi.org/10.1371/journal.pcbi.1008242

Pownall, M., Harris, R. and Blundell-Birtill, P. (2022) 'Supporting students during the transition to university in COVID-19: five key considerations and recommendations for educators', *Psychology Learning & Teaching*, 21(1), pp. 3–18. https://journals.sagepub.com/doi/pdf/10.1177/14757257211032486

Raaper, R. and Brown, C. (2020) 'The Covid-19 pandemic and the dissolution of the university campus: implications for student support practice', *Journal of Professional Capital and Community*, 5(3/4). pp. 343–349. https://www-emerald-com.edgehill.idm.oclc.org/insight/content/doi/10.1108/JPCC-06-2020-0032/full/html

Watermeyer, R., Crick, T., Knight, C. and Goodall, J. (2021) 'COVID-19 and digital disruption in UK universities: afflictions and affordances of emergency online migration', *Higher Education*, 81(3), pp. 623–641. https://doi.org/10.1007/s10734-020-00561-y

Whelehan, D. F. (2020) 'Students as partners: a model to promote student engagement in post-COVID-19 teaching and learning', *AISHE*, 12(3). https://ojs.aishe.org/index.php/aishe-j/article/view/479

Chapter 4

What the CHAMELEON Framework Taught Us About Equitable and Adaptable Pedagogy

Laura Davies and Joseph Davies

Introduction

Born out of the disruption, trauma, and immense professional challenges faced during the COVID-19 pandemic, the CHAMELEON framework for adapting to new educational conditions (see Table 4.1) has had a long-term transformative impact on English for academic purposes (EAP) teaching at a Sino–foreign joint venture university. The authors' experiences with internal and external EAP communities of practice (Wenger, 2010) for personal and professional support during the pandemic led to the CHAMELEON framework's development (see L. Davies *et al.*, 2020b; J. Davies *et al.*, 2020a). The framework's guiding principles are to show compassion and empathy in order to foster equitable and adaptable conditions for teaching and learning. As such principles have wide general appropriacy and relevance for various educational contexts beyond the confines of change management response interventions, the framework was designed with a wide and long-term scope in mind. Therefore, this chapter aims to elucidate the long-term, transformative impact the CHAMELEON framework has had on our practice. The guiding principles are used by the authors in their roles as EAP assistant directors and in their associated communities of practice. To demonstrate its applicability, the following sections will outline how the CHAMELEON framework has influenced equitable and adaptable pedagogy. Specifically, three pertinent areas will be presented: collaborative communication and the development of micro-teams, response to generative artificial intelligence (AI) models, and increased undergraduate and graduate EAP synergy. For each area, we will illustrate how key factors from the framework have been used to positively enhance and transform our teaching practice.

DOI: 10.4324/9781003503149-6

Table 4.1 CHAMELEON framework for adapting to new educational conditions (Davies and Davies, 2021)

	Factor	Explanation
C	Communicate	Communicate with colleagues and communities of practice regularly and openly. Collaborate and form teams to share and divide tasks and responsibilities where possible. Connect with your scholarly community as time allows (conferences, working groups, chats).
H	Humanise	Be kind, supportive, and responsive to learner and peer needs, interests, and capabilities and to your own! Try personalising teaching materials and class input to show you care and help reduce learner anxiety. Be patient and understanding of others' circumstances.
A	Assess	Assess the needs of your learners in this new educational context. Evaluate what has changed and how this will impact your learners. Assess your own capabilities operating under these new conditions – you must first survive before you can thrive. Assess the needs of your colleagues, offer expertise, and support where you can.
M	Motivate	Motivate students by delivering classes in a positive and dynamic way that inspires learners to take part. Develop tasks that appeal to various learning preferences and provide opportunities for autonomous learning. Motivate yourself and your team through regularly checking in with peers and developing a community of practice.
E	Engage	Actively encourage student engagement with your course and their wider interests where possible to promote a shared sense of community. Enable students to metacognitively reflect on their learning and progress to set regular learning goals. Where possible, facilitate group work and peer support, and utilise different feedback methods (peer review, voice and video feedback) to promote academic and peer engagement and a sense of connectedness.
L	Localise	Strongly consider the contextual norms and expectations of the local teaching environment. Familiarise yourself with restrictions that students, colleagues, or you may face if geographically dispersed, and ensure online tools and resources are appropriate and available to all who need them.
E	Evolve	As internal and external, personal and professional needs and circumstances change, ensure to plan for flexibility, allowing for evolving needs. Scaling back may be necessary.
O	(be) Open	Be open to new ideas; trial new tools and techniques. Use change as a learning and development process for teachers and students.
N	Negotiate	Regularly consult and discuss with learners and peers about their changing needs and expectations while studying and working in a new environment. Ensure course workloads are manageable for both you and your students, and be willing to adapt if necessary. Reevaluate priorities.

Transformations of EAP Practice: Development of EAP Micro-teams

One of the key takeaways from our collective responses to the COVID-19 pandemic was the benefit and importance of regular *communication* and collegial support from both a professional and personal perspective. For example, Shah (2012) recommends that peers talk, share, and collaborate to promote faculty wellbeing. Therefore, we have sought to enhance such collaborative communication post-pandemic. To do this, the larger undergraduate EAP teaching team of 17, despite all teaching the same courses, has been divided into four smaller micro-teams who meet weekly to provide support and increase efficiency by dividing tasks and responsibilities. Similarly, the smaller graduate teaching team of eight also meet weekly to develop curriculum and discuss any ongoing issues. This continuation of practice provides a clear example of how the CHAMELEON framework has had a positive long-term transformative impact.

Following the reflections presented by L. Davies *et al.* (2020a), the creation of micro-teams was initially intended to ensure faculty unable to return to China due to COVID-19 did not feel isolated, were able to be active members of the community, and could contribute to course development. However, continuing this practice has proved highly *motivating* for colleagues, and such regular communication has allowed teaching teams to *evolve* and remain *open* to change based on colleagues' and students' changing needs. As COVID-19 naturally resulted in higher faculty turnover, this practice has provided an important channel of support for new colleagues who may not feel comfortable speaking up in monthly whole-team meetings or even larger departmental meetings. Furthermore, in an attempt to *humanise* and show care, support, and kindness to colleagues, such micro-teams allow workloads to be shared and tasks distributed, meaning that targeted support is available when needed (for example, if colleagues are unwell).

One tangible example of how such regular collaborative communication has benefited the graduate EAP teaching team is in their *negotiated* permissions/restrictions on students' AI use. Despite working with students from different graduate programme disciplines, the EAP teaching team work towards largely the same curriculum (Davies, 2023; Davies *et al.*, 2022). As such, decisions regarding curriculum, assessment, and materials are made collaboratively during weekly curriculum development meetings. Following the responses to generative AI outlined in more detail following, the graduate EAP teaching team discuss and agree upon which AI functions will be permitted and restricted for each of the three major assignments after taking into consideration students' changing needs. Such decisions are clearly *communicated* to students, which creates equity amongst all graduate students as they all have the same opportunity to use AI tools within the same permission parameters. Avoiding a course policy and instead working on an assignment-by-assignment basis also allows us to select permissions and restrictions that best fit the desired learning outcomes of each assignment. It also allows the team to remain *open* and *evolve* as AI technologies change and results from new AI research projects are analysed. Ultimately, without the space and time the CHAMELEON framework facilitated for regular and *open* collaborative *communication* between colleagues, this approach would not be possible.

Responses to Generative Artificial Intelligence Models

Just as the higher education (HE) sector was recovering from the COVID-19 pandemic, a second major disruption was caused by the rapid emergence and development of generative AI deep learning models such as OpenAI's GPT (Generative Pretrained Transformer). As noted by Yan (2023), such tools have had a significant impact on academic writing due to their ability to understand and generate human-like text. Such models, despite their potential for increased student interaction, language accuracy, feedback, and creativity, have raised significant concerns regarding academic integrity (Dawson, 2020) and students' reduced academic writing skills (Dwivedi *et al.* 2023). Such a trend has far-reaching implications for the whole HE sector but is particularly relevant for those working in EAP contexts. Consequently, this has once again required our discipline to adapt to new educational conditions, providing an ideal opportunity to use the CHAMELEON framework to support change in a context beyond COVID-19. We will now share specific insights as to how the framework has been used to adapt equitably to the rapid increase in generative AI technology.

Regular and open *communication* is a key feature of the CHAMELEON framework, and this has been essential in our response to generative AI. For example, as policy on this matter was unclear and undeveloped, a departmental working group was established to devise and disseminate an EAP-related AI policy prior to the start of term. This created a community of practice (Wenger, 2010) of colleagues who shared a professional interest in AI and were willing to work towards the same goal for the benefit of the department. Such colleagues have continued to support one another as will be further outlined subsequently. Furthermore, in order to remain *open* and to *evolve*, it was clearly communicated to colleagues and students that the policy was just a starting point and will be regularly updated as we learn more about generative AI's capabilities.

Despite the obvious threats to academic integrity (Dawson, 2020; Dwivedi *et al.*, 2023), it is important to respond in a *humanistic* way. Rather than prohibiting the use of AI for students' academic submissions, rendering many assessment strategies invalid, we adopted a caring and supportive approach as opposed to a punitive one. For example, to *motivate* and *engage* both learners and faculty, we embedded AI tools into our curriculum and teaching pedagogy and work with students at undergraduate and graduate level. Students are encouraged and supported to interact with and, importantly, critique AI tools for functions such as sourcing literature, summarizing abstracts, comparing research papers, compiling reference lists, and paraphrasing text. Nguyen *et al.*'s (2024) research that showed increased interaction with AI tools can lead to increased academic writing performance, which would appear to support our approach.

Linking to the previously mentioned *open* and *humanistic* approach, we do not assume that students intend to cheat. Instead, to *assess* students' motivations for using AI and where it may be most appropriate to reduce their cognitive load (Dawson, 2020), members of the AI CoP have received funding to conduct a collaborative research project involving all undergraduate and graduate students at our university. Initially, a top-down approach to AI policy development was essential due to the urgency during the summer vacation. However, as the situation *evolves*, this bottom-up research project will be influential in better understanding learners' needs. The results will be used to develop more *motivating* and *engaging* AI-related class tasks and policies and demonstrate a consultative *negotiated* approach where students' voices are heard. We have also provided external expertise in the area by organising a guest lecture for the university community discussing new guiding principles from the Australian HE regulator (TESQA, 2023) that we intend to *localise*. Both internal and external *communication* is key. To that end, we have shared our pedagogical approaches to generative AI and preliminary research findings with our university community and through several external conference presentations.

Finally, as GPT is not (readily) available to mainland Chinese users, this creates a major inequity for our learners when compared to their international peers in the workplace. As such, in order to *localise* our response, and protect our users' data, university leadership invited members of our AI policy working group to participate in a trial of an internal university GPT tool, which has since been adopted. This internal interface and associated university guidelines also helped further *humanise* the transition and simplify the process for faculty and students who were not familiar with GPT access or functionality.

Increased Undergraduate and Graduate EAP Synergy

Using the framework beyond COVID-19 and learning from previous successful implementations has subsequently led to increased synergy between undergraduate and graduate EAP teaching teams. Several key examples of how the framework has opened up the space to facilitate such synergy to benefit the department as a whole will now be discussed briefly.

In response to the emergence of generative AI and in an attempt to encourage students to acknowledge and appropriately source any uses of AI within their academic submissions, the undergraduate EAP teaching team developed AI assignment cover sheets and shared this approach with graduate EAP colleagues. This simple sharing of artifacts between teams sparked further discussion and collaborative development of the documents. They were redesigned to be more *engaging* and to promote metacognitive reflection by following Bloxham and Campbell's (2010) research that found interactive feedback cover sheets can encourage students to think more carefully about their writing. Specifically, the newly designed cover sheets explicitly *communicated* which AI functions were permitted or restricted, requiring students to state which tools and functions had been used and to briefly explain how or whether they were helpful. A further function of the cover sheets supports our *open* and adaptable approach to AI within EAP. For example, when students acknowledge use of AI tools that faculty are unfamiliar with, our own knowledge and expertise in the area grows as we can then source and use such tools.

For such synergy to flourish regular *communication* and sharing of ideas and materials must be reciprocal. As such, the updated AI cover sheets were reshared with the undergraduate EAP team to further adapt for their context/course and were presented to and shared with the wider university community for use or adaptation. As mentioned previously, our approach to embedding AI within EAP pedagogy follows Nguyen *et al.* (2024) and the Australian Tertiary Education Quality and Standards' (2023) guiding principles for assessment reform for the age of artificial intelligence. Specifically, we maintain that learners should be encouraged to work *with* AI and that assessments should emphasise appropriate, authentic *engagement with* AI. To this end, the graduate EAP teaching team developed a series of *engaging* and *motivating* class task worksheets for several AI functions, scaffolding students' ability to use and interact with the university's *local* GPT tool via prompt engineering, questioning, and critical discussion. As discussed previously, such tasks were shared with undergraduate EAP colleagues initially and then with the wider university community and beyond via conference presentations. To conclude, the importance of not only developing but then sharing materials related to current AI technology is essential to ensure equity for students, ensuring that they are all exposed to and given the opportunity to appropriately use such powerful tools.

Our final example of increased synergy between EAP levels relates to external CoP *communications* that were shared across teams, leading to increased *engagement* with and *openness* to trial new EAP feedback approaches. Following a conference presentation, UK-based researchers at another university reached out to collaborate on a cross-institutional dialogic feedback project. After a successful trial of the new dialogic approach within postgraduate EAP courses, it was subsequently shared with and adopted at undergraduate level, thus increasing equity and giving students across both levels the opportunity to benefit from this new feedback approach. This project has led to an additional CoP with co-researchers at several universities around the world, sparking interest from many colleagues. The aim is to investigate whether a live dialogic feedback approach can improve feedback efficiency and efficacy. If so, we intend to *negotiate* with colleagues and learners to implement this approach more widely to potentially reduce the heavy EAP grading and feedback workload currently faced while simultaneously increasing student feedback literacy (Carless and Boud, 2018) and teacher feedback literacy (Carless and Winstone, 2023).

Conclusion

The CHAMELEON framework was initially designed to support colleagues adapting to the new educational conditions caused by COVID-19. The framework's guiding principles are to show compassion and empathy to foster equitable and adaptable conditions for teaching and learning. This chapter has outlined the longevity of the framework and the transformative impact it has had on the EAP practices at a Sino–foreign university. Specifically, the examples of collaborative communication across micro-teams, generative AI, and increased cross-level synergy have been used to demonstrate how the CHAMELEON framework has informed lasting enhancements using equitable and adaptable pedagogy. It is anticipated that the lessons learned and practices shared within this chapter can be of practical use to HE educators engaged in support across a wide range of HE disciplines, focused on writing, assessment, pedagogy, and generative AI. In particular, the chapter demonstrates how the key principles outlined in the framework offer guidance when responding to significant and unprecedented educational change.

References

Bloxham, S. and Campbell, L. (2010) 'Generating dialogue in assessment feedback: exploring the use of interactive cover sheets'. *Assessment & Evaluation in Higher Education*, 35(3), pp. 291–300. https://doi.org/10.1080/02602931003650045

Carless, D. and Boud, D. (2018) 'The development of student feedback literacy: enabling uptake of feedback'. *Assessment and Evaluation in Higher Education*, 43(8), pp. 1315–1325. https://doi.org/10.1080/02602938.2018.1463354

Carless, D. and Winstone, N. (2023) 'Teacher feedback literacy and its interplay with student feedback literacy'. *Teaching in Higher Education*, 28(1), pp. 150–163. https://doi.org/10.1080/13562517.2020.1782372

Davies, J. A. (2023) 'Understanding and crossing disciplinary boundaries: Pedagogical insights from an interdisciplinary graduate-level EAP course sequence', in L. Buckingham, J. Dong, & F. Jiang (eds.), *Interdisciplinary practices in academia: writing, teaching and assessment*. Taylor & Francis Ltd.

Davies, J. A., Carter, T. and Campbell, M. (2022) 'Building confidence, performative habits, and audience awareness through a graduate-level academic communication course', in M. Siczek (ed.), *Pedagogical innovations in oral academic communication*, University of Michigan Press.

Davies, J. A., Davies, L. J., Conlon, B. M., Emmerson, J., Hainsworth, H. and McDonough, H. G. (2020a) 'Responding to COVID-19 in EAP contexts: a comparison of courses at four Sino-foreign universities', *International Journal of TESOL Studies*, 2(2), pp. 32–51. https://doi.org/10.46451/ijts.2020.09.04

Davies, L. J., Chiocca, E. S., Hiller, K. E., Campbell, M. and Naghib, S. (2020b) 'Transformative learning in times of global crisis: reflections on collaborative working practice', *CEA Critic*, 82(3), pp. 218–226. https://doi.org/10.1353/cea.2020.0036

Davies, L. and Davies, J. (2021) 'The CHAMELEON approach to change: adapting to new educational conditions'. *Journal of Learning Development in Higher Education*, 22. https://doi.org/10.47408/jldhe.vi22.836

Dawson, P. (2020) *Defending assessment security in a digital world: preventing e-cheating and supporting academic integrity in higher education.* Routledge.

Dwivedi, Y. K., Kshetri, N., Hughes, L., Slade, E. L., Jeyaraj, A., Kar, A. K., Baabdullah, A. M., Koohang, A., Raghavan, V., Ahuja, M., Albanna, H., Albashrawi, M. A., Al-Busaidi, A. S., Balakrishnan, J., Barlette, Y., Basu, S., Bose, I., Brooks, L., Buhalis, D., Carter, L. and Wright, R. (2023) 'Opinion paper: "So what if ChatGPT wrote it?" Multidisciplinary perspectives on opportunities, challenges and implications of generative conversational AI for research, practice and policy'. *International Journal of Information Management*, 71, 102642. https://doi.org/10.1016/j.ijinfomgt.2023.102642

Nguyen, A., Hong, Y., Dang, B. and Huang, X. (2024) 'Human-AI collaboration patterns in AI-assisted academic writing'. *Studies in Higher Education*, pp. 1–18. https://doi.org/10.1080/03075079.2024.2323593

Shah, M. (2012) 'The importance and benefits of teacher collegiality in schools: a literature review', *Procedia-Social and Behavioral Sciences* 46, pp. 1242–1246. https://www.sciencedirect.com/science/article/pii/S1877042812014115

Tertiary Education Quality and Standards (TESQA). (2023) Assessment reform for the age of artificial intelligence. https://www.teqsa.gov.au/guides-resources/resources/corporate-publications/assessment-reform-age-artificial-intelligence

Wenger, E. (2010) 'Communities of practice and social learning systems: the career of a concept', in Blackmore, C. (ed.), *Social learning systems and communities of practice* (pp. 179–198). Berlin: Springer Verlag and the Open University.

Yan, D. (2023) 'Impact of ChatGPT on learners in a L2 writing practicum: An exploratory investigation.' *Education and Information Technologies* 28, pp. 13943–13967. https://doi.org/10.1007/s10639-023-11742-4

Chapter 5

What Designing Accessible Academic Development Provision Taught Me About Compassionate Education

Sean Afnán Morrissey

Background

An ongoing commitment to professional development is vital for all those who teach and/or support learning in higher education (HE). The Professional Standards Framework (AdvanceHE, 2023) defines 'enhancing one's practice through continuing professional development (CPD)' as an essential activity that underpins effective teaching practice. However, meeting this commitment can be challenging for staff. This is so due to the complex pressures faced by all academic professionals, particularly teaching staff, which are being amplified by changes in the wider context. Academics are 'busier and working faster than ever' (Berg and Seeber, 2016). In addition to 'sobering' trends in staff/student ratios (Hanna, 2023), the sector as a whole is experiencing increased job insecurity (Spence, 2019) with many teachers finding themselves on zero hours and hourly paid contracts.

Over the last few years, moreover, several factors have combined to further disrupt the policy and practice contexts in which learning and teaching take place. This 'tsunami' of drivers includes COVID-19, climate change, an unstable global political context and – more recently – developments in generative AI. It is widely accepted that the scale and nature of these changes has significantly impacted the wellbeing of staff in higher education (Dougall *et al.*, 2021; Wray and Kinman, 2021), which is perhaps unsurprising given the lessons we, as a sector, learned during the 2020 'pivot online'.

Staff Wellbeing and CPD

Due to the abrupt nature of the pandemic, many academic staff and professional services teams were unprepared for an emergency 'forced transition' to fully online teaching and assessment (Erlam *et al.*, 2021). From a professional skills perspective, the challenge of developing the many competencies and capabilities associated with the digitalisation of teaching and learning, while managing increased workloads and time demands and dealing with the challenges of the pandemic personally, was immense. It is no coincidence that in a

2021 survey of 1,200 HE employees across 92 UK universities, half said they had experienced chronic emotional exhaustion, worry, stress, and poor mental health during the academic year 2020/21 (Bassa, 2022). A 2022 survey conducted by University and College Union indicated that two-thirds of university staff were considering leaving the sector (Bassa, 2022).

Seeking help during this protracted period of disruption – both in terms of direct support for wellbeing or with the development of the new skills and competencies that are required to adapt practice to new, emerging realities – was not seen as a practical option by many due to 'heavy workloads' and 'inflexible schedules' (Wray and Kinman, 2021). Research at Strathclyde (Savage and Morrissey, 2021) used Williams and Penman's (2011, p. 212) 'exhaustion funnel' to theorise the link between 'professional burnout' and an overall decline in the engagement of teaching staff in professional and academic development activities during the period 2020–2022.

Ongoing Disruption

While many believed COVID-19 might create a space for the international academic community to pause, reflect, and prepare for a 'new normal' (Scherman *et al.*, 2023), the reality, for many, has been one of ongoing uncertainty and constant change. The 2020 pivot was followed equally abruptly by a period of hybrid teaching and learning, a return to campus, successive rounds of industrial action, a marking boycott, and the emergence from relative obscurity of generative artificial intelligence (gen-AI). According to Rudolph *et al.* (2023), 'developments in the chatbot space have been accelerating at breakneck speed'. Carrigan (2023) argues that 'even a singular system like ChatGPT encompasses a dizzying array of use cases for academics, students and administrators that are still in the process of being discovered. Its underlying capacities are expanding at a seemingly faster rate than universities are able to cope with'.

For many higher education teachers, whose wellbeing is already impacted by years of disruption within and outside of academia, the challenge of negotiating complex questions related to gen-AI, while investing time and effort into developing new skills and competencies and ultimately pivot practice is, once again, monumental. The task of supporting colleagues to navigate these challenges, while simultaneously managing the pressures of additional related work, has transformed academic development at the University of Strathclyde.

Compassionate Academic Development

At Strathclyde, a research-intensive university, academic development is conceived of as a set of interrelated processes that seek to enhance academics' professionalism (Evans, 2023). Influenced by the work of Lave and Wenger

(1991), we value informal discussions, mentoring, professional dialogues, and practice sharing, alongside formal academic credit-bearing provision and pathways to professional recognition. Since our initial response to COVID-19 – detailed in Morrissey and Savage (2021) – the work of the Academic Development team has been driven by two key questions: How to ensure timely, equitable access to CPD amidst an overall decline in staff engagement in academic development provision? And how to address serious concerns about staff wellbeing?

In seeking answers to these questions, we were drawn to work on *compassionate pedagogy*. 'Compassion', in this context, refers to the capacity to notice suffering in others and the desire to act to prevent or alleviate suffering (Hamilton and Petty, 2023). Beyond simply recognising one's duty to 'see things from the students' perspective' (Waghid, 2014, cited in Ahern, 2019), compassion here implies the motivation to act to the benefit of others. Hao (2011, p. 92) describes critical compassionate pedagogy as a framework that involves reflexivity on the part of educators and active opposition to institutional and classroom practices that disadvantage particular groups (Hao, 2011). Working within and around the same pressurised circumstances as the colleagues we supported through academic development provision, we also drew on our own lived experience as university employees to inform decision-making and practice.

In late 2020 our team undertook a staff survey and series of focus groups that highlighted three key themes of relevance to the provision of CPD. These were *time*, with many articulating perceived tensions between investing in one's own development and 'getting things done'; *access*, with flexible, agile working impacting the ability of colleagues to engage with CPD – for example, as one focus-group participant put it, 'if I'm designing a set of online activities in the middle of the night, that's when I need the training'; and *isolation*, with many feeling disconnected from work, colleagues, and their students.

In the years that followed, our team has attempted to address some of the ways in which crisis – manifest in chronic emotional exhaustion, worry, stress, and poor mental health – was impacting HE teachers and their students individually and collectively through compassionate academic development. Our provision is now underpinned by principles of accessibility and acceptance. These principles are expressed through a commitment to provide staff with regular, co-created, and flexible CPD opportunities. Formal development activities are supplemented by informal spaces that respond to staff's need for socialisation and wellbeing support.

Transformative Practices

The pillars of our approach to compassionate academic development are as follows.

Pillar 1 – MicroCPD

In response to a key finding from our 2020 staff survey that many were – as one participant put it – 'tired, burned out, and beginning to neglect my own professional development', a weekly programme of micro-CPD was initiated in April 2021. Strathclyde's micro-CPD programme was inspired by a programme developed at the University of Birmingham's Higher Education Futures Institute (HEFi). Our programme offers staff weekly access to bite-sized learning opportunities, delivered by email, that address a wide range of development needs in learning and teaching. The rationale is that no matter how busy one is, everyone can find 3–5 minutes in their working week to develop one's practice.

The programme has become a hallmark of academic development at Strathclyde. Having relied on the agency of two academic developers initially, the programme now receives the support of a digital development assistant. Topics are proposed and often authored by colleagues across Strathclyde's four faculties and professional services directorates including the Library, Disability and Wellbeing Services, Education Enhancement, and the Centre for Sustainable Development. More recently, a handful of students have contributed to the programme.

In 2022, a provisional evaluation of the programme involving 94 participants gave us strong indications that micro-CPD is positively impacting colleagues' practice: 89% of respondents felt they had been introduced to new information, approaches, and/or ideas while 76% of respondents had made, or intended to make, changes to their teaching as a result of their engagement with the micro-CPD programme. A colleague who responded to the survey commented that the programme has 'increased my knowledge base and made me think about how I deliver learning'. Others reported that 'the topics have given me a new perspective or a new way of thinking about things, which has been very useful considering the very small time investment it takes to read the Micro CPD'.

Pillar 2 – Peer Support Networks

'Belonging' is a key component of a compassionate education. Staff peer support networks (SPSNs) have become a defining feature of the Strathclyde approach to staff development and to embedding wellbeing across our portfolio, providing spaces for staff to connect, share, and support one another. Since the pandemic, our approach has been to grow our programme of networks and support them to flourish.

Currently a number of networks are thriving at Strathclyde including a Pedagogy and Publication Network; a Playful Learning Network, our Leadership in Learning and Teaching Network; the Programme Leaders Network; and the Advance HE Senior Fellows Network. SPSNs are also in place to support staff completing experiential applications for Advance HE

Fellowships through writing retreats, formal opportunities for mentoring, feedback on drafts, and access to relevant resources.

A study of SPSNs at Strathclyde and another Scottish HE institution (Savage et al., 2022) concluded that the networks promote positivity, encouragement, and resilience and operate in an atmosphere of acceptance.[1] Most research participants agreed or strongly agreed with the statement 'participating in staff peer support networks has a positive impact on my wellbeing'.

Focus group participants commented:

> Being part of these networks, knowing that people appreciate what I do, has helped me to feel connected … it gives me motivation to be brave and bold in my practice.
>
> At various stages throughout the last few years, I've felt quite isolated. These networks … have been a real source of affirmation that what I am doing with my students is working and is making a difference.

In addition to facilitating SPSNs, the Academic Development team has used a toolkit developed with funding from Advance HE to actively support colleagues across the Faculties and Professional Services directorates to establish networks for climate ambassadors, learning technologists, and videographers and an inclusive assessment community of practice.

Pillar 3 – Responsive Academic Development

A key component of our response to the COVID-19 pandemic was the roll-out of an inclusive approach to blended and online learning design (BOLD). BOLD is a holistic, evidence-based curriculum design approach accompanied by a series of related workshops and resources that can be accessed by individuals or programme teams synchronously or asynchronously. By the end of the 2019/20 academic year, an army of 350 or so early adopters were able, through these efforts, to confidently design high-quality online curricula. Yet the popularity of the workshops contrasted starkly with CPD engagement across the rest of our academic development portfolio, particularly our non-credit-bearing and Advance HE Fellowship programmes.

Thinking compassionately in this context required us to adopt a humble posture of learning. Rather than asking 'why are our numbers down?', instead we began to explore several questions designed to help us connect with our staff: are the programmes meeting our needs or our staff's needs? Do they strive for equity and fairness? Are our programmes done to staff or with staff? And does our portfolio of development provision recognise stressors and mitigate against them?

Subsequent consultations with staff, primarily those staff attending our SPSNs, highlighted widespread pragmatism in decision-making around access to CPD,

> During that first lockdown all anybody cared about was 'the pivot'. With the greatest of respect to you guys in the Academic Development Team, I just didn't have time to think about my Senior Fellowship application or attend, like, a Module Evaluation Drop-in Session.

The findings of these consultations led to a substantive, strategic realignment of our programme to better meet the needs of staff and institutional and sector-wide priorities.

One example of this has been a new development sub-theme on education for sustainable development (ESD). Consciousness of the importance of ESD rose significantly during 2021 when Glasgow hosted COP-26. It has since been adopted as a key educational priority within the university's 2025–2030 strategic plan. Another has been the development of a gen-AI knowledge hub, a series of workshops and resources that can be accessed synchronously and asynchronously. A cross-directorate team at Strathclyde recently launched a Gen-AI Expert Working Group (Learning, Teaching, Assessment) Digest. Workshops that address staff wellbeing (which has direct implications for student motivation, wellbeing, and success), such as 'Mindfulness in Learning and Teaching', 'Using Your Calendar to Claw Back Time', 'Setting Boundaries', and 'Wu Wei Teaching', are offered through the year.

Pillar 4 – Online/Hybrid the New Norm

Strathclyde's People Strategy encourages 'agile working', which generally sees academic staff working from home two days a week (pro rata). The strategy also calls for 'Meeting Free Fridays', which support staff to enjoy a 'work free weekend' as far as possible. These initiatives are sector-leading and have been recognised through various national awards and commendations. However, flexible, agile, and home-working practices practically impact the ways in which staff access on-campus training and academic development at Strathclyde.

In 2022, recognising the opportunity to increase access to our programmes, the academic development team undertook a change project in consultation with colleagues in HR, the University's Disability and Wellbeing Service, the Equality and Diversity Team, Strategic Committees, and the Associate Principal (Social Inclusion). This led us to affirm our commitment to offering an accessible and inclusive service that meets the needs of all staff. Here, our 'daily commitment to compassion' involved striving to ensure that our mode of delivery did not place additional barriers in the way of colleagues who desired access to CPD.

We concluded that online training with the option of hybrid delivery best supported the university's commitment to hybrid working. It is more accessible and inclusive, and in most cases, accessible online/hybrid delivery is further enhanced through inclusive practices such as accessible materials being provided in advance and accessible session design to account for a range of needs with shorter sessions, regular breaks, subtitles and transcripts enabled, and recordings that are made available for participants after the fact. The team also recently identified an EDI contact and set up a dedicated mailbox for confidential EDI-related enquiries.

Conclusion

Our approach to delivering learning and teaching development activities at Strathclyde has been informed by principles of compassionate pedagogy and our own lived experiences of working in a university during a period of radical change. It has involved working alongside staff and other stakeholders to identify development priorities, as well as barriers, stressors, and steps to mitigate them. We have sought to identify practical strategies for supporting the 'whole selves' of academic professionals and develop staff resilience at times and in spaces that work for them while continuing to enhance academic professionalism across the institution. These are underpinned by a commitment to offering regular, responsive, and flexible CPD opportunities, informed by the voices of our colleagues.

Taken in isolation, changes such as the adoption of hybrid delivery, the development of a micro-CPD programme, staff peer support networks, and a commitment to wellbeing are not necessarily revolutionary. However, a compassionate approach to education is not only about *what* we do by also *why* and *how* we do it. Compassion is an inner quality that, as Sam Ahern (2019) puts it, requires 'innate motivation' on the part of 'compassionate pedagogues' rather than merely 'a formal framework or policy requirement'. Thinking and acting with compassion is the moral duty of all those with responsibility for supporting staff and students through the current period of change, disruption, and uncertainty in HE, regardless of the disciplinary or institutional contexts in which they operate.

Note

1 The peer support network study discussed in this chapter received ethical approval and the evaluation quotes are shared with permission from the respective sources. The author wishes to express gratitude to the participants who graciously allowed the use of these quotes to provide illustrative examples and insights related to the discussion.

References

AdvanceHE. (2023). Fellowship. Available at: https://www.advance-he.ac.uk/fellowship#psf2023

Ahern, S. (2019). 'Compassionate pedagogy in practice'. *LSE Blog*, 3 July. Available at https://blogs.ucl.ac.uk/digital-education/2019/07/03/compassionate-pedagogy-in-practice/ (Accessed 22 April 2024).

Bassa, B. (2022). 'Pouring from an empty cup: poor university staff wellbeing is an impossible ground for high quality teaching'. *Advance HE Blog*. Available at https://www.advance-he.ac.uk/news-and-views/pouring-empty-cup-poor-university-staff-wellbeing-impossible-ground-high-quality (Accessed 20 February 2024).

Berg, M. and Seeber, B. K. (2016). *The slow professor: challenging the culture of speed in the academy*. Toronto, ON: University of Toronto Press.

Carrigan, M. (2023). 'Are universities too slow to cope with generative AI?' *LSE Blog*, 14 April. Available at: https://blogs.lse.ac.uk/impactofsocialsciences/2023/04/27/are-universities-to-slow-to-cope-with-generative-ai/ (Accessed 20 February 2024).

Dougall, I., Weick, M. and Vasiljevic, M. (2021). 'Social class and wellbeing among staff and students in higher education settings: mapping the problem and exploring underlying mechanisms'. *Journal of Applied Social Psychology*, 51, pp. 965–986.

Erlam, G. D., Garrett, N., Gasteiger, N., Lau, K., Hoare, K., Agarwal S. and Haxell, A. (2021). 'What really matters: experiences of emergency remote teaching in university teaching and learning during the COVID-19 pandemic', *Frontiers in Education*, 6, p. 639842.

Evans, L. (2023). 'What is academic development? Contributing a frontier-extending conceptual analysis to the field's epistemic development', *Oxford Review of Education*. https://doi.org/10.1080/03054985.2023.2236932

Hamilton, L. G. and Petty, S. (2023). 'Compassionate pedagogy for neurodiversity in higher education: a conceptual analysis', *Educational Psychology*, 14, p. 1093290.

Hanna, L. (2023). 'We need to talk about staff retention in the sector', *HEPI Blog*, 28 November. Available at https://www.hepi.ac.uk/2023/11/28/we-need-to-talk-about-staff-retention-in-the-sector/ (Accessed 16 February 2024).

Hao, R. N. (2011). 'Critical compassionate pedagogy and the teacher's role in first-generation student success', *New Directions for Teaching and Learning*, 127, pp. 91–98.

Lave, J. and Wenger, E. (1991). *'Situated learning: Legitimate peripheral participation'*. Cambridge University Press. https://doi.org/10.1017/CBO9780511815355

Morrissey, S. A. and Savage, K. (2021). 'Reconceptualising learning and etaching staff development at Strathclyde: supplementing formal provision with informal spaces', *Journal of Learning Development in Higher Education*. Special Issue 22: Compendium of Innovative Practice, pp. 1–6.

Rudolph, J., Tan, S. and Tan, S. (2023). 'War of the chatbots: Bard, Bing Chat, ChatGPT, Ernie and beyond: the new AI gold rush and its impact on higher education', *Ed-Tech Reviews*, 6(1), pp. 364–389.

Savage, K. and Morrissey, S. (2021). 'Keeping well, teaching well: supporting staff wellbeing', *Journal of Learning Development in Higher Education*, 22, pp. 1–6.

Savage, K., Willison, D. and Morrissey, S. A. (2022). 'Strathclyde leadership in learning and teaching network: a reflective case study', QAA Scotland Programme Leader's Cluster. Available at: https://pure.strath.ac.uk/ws/portalfiles/portal/135364507/Savage_etal_QAA_2022_Strathclyde_leadership_in_learning_and_teaching_network_a_reflective_case_study.pdf (Accessed 15 August 2024).

Scherman, R., Misca G., Walker, D. and Pagè, G. (2023). 'Editorial: COVID-19 and beyond: From (forced) remote teaching and learning to "the new normal" in higher education', *Frontiers in Education*, 8, 8–11.

Spence, C. (2019). 'Judgement' versus "metrics" in higher education management'. *Higher Education*, 77, pp. 761–775.

Williams, M. G. and Penman, D. (2011). *Mindfulness: the eight-week meditation programme for a frantic world*. London: Hachette Digital.

Wray, S. and Kinman, G. (2021). 'Supporting staff wellbeing in higher education', *Education Support*. Available at https://www.educationsupport.org.uk/media/x4jdvxpl/es-supporting-staff-wellbeing-in-he-report.pdf (Accessed 16 February 2024).

Chapter 6

What a Compassionate Approach to Transforming Practice Taught Me About Driving Institutional Change

Martin Compton

Introduction

This chapter is built on my experiences as a teacher trainer and academic developer across a range of settings, including schools, further education institutions, and various universities in the UK. The rapid transitions necessitated by COVID-19 meant that these experiences were particularly focused on managing sudden, widespread changes in educational practices and environments.

The consequent articulation of a framework for compassionate academic development is explored below. Two significant subsequent inflection points for the universities I worked at in respect to HyFlex teaching modalities[1] and, most recently, the implications of generative AI show the transferability of the framework's application. During COVID-19 I deliberately centred a successful compassionate approach to the pandemic response work despite significant pressure from the senior leadership team to take a very different approach. This decision reflects my professional manner and values that have long shaped the way I work, as well as my understanding of the challenges and tensions common in this type of role. The broad principles of my compassionate approach are rooted in fundamental values but evolved to something more coherent during the pandemic. As a result, a framework began to emerge that supports sustained impact at scale and is also transferable. It challenges conventional tech-focused training approaches by deemphasising technology and prioritising compassion and human elements. The approach was borne from the practice of academic development during a time of crisis, trauma, and significant change but has applicability across any educational context.

I have always seen academic development as a privilege due to the position it affords. In multiple roles across further education (FE) and higher education (HE) I have benefitted from a central position that enabled me to engage with a wide array of disciplines and individuals from across all faculties. A critical aspect of this role concerns facilitating support for and development of colleagues. It is rewarding work, especially when the impact on new educators can be visible and swift. Of course, the role can also come with significant challenges. We often need to navigate fractious tensions between the needs of individuals or departments and those of senior leaders and policymakers who are themselves pressured by the impact of crude but nevertheless popular evaluation metrics applied at institution and programme levels. Perhaps the most challenging aspect for me is the commonly cited phenomenon where the inclusive and developmental values that underpin my broader approach are challenged by policy and practice that errs towards interventionist academic development practices (Brew, 2011) such as targeting teams with low National Student Survey scores for 'remedial' work. The values underpinning my work, encapsulated by 'reflective practitioner' and 'interpretive hermeneutic' orientations to academic development (Land, 2001, p. 6), often jolt against the technicist and managerial roles ascribed to academic development teams. We thereby risk being 'misperceived' by faculty colleagues as instrumental agents of compliance rather than committed educationalists engaged in nuanced 'cultural work' (Stensaker, 2018, p. 277).

COVID-19 magnified the inherent advantages of the academic development role while simultaneously expanding its reach in unprecedented ways. The crisis centred academic developers deeply within the institutional response, highlighting our importance in navigating this abrupt transition, which led to incredible demands on our time and an increased amount of emotional labour (Trotter *et al.*, 2022; McSweeney and Moore, 2023). The pandemic amplified the positive aspects of our work, and it underscored our pivotal contribution to the university's broader response. However, it also aggravated the tensions and necessitated articulation of a rationalised approach that countered much of the instinctive thinking from both senior leaders and the academic colleagues we are committed to supporting (Compton and Gilmour, 2022). The following framework grew out of a teaching-focused UK university context, but it has since seen equal applicability in two research-intensive university contexts and has much wider application.

A Framework for Compassionate Academic Development

The compassionate approach to development is rooted in a values-driven philosophy and reflects a broader, long-standing commitment to staff development and teaching that is not defined by finding fault, monitoring, or 'gate-keeping' but is supportive instead. In my role as an academic developer, I have long endeavoured to shift emphases where they exist from monitoring competence to providing space and scaffolding for colleagues to evolve and grow as educators (Compton, 2019). At its core, this compassionate framework embodies principles of empathy, inclusion, and practical engagement, mirroring inclusive values and learner-centredness. Such inclusive values sit at the heart of many, if not all, institutional teaching and learning policies but are too often subsumed by external drivers and local or institutional cultural factors. In the post-lockdown period as universities struggled to navigate the liminal space between emergency remote teaching and the drive to return to campus and get back to 'normal', I articulated the factors I found to be the most impactful (Compton, 2021), and these are explored in more depth in the following sections.

Respond to Immediate Needs

It may seem self-evident to tailor activities and events to directly address the most pressing needs or concerns of the audience. However, when those needs are affective and misalign with assumptions that prioritise cognitive demands, more immediate needs can be masked, particularly when people are operating in crisis mode. When the realities of the lockdowns became apparent, my institution swiftly rolled out Microsoft Teams as the primary mechanism for synchronous communication. Few people in the institution had experience using this tool, and the assumption was that the key priority should be on technical upskilling. While this was essential, the reality was that this was also a time of huge anxiety and trauma. Colleagues needed time to connect and space to surface their emotional needs.

For my team, our paramount concern became facilitating this time and space for emotional connection and expression. We recognised that addressing these affective needs was crucial for our colleagues' wellbeing and ability to adapt to the new circumstances. This approach of prioritising emotional needs over immediate technical skills challenged the conventional wisdom of crisis management in education. Transferring this approach to times of less evident crisis requires us to deliberately challenge our own concerns about optimising time. It necessitates dedicating time to connect and surface the rationale for this approach with any group of colleagues or students. This focus on affective needs and human connection pushes against the transactional norms that have become prevalent in massified higher education (Denial, 2020).

Prioritise Compassion, Inclusion, and Equity

As a first-generation and mature graduate with fifteen years of experience working on widening access to HE programmes, I developed an approach to teaching that prioritises humanising the experiences of my students. This approach underpins the compassionate framework, which emphasises empathy, kindness, and inclusivity in all interactions and teaching practices. Adults returning to education after a long absence often have traumatic educational histories. It would be illogical and self-defeating to replicate the formal norms of conventional schooling. While the necessity of this approach may not be immediately visible in all contexts, taking an equity-centred approach can help realise preexisting policy goals. It also acknowledges the extent to which trauma impacts one's ability to study within more conventional academic cultures (Venet, 2023). This recognition aligns with hooks' (1994) assertion that intellectual endeavour should not be separated from our emotional selves.

The compassionate framework does not dictate a particular teaching style, but it does advocate for the elevation of certain values in all educational interactions. In respect to the collective, traumatic experiences of the pandemic, I found my approach to teaching needed to recognise the value of, and advocate for, empathy, kindness, and inclusivity more than ever. These values became catalysts for transforming educational practices during this challenging time (Denial, 2020).

By connecting my personal experience and teaching philosophy to the compassionate framework, I've found a theoretical underpinning that supports and validates my approach. This framework provides a structure for understanding why humanising education and prioritising affective needs are crucial, especially in times of crisis or when working with students who may have had negative educational experiences in the past.

Model Practical Application

In my experience across a range of development programmes in several universities and multiple PGCE programmes in FE colleges, I have witnessed (and no doubt contributed to) a tension between the credibility-affirming theoretical content and the practical needs of participants. We design curricula as a way of establishing credibility through expertise (Little and Green, 2022) because credibility is essential to enable those in academic development to effect change. Practical expertise does not often inhabit the same space as theoretical or research focused expertise, but it is invariably practical applications of theory and research that are sought and highly valued by participants. While rooting practice in evidence is key, starting with theory alone can often feel disconnected from the immediate needs of practitioners. To bridge this gap, in all my resources and workshops I strive to model approaches that provide a template for the practical integration of methodologies or technologies. This modelling directly links to the most common anxieties and challenges faced by the colleagues I work with. As I write, I am reminded of a day long workshop I attended many moons ago titled 'Teaching without talking' where the facilitator barely paused for breath all day.

Moving Beyond Procedural Training

A critical, yet often overlooked, element in academic development is the creation of space for emotions and anxieties to surface. This approach is fundamental to genuine engagement and sustained change. By allowing time for participants to express and process their feelings, we establish a foundation for meaningful dialogue and transformation. Employing a 'click here, click there' approach has never been a way of working I recommend (Compton and Almpanis, 2018) as it limits, almost by design, opportunities for dialogue. Resisting the pressure to scale technical training of that nature meant embedding procedural fundamentals in synchronous sessions and asynchronous materials but also, as already highlighted, centring acknowledgement of anxiety and the human implications of the crisis. Not only that, existing and increasingly familiar compliance and induction training is often engaged with cynically or strategically (Antoniadou and Quinlan, 2022) and is easily conflated in the minds of colleagues with change initiatives. Surfacing an acknowledgement of such issues and contrasting in form and style is a key element to engender engagement. Finally, and most importantly, granting space for ongoing dialogue (both asynchronous and synchronous) is critical to enabling sustained change in practice and in signifying a shift from unidirectional to multidirectional engagement.

Transparency in Approach and Rationale

Being open about chosen pedagogical methods and clearly explaining the reasons behind them fosters understanding of their effectiveness and helps challenge strongly held beliefs and expectations. This transparency is crucial in building trust and engagement. Critical in my discussions about challenging perceptions is to preempt them and find space to surface expectations. I often hear colleagues say that their students do not respond well to nontraditional approaches, eschewing 'active learning' and insisting lectures suit them best. Whilst it is easy to hear those voices, they should not trump decades of pedagogic research or the voices of those less inclined to speak their minds. Above all, sharing rationales for approaches taken is key to fostering understanding and buy-in.

During the pandemic, I applied this transparent approach to online learning. While many worried about students not turning on their video cameras, in synchronous online workshops I clearly stated that I sought interaction and connection by text, audio, or video, acknowledging that some people would not have the bandwidth (technically or emotionally) to connect by video but expressing that seeing at least one or two people really helped me as a facilitator. This openness about my needs and understanding of the situation created an environment of mutual respect and flexibility. Countless colleagues reported that adopting this same approach transformed their synchronous sessions. Managing expectations in this way can be further buttressed by including a rationalised approach in presession materials, ensuring learners come to sessions with a clear understanding of the pedagogical approach and its benefits.

Encourage Reflective and Meta-Level Thinking

Related to the need for transparency outlined above, it is important to integrate opportunities for participants to reflect on and discuss the methods and techniques used, particularly in relation to their own practice. Making this deliberate and an essential part of my session design enables me to challenge what might be tacit; surfacing otherwise hidden aspects of the way I design teaching and learning. Disciplinary expertise and pedagogic conventions within disciplines cannot be swept away (even if that was desirable) in a workshop, but by stepping aside from the content, making space for reflection, and signalling the modelling embedded within a session, these techniques elevate recognition of how different approaches could work in different contexts. Questions like: 'How did I get people to contribute on mic?' and 'What strategy did I use to …?' remain staples of workshops I facilitate. These questions change the focus from what is being taught/learnt to how it is being conveyed/processed.

Create Safe and Flexible Learning Environments

In many ways, this final component is a consequence of putting 1–6 in place. It is about the deliberate design of learning spaces that are accommodating, safe, and flexible. It necessitates offering various ways to participate and interact while respecting personal preferences. This may include sensitivity when organising and managing both physical and digital environments. For instance, during every synchronous event, colleagues are provided with options to raise questions or offer comments either anonymously or openly. Additionally, channels are made available for participants to contribute their thoughts after the events have concluded. This approach ensures that all participants have multiple avenues for participation, catering to different comfort levels and ways in which they engage with the materials and activities.

Transferability and Transformation

The opportunity to reflect (Compton, 2021) really helped me to pull together and articulate this compassionate framework and to exemplify its key aspects. Events and work across two other institutions has subsequently shown me with clarity the transferability of this approach. I will outline this briefly in relation to two pivotal phenomena: HyFlex teaching and generative AI.

In my approach to supporting HyFlex teaching and the transition back to campus, I was once again guided by the necessity to centre compassion as the shift back was fraught with anxieties for both staff and students. In contrast to the online interactions, anxieties about this approach to teaching, which connoted significant cognitive labour and technical expertise, were more visceral. I made a conscious effort to assuage these fears by centring them and allowing space to surface them while drawing on both lockdown experiences and a wider approach to staff development work. I recognised the importance of operating at a metacognitive level and deliberately designed support to parallel the approach taken during the online teaching phase. Again, I deliberately avoided a prescriptive 'training' approach and instead fostered an environment that illuminated theory through practice, encouraging a more reflective and thoughtful adaptation to another 'new normal'. Every live session was itself in

HyFlex mode, facilitated by me and a designated 'co-pilot' colleague who took on predefined responsibilities such as online chat monitoring and/or discussion or group activity facilitation. Team teaching was a deliberate challenge to the ways in which teaching had previously been resourced, but it provided a critical point of leverage for colleagues who were concerned about undertaking teaching in this way. Instead of transactional 'how to' training, they experienced allyship, advocacy, and a pooling of resources to support pedagogic arguments and assuage wellbeing anxieties.

Moving to the challenges presented by the proliferation of generative AI, I like many in similar development roles have found myself confronting a landscape saturated with noise – some of it cautious and measured, but much of it driven by anxiety and panic. The rapid evolution of AI presents a multifaceted challenge with profound yet uncertain implications for education. For most, AI is uncharted territory, with limited direct experience in utilising these emergent tools for teaching, assessing, and defining appropriate use. Recognising the complexity and contention within this landscape is crucial. A one-size-fits-all training or workshop approach clearly would not suffice, particularly in a large, multifaculty institution. To effect change at scale, space for expressing anxieties needs to be made. In this way, competing perspectives can be surfaced, and colleagues can then become engaged in varied ways, recognising that there is diversity of experience and they might learn according to their need and current comfort level. I have facilitated workshops that not only raised awareness and provided reassurance but also offered experimental, hands-on opportunities for staff to express personal anxieties and discuss complex implications, with space to ask any questions in a range of formats. In addition, I led on the production of an accessible, AI literacy-focused online course, aiming to inspire critical engagement with generative AI in HE across the sector. Designed not just for academic and professional services staff but also for students, this resource has seen global engagement, and much of the positive feedback received focuses on the empathetic, nontechnical, and applicable design. The content, featuring contributions from a cross-section of the university, emphasises dialogue and debate, particularly in applying generative AI creatively but responsibly in teaching, learning and assessment activities.

In lockdown and in the transition back to campus period my personal facilitation of workshops reached an unprecedented number of colleagues in a short time frame, but it was evident that there was a need to reach wider and deeper. Differentiating the 'offer' from the academic development team from 'compliance' training to an overtly compassionate approach has been critical. The framework presented here is itself a practical manifestation of that approach in the pivot online, as we adapted to HyFlex teaching and as we respond to the implications of AI advances. In all three examples, technical upskilling was essential, yet the deeper issue was more than just a skills deficit. Institutional change necessitated space for critical engagement and genuine agency as implications unfolded and continue to unfold. Institutional transformation requires creating space for critical thinking and genuine agency as we navigate evolving implications. To achieve this, we need to give equal weight or priority to dialogue over technical skills development. This approach allows educators to express their anxieties, which, if left unaddressed, can significantly hinder progress and development. Varied and sustained points of contact are more effective than approaches that privilege efficiency.

Perhaps most importantly, I have seen that compassion is essential – not just during obvious crises but as a constant approach. This means showing understanding for diverse ways of being, acknowledging personal challenges, and recognising the risks of excessive workload and burnout. By embodying this compassionate approach, we create an environment where colleagues can truly connect, collaborate, and grow. This, in turn, means academic developers can better forge a credible reputation as allies and champions of the colleagues we are tasked with developing. By being overtly compassionate in our approach we acknowledge the reality of the working lives of our colleagues and are able to signal pedagogic practices that challenge some of the more negative manifestations of teaching in massified institutions by modelling and showcasing the value of compassionate strategies.

Whether institutional change is imperative, reactive, and transitional or an element of a permanent shift in practices, a compassionate approach is about showing care and valuing the affective at least in equal measure to skills and knowledge development. It challenges the primacy given to content coverage in teaching and in the ways we do development work and is a provocation to reflect on current pedagogies and the impact they have on both staff and students.

Note

1 Often also called 'hybrid' teaching, *HyFlex* here refers to simultaneous in-person and online teaching that became common during the transition from COVID-19 lockdowns and the return to on-campus teaching as default.

References

Antoniadou, M. & Quinlan, K. M. (2022) 'Holding true or caving in? Academics' values, emotions, and behaviors in response to higher education reforms'. *Higher Education Policy*, 35, 522–541. https://doi.org/10.1057/s41307-021-00225-1

Brew, A. (2011) 'Foreword', pp. 127–132, in L. Stefani (ed.), *Evaluating the effectiveness of academic development: principles and practice*. Oxon: Routledge.

Compton, M. (2019) 'Purpose, process and perception: rethinking PGCert HE teaching observations'. *Educational Developments*, 20(3), 18–21.

Compton, M. (2021) 'Sell them what they want; give them what they need: managing tensions and competing expectations in live online lecturer development workshops'. *Journal of Learning Development in Higher Education*, 22. https://doi.org/10.47408/jldhe.vi22.695

Compton, M. & Almpanis, T. (2018) 'One size doesn't fit all: rethinking approaches to continuing professional development in technology-enhanced learning'. *Compass: Journal of Learning and Teaching*, 11(1), 10. https://doi.org/10.21100/compass.v11i1.708

Compton, M. & Gilmour, A. (2022) 'Walking the tightrope: enabling mindset and practice transformation at scale through compassionate academic development'. *International Journal for Academic Development*, 27(2), 203–206. https://doi.org/10.1080/1360144X.2022.2066674

Denial, C. (2020) 'A pedagogy of kindness', in J. Stommel, C. Friend, and S. Morris (eds.), *Critical digital pedagogy: a collection* (pp. 212–218). Washington: Hybrid Pedagogy Inc.

hooks, b. (1994) *Teaching to transgress: education as the practice of freedom*. New York: Routledge.

Land, R. (2001) 'Agency, context and change in academic development', *International Journal for Academic Development*, 6(1), 4–20. https://doi.org/10.1080/13601440110033715

Little, D. & Green, D. A. (2022) 'Credibility in educational development: trustworthiness, expertise, and identification'. *Higher Education Research & Development*, 41(3), 804–819. https://doi.org/10.1080/07294360.2020.1871325

McSweeney, J. & Moore, R. E. (2023) 'Understanding the impact of a pandemic on the work of educational developers'. *International Journal for Academic Development*. https://doi.org/10.1080/1360144X.2023.2297412

Stensaker, B. (2018) 'Academic development as cultural work: responding to the organizational complexity of modern higher education institutions'. *International Journal for Academic Development*, 23(4), 274–285. https://doi.org/10.1080/1360144X.2017.1366322

Trotter, H., Huang, C.-W. and Czerniewicz, L. (2022) 'Seeking equity, agility, and sustainability in the provision of emergency remote teaching during the COVID-19 pandemic: a center for teaching and learning takes an expanded role'. *Higher Learning Research Communication*, 12(0), 1–24. https://doi.org/10.18870/hlrc.v12i0.1280

Venet, A. S. (2023) *Equity-centered trauma-informed education*. New York: Routledge.

Section 2

Building Connections to Transform Practice in Higher Education

Alicja Syska

It is a truth pretty universally acknowledged that to build connections with others, one must have opportunities to meet them in a climate that allows those connections to be built. The 2020 pivot to remote teaching and learning denied us many of these opportunities, instead demanding that we either surrender to the limitations of the less familiar online environment or use our creativity to urgently construct new and innovative building blocks for forming those connections. The chapters in this section show us not only how the authors unleashed their creativity to build meaningful links and relationships in the emergency of the pandemic but also how their innovations and interventions ultimately improved their ability to facilitate and sustain more durable and more compelling connections with and for their colleagues, their students, and even themselves in the long term.

We all know of the value of connections, but what does it mean to build them, and how do we create the right climate for them to form? Indeed, what do we mean by 'connections' in the first place? Connections involve forming bonds with others in a way that makes those interacting feel seen and heard, respected and supported. They do not have to be strong or deep; indeed, even the most basic attempts at connecting can make a difference to how all those involved feel (Sandstrom and Dunn, 2014). Connections can be relations, bridges, networks, or partnerships, developed either through complex and deliberate exchanges or via chance conversations and encounters. We can make efforts to connect with others as much as we might feel the need to connect with ourselves. What forming connections requires is an appreciation of their value and readiness to open up, as well as a good dose of empathy and vulnerability, courage and freedom, much pride in the effort, and little to no prejudice.

What emerges from the discussions our readers are about to partake in is that building connections in higher education (HE) can happen on many different levels and take a range of shapes and features. Connections can be forged by opening a genuine dialogue and reducing power distances; by creating informal and creative spaces for staff and students to interact freely; by rethinking assessment and feedback; and by embracing new modes of scholarly communication while also welcoming, perhaps surprisingly, the vulnerability and authenticity that come with establishing radically new, often more authentic and more inclusive, connections. These can be either spontaneous in the way they occur or deliberately planned, designed, and tested with the intention of increasing the sense of belonging in an environment that does not lend itself to belonging naturally.

None of these ideas and provocations might be new to the well-informed and experienced reader. After all, Freire's seminal work (1970) critiquing what he called the 'banking model' of education that reinforces traditional hierarchies and power structures in HE has already allowed us to appreciate the value of engaging students and colleagues in a constant dialogue that is meaningful to their daily existence and values. bell hooks's (1994) elaboration on these 'transgressive' practices has reinforced our commitment to bringing our true selves into the classroom and staying actively involved with students in the learning process. Both thinkers' emphasis on education as a practice of freedom transpires across this section's chapters as their authors freely reimagine HE in more open, collaborative ways.

This freedom to reimagine cuts across multiple layers of the HE landscape. We can see references to assessment and its potential to not just measure learning but actively contribute to it (Boud, 2000) as well as examples of advocating for practices that position students as active agents in the feedback process, not just its passive recipients (Carless and Boud, 2018). We can appreciate nods to the concept of academic and social integration that brings a sense of belonging (Tinto, 1997), particularly relevant in the context of the post-pandemic university, which is still suffering from disrupted traditional modes of academic and social integration and requires new strategies to foster belonging and community (Syska and Pritchard, 2023). The long-standing calls for a fundamental reorientation of education around the concept of care (Goldstein, 1999; Noddings, 2012) have been just as influential, especially in promoting a more holistic view of education that goes beyond cognitive development to include emotional and moral dimensions. This human, embodied aspect of education, even as we increasingly rely on technology to facilitate teaching and learning, is equally pertinent to the discussion of new modes of scholarly communication, especially new forms of publication, collaboration, and dissemination of knowledge (Weller, 2011). Indeed, networked practices are critical to establishing novel ways of measuring academic impact that go beyond traditional citation counts, including measures of online engagement (Veletsianos, 2016). The creation of these new opportunities for connection and learning among our authors is facilitated by the relative ease with which boundaries can be crossed in Third Space work (Whitchurch, 2012) that flows between traditional academic and professional roles and structures.

The way our authors have brought all these ideas into their practice is what makes their chapters so compelling and valuable as an educational resource. In the opening piece, Carina Buckley and Rebecca Cohen (Chapter 7) bring our attention to the unheralded virtues of relational working and positioning Third Space teams as 'network hubs' to connect different parts of the university community. The chapter illuminates how informal online tea breaks during the pandemic allowed for more authentic, free-flowing conversations, which in turn affected the quality of interactions among team members, underscoring the extent to which the world of work is shaped by meaningful and reciprocal relationships. Much research had been done on this issue before 2020 by Blustein (see 2011, among other publications) but the post-pandemic educational landscape for the first time provided a context that allowed us to experience the artificial splits between work and relationships more acutely and to truly appreciate the kind of isolation that relational working has always argued against.

Adding another layer to Chapter 7's focus on team building and de-siloing working relationships, Chapter 8 expands the same concern onto the larger community. Lee Fallin's reflection on how the pandemic ironically allowed him to move beyond his immediate team and become part of the cross-institutional research and scholarship scene has the power to provoke important questions around what it takes to be connected and to what extent our own agency limits or expands our networks. Fallin's story is an apt illustration of the interplay between the 'protean' and 'boundaryless' careers (Briscoe *et al.*, 2006) that characterise many Third Space values-driven and self-directed professionals in HE. Such careers often depend on one's ability to proactively develop relationships beyond organisational boundaries and build networks of opportunity that lead to new communities of practice and new modes of connection and collaboration.

Chapters 9 and 10 shift the conversation to the challenge of connecting with students and may have been just as well written as a dialogue. They both highlight the importance of creating more dialogic, collaborative learning spaces that reduce the traditional power distance between educators and students. In Chapter 9, Lynn Gribble and Janis Wardrop reveal the ways they used learning management system tools to provide personalised support and nudges to students, while Lucinda Becker in Chapter 10 explores how shared online reading spaces can give students more ownership over their learning. These innovations suggest new approaches to assessment that foster more connection, including using learning analytics to provide more personalised, timely feedback and promoting collaborative reading practices as a form of formative assessment.

The final two chapters discuss podcasting as a disruptive tool that can be used to build connections not only with students but also – perhaps more surprisingly – with our professional selves. Although the authors of both pieces deal with the same mode of expression, they differ in their approaches to podcasting and its affordances. While Julia Bohlmann and Micky Ross in Chapter 11 use their dialogue as an opportunity to promote more accessible and inclusive teaching practices, Alicja Syska in Chapter 12 draws out a series of revelations about the insights podcasting can give into writing. What connects them is that for both chapters' authors, podcasting is a liberatory practice that reveals the potential of unconventional and disruptive pedagogies to create more conversational, accessible, and authentic modes of academic discourse. As such, the authors frame podcasting as part of reimagining academic communication in more open, dialogic ways and rethinking our relationship with more traditional modes of expression, such as writing. In revealing how podcasting requires embracing imperfection and authenticity, the closing chapter effectively connects back to the opening one that encourages us to use informal spaces as a way of showing more of our authentic selves, thus closing the conceptual loop of this book section.

What is clear throughout is that, altogether, the chapters unveil the hidden community of practice (Wenger, 1998) we are all part of in HE but do not always recognise or draw on. Wenger's concept reconsidered allows us to see the post-pandemic university as a more distributed network of learning communities, connected through both physical and virtual spaces, and relying on these connections to sustain meaningful worlds of work. The practices described in the chapters – from informal gatherings to collaborative podcasts – can be seen as ways of weaving these distributed communities together. At the same time, the emphasis on authenticity, vulnerability, and care across these discussions suggests that technology alone is not enough to build productive connections. Rather, it's about using a range of means in intentional ways to foster genuine human connection and a sense of shared purpose in learning and scholarship. As such, their approaches can be seen as the epitome of Parker Palmer's (2007) legendary advocacy of teaching integrity: 'Good teachers possess a capacity for connectedness. They are able to weave a complex web of connections among themselves, their subjects, and their students so that students can learn to weave a world for themselves.'

This shift towards more critical, dialogic pedagogies to foster connections is not without challenges, however. It requires educators to relinquish some traditional forms of authority and be open to uncertainty, self-doubt, and potential risks. It also raises questions about how to balance this approach with institutional requirements and expectations. Nevertheless, the examples in this section suggest that taking these risks, embracing vulnerability and uncertainty, and working through self-doubt brings rewards beyond the immediate context of the practitioner and their classroom or team. What all the authors in the chapters that follow collectively paint is a picture of a university that has the potential to be more open, more collaborative, and more attuned to the relational aspects of teaching and learning. While challenges remain, the practices shared here bring a lot of promise.

References

Blustein, D. L. (2011). A relational theory of working. *Journal of Vocational Behavior*, 79(1), 1–17. https://doi.org/10.1016/j.jvb.2010.10.004

Boud, D. (2000). Sustainable assessment: rethinking assessment for the learning society. *Studies in Continuing Education*, 22(2), 151–167.

Briscoe, J. P., Hall, D. T. and DeMuth, R. L. F. (2006). Protean and boundaryless careers: an empirical exploration. *Journal of Vocational Behavior*, 69(1), 30–47. https://doi.org/10.1016/j.jvb.2005.09.003

Carless, D. and Boud, D. (2018). The development of student feedback literacy: enabling uptake of feedback. *Assessment & Evaluation in Higher Education*, 43(8), 1315–1325. https://doi.org/10.1080/02602938.2018.1463354

Freire, P. (2000 [1970]). *Pedagogy of the oppressed* (30th anniversary ed.). New York and London: Continuum.

Goldstein, L. S. (1999). The relational zone: the role of caring relationships in the co-construction of mind. *American Educational Research Journal*, 36(3), 647–673. https://doi.org/10.3102/00028312036003647

hooks, b. (1994). *Teaching to transgress: education as the practice of freedom*. Routledge. https://doi.org/10.4324/9780203700280

Noddings, N. (2012). The caring relation in teaching. *Oxford Review of Education*, 38(6), 771–781. https://doi.org/10.1080/03054985.2012.745047

Palmer, P. J. (2007). *The courage to teach: exploring the inner landscape of a teacher's life*. San Francisco: Jossey-Bass.

Sandstrom, G. M. and Dunn, E. W. (2014). Is efficiency overrated? Minimal social interactions lead to belonging and positive affect. *Social Psychological and Personality Science*, 5(4), 437–442. https://doi.org/10.1177/1948550613502990

Syska, A. and Pritchard, C. (2023). Blended learning as a site of struggle: a critical realist analysis of students' perceptions of blended learning and its impact on their sense of belonging, *Journal of University Teaching & Learning Practice*, 20(6). https://doi.org/10.53761/1.20.6.15

Tinto, V. (1997). Classrooms as communities: exploring the educational character of student persistence. *The Journal of Higher Education*, 68(6), 599–623. https://doi.org/10.1080/00221546.1997.11779003

Veletsianos, G. (2016). *Social media in academia: networked scholars*. New York: Routledge.

Weller, M. (2011). *The digital scholar: how technology is transforming scholarly practice*. London: Bloomsbury Academic.

Wenger, E. (1998). *Communities of practice: learning, meaning, and identity*. Cambridge: Cambridge University Press.

Whitchurch, C. (2012). *Reconstructing Identities in higher education: the rise of 'Third Space' professionals*. London: Routledge.

Chapter 7

What an Online Tea Break Taught Us About Collaboration

Carina Buckley and Rebecca Cohen

Introduction

Serendipitous conversations – those 'that lead to unexpected yet fortunate discoveries' – can be a valuable and significant feature of 'knowledge work' (Olshannikova *et al.*, 2020, p.1). Knowledge is often initially shared within 'small, tightly knit, local networks' or 'microcultures', with the concomitant risk that it remains there (Taylor *et al.*, 2022, p. 279). However, when serendipitous, knowledge-producing conversations occur between members of different microcultures as part of a wider network, those people who straddle disparate groups may find themselves 'at higher risk of having good ideas' (Burt, 2004, p. 349). Conversations under these conditions provide fertile grounds for innovation and creativity and can be a valuable dimension of university working life (Brown *et al.*, 2014). This chapter explores the microculture of a Learning Design team working within and across third space and their capacity to network with other institutional microcultures. In doing so, it asks how microcultures allow for the effective sharing of knowledge through informal conversation. The lockdown of March 2020 put out of bounds the corridors and kitchens where these conversations would often take place and risked fracturing the team's established, dynamic interplay of the personal and professional into a reductive, work-focused dimension. To counter this, we established a channel through which conversations and ideas could continue to organically flow in the guise of a daily online tea break. Formalised through a calendar invitation but otherwise informal, this free-wheeling, agenda-less, liminal space served as a point of connection, a replacement for the 'social glue' (Churchill, 2010) through which our group was bound and held in relation, and where serendipity could find us again.

Upon our return to campus, we realised that something had fundamentally changed in the way we approached our work and each other. Our working practices had undergone a transformation, provoked by the authenticity and fluidity we had found in the online environment to become inherently collaborative. In this chapter, we outline and explore how the ethos of valuing people over output has influenced our expectations around collaboration,

DOI: 10.4324/9781003503149-10

grounding it in problem-solving, personal authenticity, and connection. This ethos and the approach it shaped has transformed the wider Education Office and the way we work with colleagues across the university by helping us to question what it means to collaborate and how we keep sight of each other in an increasingly output-oriented environment.

Structureless Structures and Open Networks

The Learning Design team at Solent University is part of the Education Office and is responsible for advising and mentoring course teams on enhancing and innovating their learning and teaching (L&T) practices. The ways of working we learned during lockdown and developed through our online tea break directly govern how we now support and interact with colleagues. Following our return to campus, the daily tea break, so vital during lockdown, has ceased to exist. Instead, the strong personal connections it facilitated between us have been carried into scheduled 30-minute team meetings: online on Mondays and Thursdays, and in person on Tuesdays and Wednesdays, accounting for working patterns, creating space for serendipity. While this amount of contact between team members might seem unnecessary, even excessive, these regular connection points serve a vital purpose beyond updating colleagues on work in progress. Within the structure of the meetings lies a structureless, person-centred approach (Coghlan, 1993) that has transformed the operational tasks of planning and reporting into curiosity-driven problem-solving and positive inquiry: the foundation of our collaborative dynamics. In practice, this involves cultivating a sense of ownership over projects, with team members empowered to make decisions and find support in their implementation according to the paradigms of the various local course-based contexts they encounter. The person, as opposed to what they produce, is paramount, and therefore their knowledge, identity, and positionality are central to the collaborative process.

The discipline, as 'the central organising vehicle in higher education' (Jawitz, 2009, p. 242), acts as a site for the formation and negotiation of members' professional identity through its contextualisation as a community of practice. Learning design is part of third space in that, while often positioned within professional services, it is nevertheless based on expertise in teaching and learning (Whitchurch, 2008; White and White, 2016). It is not institutionally configured as a discipline (defined here as an ontological framework for 'organising learning' and 'the systematic production of new knowledge' [Barrow, 2023, p. 640]), but it does act as an organising concept for team members: a shared space where knowledge is exchanged, individuals participate, and agency is exercised. The team therefore also becomes an arena for the shaping of professional identity, and the team meeting, in how it effectively nurtures a 'disciplinary tradition' (Roxå and Mårtensson, 2009, p. 548) that informs and is informed by the sociocultural contexts in which the individual team members work, is the location for the social engagement that underpins this activity.

Most importantly, social engagement is not confined to our team's meeting space or the people within it. Just as the team itself is a 'microculture' (Roxå and Mårtensson, 2011), so, too, do the individual members belong to and straddle other microcultures across the university as part of a boundless set of institutional networks engaging in 'significant conversations' (Roxå and Mårtensson, 2009, p. 555) with academic colleagues. Significant conversations are characterised as being trustful, private, and intellectually intriguing, and as such tend to be of a less restricted nature than more formal, minuted conversations might allow. Their significance lies in the way they are focussed on exploring and constructing the conversational partners' understanding of learning and teaching, and then incorporating subsequent adjustments to that understanding into their practice (Roxå and Mårtensson, 2009). This mode of working for the learning designers is exemplified by each of us having 'our' academics with whom we work, often based on connections extended from previous collaborations. These relationships have been accelerated and strengthened by extending our team meeting model to all those we encounter throughout the university community.

The information, ideas, and experiences encountered in these wider microcultures – the engineering course team or two adult nursing colleagues, for example – are then brought back to the learning design team, where they may spark inspiration for their repurposing in conversations and development with the marketing course leader, perhaps, or the apprenticeships provision. In this way, each learning designer acts as a network node, or 'hub' (Taylor et al., 2022, p. 279), through which knowledge can readily flow from microculture to microculture, indirectly connecting the wider university community and thereby overcoming the risks of silo thinking while providing space for serendipitous discovery. In their role as 'knowledge catalysts' (Fields et al., 2019, p. 218), the learning designers add to institutional knowledge and facilitate change by supporting the cross-pollination of ideas between colleagues who do not know each other and would be unlikely to work together spontaneously. Through our dual roles as individual 'hubs' and members of a (team-based) community of practice, we actively work to make connections, share learning and resources, and facilitate integration of our networks (Taylor et al., 2022). The key strength of the hub approach is therefore the synergy of connection enabled by the microculture of the freely structured meetings. Together, we can achieve more than would be possible as individuals.

The Person in the Centre

Any collaboration thrives on personal relationships, and its success is dependent on the quality of those relationships. In recognising that we are working in a deliberately person-centred way with our conversational partners and networks, we are able to draw upon this model to transform the team meeting – and then our significant conversations – into a collaborative, identity-building sphere. Taking a person-centred approach to the team and our broader networks means adopting the 'congruence' or authenticity, the 'unconditional positive regard', and the 'empathetic understanding' originally identified by Rogers (Coghlan, 1993, p. 12) as being central to effective facilitation. These are mediated by five key factors at play in this process (Clouston and Whitcombe, 2005, pp. 267–269), all of which speak to the way in which we use our meeting time together.

The *environment* encompasses both the physical place, whether that is the campus or individual working spaces at home, and the organisational norms and expectations that regulate how the setting is used. Our team meeting was established with and is guided by expectations around attendance, attention, and contribution. Absence is exceptional and attendance is active; all members are expected to contribute to the discussions that emerge, whether that contribution is in the form of conversation during the meeting or the sharing of ideas or resources in the chat afterward. No one dominates, and no one is forced to speak for the sake of it. As a result, *group dynamics* are central. While we have a strong team identity, within that we recognise individuality through understanding our different strengths, preferences, experiences, responsibilities, and constraints. These elements of ourselves are brought to light through free-wheeling conversation, initiated with an open invitation to raise any issues and then lightly facilitated to ensure all members of the team have the opportunity to learn from each other.

To do so effectively, clear *communication* is vital. Team members bring conversations, issues, and problems back from their networks for exploration and review, trusting in each other's abilities to offer possible solutions that will meet wider needs. The team meeting also holds the prospect of disseminating outcomes from one microculture to another, connecting colleagues and strengthening collective institutional knowledge. In their *readiness* to learn, team members take on the role of facilitator, able to recognise and value the contributions of others and support academic colleagues' ongoing sense of ownership over their learning and teaching materials. The final component of our collaborative approach is therefore *congruence*, in that we exercise flexibility in modifying tested and established methods or interventions for new contexts and specific needs, including those we have not encountered before. Our priority – within the team and when collaborating with colleagues – is to focus on the individual, acknowledging where they are in that moment, and responding with empathy and support.

Case Study: A Learning Designer as an Active Hub

During one team meeting, a colleague inquired about a new teaching group I (RC) had recently taken on. At the time, I was in the process of designing and producing learning content for each week, which involved engaging students with the virtual learning environment (VLE) and guiding them through the foundational knowledge, key concepts, and theoretical frameworks within the subject's professional context. My main aim was to find a way to engage students in the site, with the content and each other, as engagement levels were currently less than ideal. As I began explaining my approach, the conversation organically evolved into a collaborative brainstorming session. Without the constraints of a formal agenda, I had the freedom to bring this issue to the meeting, where space was made for us to bounce thoughts off one another. We all come from different disciplines, so when we share our perspectives we are drawing from our diverse experiences and expertise. The organic nature of our discussion allows us to explore alternative viewpoints and consider unconventional solutions. This, in turn, facilitates more effective collaboration and problem-solving, as we all feel empowered to contribute our unique insights without anxiety. We question our assumptions, challenge each other's thinking, and collectively arrive at innovative strategies for enhancing the online learning experience. For instance, when discussing ways to engage students, I suggested adding a forum as a potential tool. My colleague, who had successfully used forums before, modelled how they could be effectively utilised from the introductory session onwards. She walked me through examples of well-designed forum activities, helping me situate this approach within my own learning context, and not only convincing me but giving me the confidence that it could work with these students.

Later, I had an opportunity to return the favour. My colleague brought a request to the team meeting from a conversational partner in business management to develop a workshop for staff who teach apprentices. The problem was that few staff had direct experience of teaching those apprentices, who are also returners to education and who have extensive professional knowledge but often little academic confidence. There were concerns that the apprentices' learning was not as scaffolded as it needed to be. With a background in film, I was familiar with the framework of the 'hero's journey' as a storytelling device (Campbell, 2008), and I suggested that this metaphor would help staff in visualising how their students progressed through their course, the types of obstacles they faced, and how these could be overcome. My colleague and I set up a shared file in our Teams space to gather ideas together, and the rest of the team also added to it over the next week until we had produced an adapted model and workshop outline. My colleague then presented the outline to her contact in business, who liked the metaphor so much she organised an afternoon for all apprenticeship staff to learn together through this workshop. Now, not only do all business colleagues have the same understanding of how to support their students, but they have also now formed a community of practice together.

Taking the Principles Further

Our person-centred approach to collaborative problem-solving is one of connection and serendipity. Its impact has been transformative for our team and for the Education Office as a whole, which has undergone a cultural shift as a result. We now model this collaborative ethos when working with course teams across the university, empowering colleagues to take ownership of their challenges and co-create solutions through positive, forward-facing dialogue. In embracing fluidity and uncertainty, we have cultivated a culture that values people over output and recognises the power of serendipitous conversations in fostering innovation and collective growth (Roth, 2021). Our team attitude is one of curiosity: We do not consider ourselves to be the solvers of other people's problems or those who answer their questions; rather, we come together in mutual inquiry so our colleagues feel empowered to solve their own problems. In prioritising the personal authenticity that emerges in the purposefully structured unstructured time to connect, we create an environment where trust and psychological safety thrive (Edmondson, 2018). Under these conditions, there is more room for serendipity to drop in.

The transformation in our practice lies in the strength of our networks and the social capital they nurture. Our Learning Design team is a community of practice in that we learn from each other through participation in conversations that are themselves transformational in their character and expression. The environment in which this transformation occurs rests on five foundational principles:

- Within the structure of the team, we keep our meetings open and unstructured so we can respond to emergent issues and give space for leaps of imagination and inspiration.
- We bring our whole selves to these meetings, acknowledging our positionality, and knowing we can share ideas without judgment.
- The meetings function as a hub through which knowledge from external sources can flow. The 'trusting relationships' (Fields *et al.*, 2019, p. 225) we build form the basis of the networks we have constructed, *one conversation at a time*, around the university.
- In our significant conversations we earn trust through mutual inquiry and take on the position of learners. Only by understanding the cultural norms we encounter can we facilitate effective and long-lasting change.
- Between us, we reach all departments – which means we *all* reach all departments and therefore have an impact on the learning and teaching culture of the university.

Above all, we embrace uncertainty – which feels less risky with the certainty of peer support and connection. It is too easy to focus on the aspects of our work that can be counted and ranked and make those our criteria for success, such as the number of staff we have met with or how many colleagues came to a workshop. We can measure the number of students an intervention reached; we can list the courses and departments we have directly worked with; we can even run reports on how many people – both staff and students – have accessed our online resources or watched our videos. But ultimately, these are not indicators of the true impact of successful collaboration. We have learned, thanks to our online tea break, that the value of human connection is uncountable but vital; that where we come from is central to where we are going; and that sometimes not having a structure can be the best structure of all.

References

Barrow, M. (2023) 'Ontological congruence, discipline and academic identity in university schools of nursing'. *Higher Education*, 85, pp. 637–650. https://doi.org/10.1007/s10734-022-00858-0

Brown, C., Efstratiou, C., Leontiadis, I., Quercia, D. and Mascolo, C. (2014) 'Tracking serendipitous interactions: How individual cultures shape the office'. In *Proceedings of the 17th ACM conference on Computer supported cooperative work & social computing*, pp. 1072–1081. https://doi.org/10.1145/2531602.2531641

Burt, R. S. (2004) 'Structural holes and good ideas'. *American Journal of Sociology*, 110(2), pp. 349–399, http://www.jstor.org/stable/10.1086/421787

Campbell, J. (2008) *The hero with a thousand faces* (3rd ed.) Princeton University Press.

Churchill, E. F. (2010) 'Introduction: social glue', in K. S. Willis, G. Roussos, K. Chorianopoulos and M. Struppek (eds.), *Shared encounters* (pp. 229–233). Dordrecht: Springer.

Clouston, T. J. and Whitcombe, S. W. (2005) 'An emerging person centred model for problem-based learning', *Journal of Further and Higher Education*, 29(3), pp. 265–275, https://doi.org/10.1080/03098770500166926

Coghlan, D. (1993) A person-centred approach to dealing with resistance to change. *Leadership & Organization Development Journal*, 14(4), pp. 10–14. https://doi.org/10.1108/01437739310039433

Edmondson, A. C. (2018) *The fearless organization: creating psychological safety in the workplace for learning, innovation, and growth*. John Wiley & Sons.

Fields, J., Kenny, N. A. and Mueller, R. A. (2019) 'Conceptualizing educational leadership in an academic development program', *International Journal for Academic Development*, 24(3), pp. 218–231. https://doi.org/10.1080/1360144X.2019.1570211

Jawitz, J. (2009) 'Academic identities and communities of practice in a professional discipline', *Teaching in Higher Education*, 14(3), pp. 241–251. https://doi.org/10.1080/13562510902898817

Olshannikova, E., Olsson, T., Huhtamäki, J., Paasovaara, S. and Kärkkäinen, H. (2020) 'From chance to serendipity: knowledge workers' experiences of serendipitous social encounters'. *Advances in Human–Computer Interaction*, 2020, pp. 1–18. https://doi.org/10.1155/2020/1827107

Roth, P. (2021) 'Why serendipitous informal knowledge sharing interactions are key to boundary spanning and creativity', *Work*, 72, pp. 1673–1687, https://doi.org/10.3233/WOR-211275

Roxå, T. and Mårtensson, K. (2009) 'Significant conversations and significant networks – exploring the backstage of the teaching arena', *Studies in Higher Education*, 34(5), pp. 547–559. https://doi.org/10.1080/03075070802597200

Roxå, T. and Mårtensson, K. (2011) *Understanding strong academic microcultures – An exploratory study*. Lund University. http://lup.lub.lu.se/search/ws/files/55148513/Microcultures_eversion.pdf (Accessed 28 October 2019).

Taylor, K. L., Kenny, N. A., Perrault, E. and Mueller, R. A. (2022) 'Building integrated networks to develop teaching and learning: the critical role of hubs', *International Journal for Academic Development*, 27(3), pp. 279–291. https://doi.org/10.1080/1360144X.2021.1899931

Whitchurch, C. (2008) 'Shifting identities and blurring boundaries: the emergence of third space professionals in UK higher education', *Higher Education Quarterly*, 62(4), pp. 377–396. https://doi.org/10.1111/j.1468-2273.2008.00387.x

White, S. and White, S. (2016) 'Learning designers in the 'third space': the socio-technical construction of MOOCs and their relationship to educator and learning designer roles in HE', *Journal of Interactive Media in Education*, 2016(1), pp. 1–12, http://doi.org/10.5334/jime.429

Chapter 8

What Active Engagement with My Community Taught Me About Driving Professional Scholarship

Lee Fallin

Professional Scholarship and Engagement as Transformative Practices

The need to continue education throughout the COVID-19 pandemic afforded new opportunities for professional scholarship, open publishing, and institutional collaboration to address the shared challenges of lockdown teaching, learning, and assessment. While collaboration has long been an established aspect of higher education (HE), the increasing marketisation of the sector in the United Kingdom (UK) combined with workload pressures has eroded such opportunities. Since 2012, UK governmental policy has explicitly led HE into a market-based environment requiring students to become significant investors in the cost of their education (Tomlinson, 2016). These changes have reframed the relationships between institutions and students, with a growing narrative of students as 'customers'. Moreover, these changes have impacted the relationship between universities and other HE providers as they became competitors (Palfreyman and Tapper, 2014). This 'academic capitalism' (McNay, 2022, p. 780) has been further driven by competitive measures for teaching, research, and knowledge exchange, each measured via their respective excellence frameworks. Universities now compete for students, funding, academic staff, research grants, and research publications (Hart and Rodgers, 2023). The competitiveness, however, is juxtaposed with cultural demands for open scholarship, shared practice, and institutional collaborations that characterise 'good' HE practices. In this competitive environment, open scholarship is both a duty to be equitable and also a risk as educators share the secret to success with both their peers and competitors.

The pandemic showed us it does not have to be like this.

In this chapter, I advocate pushing against these neoliberal trends, with a call for open engagement and scholarship within our professional communities. If we cast aside the pressure to compete and instead focus on how we can connect, collaborate, and learn from one another for the benefit of our wider practice, this will have a more positive impact on us and those we work with. Connection, collaboration, and shared learning were signatures of practice

DOI: 10.4324/9781003503149-11

within the COVID-19 pandemic, and these transformative opportunities for connection must continue to be nurtured. Although the HE sector in the UK has experienced a never-ending series of policy changes and increased financial pressures that reinforced competition between providers (McNay, 2022; Palfreyman and Tapper, 2014), the COVID-19 pandemic proved a significant turning point as a shared endeavour for the whole HE sector at a global scale (Gamage, 2023; Hodges *et al.*, 2020; Sezen-Barrie *et al.*, 2023). As a complex, nonlinear, and unique issue within the context of HE, the COVID-19 pandemic presented a 'wicked problem' to the entire sector (Sezen-Barrie *et al.*, 2023), and the solution to such problems must be *collective*. In times of challenge, scholarly and learned societies possess much potential to advocate for connection, collaboration, and open scholarship – but this must be driven by respective members.

The pandemic presented a transformative opportunity for all areas of my practice. Like many other educators, the realities of the lockdowns and campus closures gave me time to think, time to collaborate with peers, and time to share my practice through scholarship. The 'Compendium of Innovative Practice' published by the *Journal of Learning Development in Higher Education* (*JLDHE*) in 2021 was a concrete example of pandemic-based open scholarship, with real stories of challenge and success shared for the benefit of everyone (*Journal of Learning Development in Higher Education*, 2021). My comprehensive analysis (Fallin, 2023) of all 102 articles published in the collection identified five key themes: emergency remote teaching, course design for the long term, pedagogy and technology support, reflective practice and evaluation, and collaboration and shared practice. These final two themes strongly highlight the value of sharing practice and engaging in continuous evaluation to address collective challenges in HE. While disruptive to education, the pandemic also effectively disrupted the neoliberal machinery within HE as the challenge of moving teaching online presented a collective problem for the entire sector. A community of practice is a group of people who share a common problem or concern (Wenger, 1998; Wenger-Trayner *et al.*, 2023), and during the pandemic, all HE practitioners were bound by the same problems and challenges with respect to teaching, learning, and assessment; we thereby became one big community of practice.

The term 'community of practice' has long been used to describe professional associations like the Association for Learning Development in Higher Education (ALDinHE), the Staff and Educational Development Association (SEDA), and the Association for Learning Technology (ALT). These spaces are particularly important for professionals to connect, share practice, and empathise with the challenges they face. Before the pandemic, I was an active member of several such associations, but the level of my activity and engagement was low – generally attending a few events and reading publications. In the run-up to the pandemic, I had joined a few associations, but in hindsight, I had never taken full advantage of both my membership and the learning to be gained for the broader community of professionals. Driven by the unsought opportunity of some free time, a desire for professional networking, and a need to adapt my practice during the pandemic, I made a conscious decision to reframe my participation in these communities.

The Transformative Journey Towards Community Engagement: Nurturing a Seedling of Scholarship

A reflection on the series of rapid developments in my scholarly activity over the course of the pandemic-driven pivot in HE sheds some light on the opportunities for growth and engagement that this challenging time offered. As the first lockdown hit, one of my initial acts was to lead the development of a self-help guide for students. My *Remote Learning SkillsGuide* (University of Hull, 2021) covered vital technologies and the basics of eLearning, which was a new paradigm for most students. I quickly realised how helpful this would be to other professionals, and so I sought permission to open source the guide with a Creative Commons Licence (Fallin, 2021a). This project stands as the first time I was allowed to apply the licence on my work, allowing other institutions to use, adapt, repurpose, and reuse the guide. Such licensing can allow legal reuse, recognising the original author and giving freedom to adapt the resources to their own needs, serving as a vehicle for scholarly reach and impact (Misra, 2020). Due to the openness and reusability of my work in this area, I was then invited to collaborate on an article for ALDinHE's official blog *Take 5* to share my practice (see Fallin and Sinfield, 2020). This was my first experience of collaborative writing within ALDinHE, and the conversations it prompted paved the way for further engagement. Contributing to the support needed at this time gave me confidence about the value my input could have. I recognised the importance of open scholarship and licensing in my own practice and was inspired to volunteer formally for the *LearnHigher* working group to champion this work to others. Once appointed, I had the opportunity to lead on updating the licence used and better supporting *LearnHigher* contributors to engage with the process. This one example demonstrates that tiny seeds of participation in a community of practice can rapidly grow towards more active scholarly involvement.

My fledgling work with ALDinHE built my confidence to get involved further, so when the call for contributions to the *Journal of Learning Development in Higher Education* (*JLDHE*) Compendium of Innovative Practice was announced, I sought further opportunities to engage with the community. The format of short, structured academic reflections for the contributions felt like an approachable opportunity to engage in scholarship, allowing me to formally capture some of the work I was doing without committing to extended research and writing. I submitted two reflections to the Compendium (Fallin, 2021b, 2021a), and these publications helped me to develop further confidence as a writer and producer of knowledge. One of the articles focused on my *Remote Learning SkillsGuide* and provided an opportunity for me to build upon my work with licensing (Fallin, 2021a), helping me further recognise a clear area where I could make a valuable contribution to ALDinHE as a whole.

Scholarship goes far beyond just authorship, and the scale of the Compendium also afforded a significant opportunity to engage in the process of peer review. As Syska (2022b) argues, peer review itself builds community, and in the case of the Compendium, I immersed myself in the reviewer role. Participating in the Learning Development community by reviewing the work of my peers helped to facilitate a sense of belonging, particularly in the context of isolating lockdowns. Through my review work, I felt a connection to the anonymous authors as they shared their experiences of pandemic life through their contributions to the Compendium. For some articles I provided extensive feedback, which becomes dialogical when revised submissions are submitted and you see how authors have developed their work in response. In the isolation of the pandemic, I valued this connection and was surprised by how rewarding a community-building anonymous review process could feel. My active contribution in supporting the work of others undoubtedly enhanced my own scholarship as it exposed me to a wide variety of approaches to scholarship and different writing styles. As a reader, I only ever saw perfected, peer-reviewed and copyedited published works. As a reviewer, I gained insight into work that was in progress, and it helped me recognise the value of peer review in the context of my own work. An unexpected benefit also came in the context of my own written contributions to the Compendium. Like everyone else, I had no frame of reference when I submitted my articles, but seeing the work of others gave me confidence that I had interpreted the brief appropriately.

This engagement with scholarship, publishing, and reviewing did not only develop me as a scholar but also brought unexpected accolades. My contributions to the *JLDHE*, and especially to the Compendium, earned me an award in 2022 for the Reviewer of the Year. While I appreciated the recognition, the real transformation in my participation happened when I was approached to become a guest editor for the journal's collaborative conference proceedings (Syska, 2022a). Prior to this, it would have never crossed my mind to become an editor, but the direct invite gave me the confidence to increase my involvement with the journal and further build on my role in furthering and supporting scholarship.

Serving as a guest editor was a fantastic opportunity to get immersed in the Learning Development community of scholars, and it gave me a whole new experience in what it is to write collaboratively. The collaborative proceedings combine conference abstracts, community reflections, and author responses. Partnered with an experienced *JLDHE* editor, I was responsible for bringing together all three elements of the article into a coherent narrative. In our guest editorial meetings, we discussed key issues – such as how much liberty there is in editing and how to form a narrative through each article (Syska, 2022a). The end result is a 'beautifully eclectic' collection of articles that capture the in-the-moment scholarship, and I found great pride in seeing the articles I edited move through to publication. When invited to interview for a standing editor role, I jumped at the opportunity and was glad to be accepted.

Over two years later, it is fair to say that being a journal editor has been transformative to my practice and that it is the embodiment of my active community engagement. Through editing, more than anything else, I feel like I am making a contribution to the Learning Development community. This is particularly poignant for me, as at the same time I started work as an academic, serving as a lecturer in education studies. My scholarship became one of my unique research perspectives, but more importantly, it keeps me connected to Learning Development. It is perhaps with some irony that I feel I have more time for Learning Development scholarship now I have left Learning Development. Being an editor has become one of the driving forces behind my professional scholarship, and it has also empowered me as a writer. I relate to the work of Syska and Buckley (2022), who argue that writing is a liberatory practice. In writing as Learning Developers, we are liberated from self-explanation, self-justification, self-doubt, and even the self. It is immensely empowering to be part of a profession that is writing itself into existence. This act also brings legitimacy to Learning Development, as it is research that brings a form of academic legitimacy to an association (Benade, 2016). This mindset has afforded new partnerships, and through *JLDHE* regular issues and conference proceedings, I have found the opportunity to collaborate further with other authors (Fallin *et al.*, 2023; Buckley *et al.*, 2023; Beeson *et al.*, 2023). This growth in scholarship was directly driven by those initial seeds of participation, and even in my *JLDHE* role, I've led updates to licensing and copyright, which are now part of every published article, continuing to drive my impact in this area.

I hope this reflexive account of my personal journey into scholarship brings to light a surprising range of activities one can undertake to grow as a scholar, particularly if it can also serve as a doorway to participation for others, as is the case with my role in the journal's innovative collaborative proceedings.

Starting Your Scholarly Transformation: Reflection, Learning, and Transferability

Networking, participation, and learning from others may seem like an obvious way to gain inspiration for enhancing practice and to develop scholarship, but reflecting on the last decade, I can say with some certainty that it is actually quite hard to get started. My journey is perhaps characterised by two key revelations: first, a recognition of what I could contribute, and second, working towards receiving invitations to participate. To return to the theme of my guiding principle, it was through active engagement with my community that my professional scholarship developed. In increasing my engagement, I had to transform how I valued and prioritised discrete activities at work, which is a valuable learning point for other Third Space professionals (Whitchurch, 2008). The space created by the pandemic lockdowns gave me an opportunity to engage in new ways with the Learning Development community. In the post-pandemic world, I continue to work hard to safeguard that time to ensure I keep scholarship time in my diary.

Deep engagement, scholarship, and publication do not happen overnight. As my story has shown, it all starts with a seedling. The capacity for those seeds to grow into an established record of action and change depends on how much we nurture them. This takes time – and so it is essential to safeguard time for development and scholarship in work life. My experience shows that it is worth carefully considering where first to plant those seeds, and here are some ideas that might help anyone interested in developing their scholarship to get started:

1 *Reflect on your contribution*: Think about your practice and what potential contributions you could make to the broader community.
2 *Get blogging*: In the same way that my journey started with *Take 5*, you could identify relevant blogs in your field and volunteer to contribute.
3 *Start reviewing*: Established associations and fields often have peer-reviewed journals. Check out their websites and see how you can get involved as a reviewer. There may be other opportunities for reviewing, from funding bids to professional development schemes and books – check out opportunities in your network.
4 *Be social*: Join social networks and connect with other professionals in your area. Social media can be a great space to find future collaborators, and it is helpful to identify relevant groups, users, and accounts in your field.
5 *Give it a go*: Most professional associations offer opportunities to get involved. From special interest groups and online communities to funding pots and informal publications, there are multiple ways in. Experiment with your participation to try new things out.
6 *Take a role*: Check out what roles and responsibilities are required for any professional associations you are a part of. Smaller roles are likely to make a great starting point, and speaking with membership leads is usually a great place to begin.

This chapter is a rallying cry for action. If you are someone who is attending conferences, reading articles, and has made it to the end of this chapter – think about what you can contribute to your networks. If you want to develop your scholarship and build a record of action and change, you have to start somewhere, and I hope the foregoing list serves as a motivation to begin this journey, if you have not already. If you are someone already involved, the most significant action you can take is to start a conversation with someone new and invite them to participate. As my story shows, so many of the actions I took were at the invitation of others.

References

Beeson, H., Dettmer, J., Fallin, L., Key, L. and Ramakrishnan, S. (2023) 'Co-creating LearnHigher: demystifying and shaping what we do', *Journal of Learning Development in Higher Education*, 29, pp. 1-12.

Benade, L. (2016) 'Learned societies, practitioners and their 'professional' societies: grounds for developing closer links', *Educational Philosophy and Theory*, 48(14), pp. 1395-1400.

Buckley, C., Holley, D. and Fallin, L. (2023) 'A manifesto for the metaverse: opportunities and challenges for learning development', *Journal of Learning Development in Higher Education*, 29, pp. 1-13.

Fallin, L. (2021a) 'Developing online content to support students: the Remote Learning SkillsGuide', *Journal of Learning Development in Higher Education*, 22, pp. 1-5.

Fallin, L. (2021b) 'Teaching academic software via YouTube videos in the Covid-19 pandemic: potential applications for learning development: the challenge', *Journal of Learning Development in Higher Education*, 22, pp. 1-5. https://doi.org/10.47408/jldhe.vi22.679

Fallin, L. (2023) 'Learning development in a time of disruption', *Journal of Learning Development in Higher Education*, 29, pp. 1-10. https://doi.org/10.47408/jldhe.vi29.1078

Fallin, L., Davison, E., Spencer, G. and Tomlinson, T. (2023) 'Supporting inclusive learning resource design with designing for diverse learners', *Journal of Learning Development in Higher Education*, 26, pp. 1-8. https://doi.org/10.47408/jldhe.vi26.924

Fallin, L. and Sinfield, S. (2020) '#Take5 #42 The best way for Learning Development to tackle #Covid19?', *Take 5*. Available at https://lmutake5.wordpress.com/tag/lee-fallin/ (Accessed 16 January 2021).

Gamage, K. A. A. (ed.). (2023) *Reshaping higher education for a post-COVID-19 world: lessons learned and moving forward*. Basel: MDPI - Multidisciplinary Digital Publishing Institute.

Hart, P. F. and Rodgers, W. (2023) 'Competition, competitiveness, and competitive advantage in higher education institutions: a systematic literature review', *Studies in Higher Education*, 49(11), pp. 2153-2177.

Hodges, C., Moore, S., Lockee, B., Trust, T. and Bond, A. (2020) 'The difference between emergency remote teaching and online learning', *Educause Review*, 27, pp. 1-12.

Journal of Learning Development in Higher Education (2021) 'Special edition, compendium of innovative practice: learning development in a time of disruption', *Journal of Learning Development in Higher Education*, Issue 22.

McNay, I. (2022) 'Academic capitalism, competition and competence: the impact on student recruitment and research assessment', *Journal of Further and Higher Education*, 46(6), pp. 780-792.

Misra, P. K. (2020) 'Creative Commons licenses: benefits and implications in teaching and research', *Research Journal Social Sciences*, 28(1), pp. 1-21.

Palfreyman, D. and Tapper, T. (2014) *Reshaping the university: the rise of the regulated market in higher education*. Oxford University Press.

Sezen-Barrie, A., Carter, L., Smith, S., Saber, D. and Wells, M. (2023) 'Research and scholarship during the COVID-19 pandemic: a wicked problem', *Innovative Higher Education*, 48(3), pp. 501-525.

Syska, A. (2022a) 'Editorial: beautifully eclectic: collaborative conference proceedings and reflections', *Journal of Learning Development in Higher Education*, 25.

Syska, A. (2022b) 'Peer reviewing as community building', *Journal of Learning Development in Higher Education*, 25, https://doi.org/10.47408/jldhe.vi25.960

Syska, A. and Buckley, C. (2022) 'Writing as liberatory practice: unlocking knowledge to locate an academic field', *Teaching in Higher Education*, pp. 1–16.

Tomlinson, M. (2016) 'The impact of market-driven higher education on student-university relations: investing, consuming and competing', *Higher Education Policy*, 29(2), pp. 149–166.

University of Hull. (2021) *Remote learning SkillsGuide*. Kingston Upon Hull: University of Hull. Available at https://libguides.hull.ac.uk/remote/home (Accessed: 23 April 2021).

Wenger-Trayner, E., Wenger-Trayner, B., Reid, P. and Bruderlein, C. (2023) *Communities of practice: within and across organizations*. Portugal: Social Learning Lab.

Wenger, E. (1998) *Communities of practice: learning, meaning, and identity*. Cambridge: Cambridge University Press.

Whitchurch, C. (2008) 'Shifting identities and blurring boundaries: The emergence of Third Space professionals in UK higher education', *Higher Education Quarterly*, 62(4), pp. 377–396.

Chapter 9

What Personalisation at Scale Taught Us About Student Belonging

Lynn Gribble and Janis Wardrop

Introduction

Learning management systems used in higher education often have greater capability than is deployed. As such our innovative practice was to harness these underutilised functions, the 'tools hidden in plain sight', to create connections with and a sense of belonging for our international cohort of students in a large compulsory core course during the COVID-19 pandemic. Teaching large classes has particular challenges, including ensuring that students are not lost or unheard, and during the pandemic, when students were working remotely, these challenges were exacerbated. Giving voice and support to assist students to navigate the university learning environment can be done at a course level by interpersonal connection and personalisation. We initially did this using emojis as a means of engaging with students online, gathering sentiment, and providing quick feedback (Gribble & Wardrop, 2021). As the pandemic lockdowns continued, the literature on belonging (for example, Delahunty *et al.*, 2014) guided further exploration to support students in developing successful behaviours in the (online) 'classroom'. The literature advocates belonging to develop students' efficacy in their studies and reduce isolation (Freeman *et al.*, 2007). Our focused attempts at building belonging required us to commence a process of unlearning, that is, to consciously give up ways of the past (Hislop *et al.*, 2013) to adopt new practices to support this group and future groups of students who had been exposed to prolonged periods of isolation and online learning. With the return to face-to-face teaching, we have remained open to unlearning previous teaching practices in our quest to create a sense of belonging and support students' transition into the academic environment for these commencing postgraduate studies, who may be new to the institution and often to the country.

Our Innovative Practice

Belonging and learning efficacy are particularly crucial given our student cohort. They are part of a large compulsory core course in a postgraduate

DOI: 10.4324/9781003503149-12

coursework programme (c. 450 students per term in 2020 and expanded up to c. 1,350 students per term in 2024) of mainly international students, the majority of whom are studying quantitative majors. This compulsory core course focuses on ethics and sustainability as part of the faculty's commitment to the principles of responsible management education (PRME). In teaching these students, we recognise the challenges of being new to the discipline and the learning environment as well as possible feelings of dislocation and culture shock studying in a foreign country. Thus, to build belonging for this cohort during the pandemic we commenced a process of exploring what the students needed and what could be offered to address those needs. In the process, we recognised that for change to occur, both instructors and the students needed to unlearn ways of the past.

In 2020, when the lockdowns across cities (and countries) hit, our students, many of whom had only just arrived 'onshore', were encouraged to return to their homes overseas to continue their studies online. The confusion and disruption of the early weeks as an international student were then compounded as they now faced a very different learning environment. When this class first moved to online learning, our initial concern was to keep our students engaged in learning and connected to their Australian learning experience. We did this through simple engagement methods such as posting emojis in the chat during synchronous classes (Gribble & Wardrop, 2021). Over time we wanted to do more to better support our students in this unfamiliar learning environment. Learning online requires a degree of educational capital (after Bourdieu, 1986), and efficacy: With the move to online learning and everyone 'behind' screens (that is, cameras off, and not visible in the online classroom), the opportunity to be lost, voiceless, and faceless was ever present. This is why building belonging was important.

The move to a fully online learning environment required us to consciously stop doing what we had done previously and explore what we could do now online to create belonging and provide support to every student. We needed to unlearn practices that had supported student belonging in the past. With our extensive experience in teaching such cohorts and our previous comfort in social learning (Bandura, 1977), we now needed to find a way to connect through personally reaching each student with just-in-time support and advice. With no requirement to have cameras on, there were few visual cues and clues to read and interpret how students were feeling; instead, we were left to interpret blank screens, the absence of completed learning activities, and silence. Our quest was to explore how we could make personal and approximate connections as we might in the corridors before and after class. Further, what could we do for the students who had felt lost, were failing to engage in the opportunities of online synchronous learning, and had little social interaction? In our process of unlearning, we needed to be mindful of the constraints – learning tools needed to be time efficient, traceable, and at no additional cost to students or faculty, while adding no to low additional cognitive load for the instructors and the students. Most importantly, they had to be personal enough to tell the students we 'see' them, and will 'find' them, when they were silenced or lost. No student was left alone (after Brunton *et al.*, 2022; Dennen, 2008).

The process of unlearning became our guide in understanding that old assumptions about 'the learner' and our 'learning environment' may no longer be relevant or effective. We needed to find new approaches and mental models that would support our desire to build belonging and connection in this somewhat isolated learning environment. Rather than expecting students to learn from us and each other as Bandura (1977) might suggest through social learning, we reimagined our roles as navigators, advisors, and guides. Going from class facilitator to class navigator and primary supporter required an identity shift. It meant that we needed to expand our focus beyond content and learning process to being the guide to everything learning, including belonging in a new academic environment. To do this, with the constraints of time and resources, we turned to tools 'hidden in plain sight', that is, embedded within the technology we already had and used.

With innovation front of mind, we explored and deployed nudge theory (Thaler & Sunstein, 2008) to guide our students to undertake specific activities that would support their learning. These activities, such as reading the assessment booklet or viewing their tutorial class materials, we know are required and necessary to be successful in an academic environment. However, what was new was that these nudges had to be instigated by the technology at hand, which was the Moodle learning management system (LMS) and Blackboard Collaborate Ultra (BB Collaborate), our synchronous online class delivery platform.

Our focus on belonging was through the lens of navigating the academic environment, wanting every student to feel seen through tailoring communications by activity or interaction with the learning system. Harnessing the power of the Personalized Learning Designer® (PLD) function meant we could 'greet' every student by name when they accessed the LMS and hold their hands 'virtually' to navigate this new academic environment of online learning, providing each student with personalised support in their studies.

Transformative Impact

We sought innovation through wanting to create belonging for our students. The literature on belonging (Freeman *et al.*, 2007) focuses on the need to find support groups, navigate the environment, and perhaps deal with a sense of loss of the past. Belonging supports students in their motivational behaviours and their ability to undertake learning tasks (Hislop *et al.*, 2013). In addition, a caring environment is seen as fulfilling a student's need to fit and, in doing so, the interactions with the instructor have positive outcomes on academic results (Freeman *et al.*, 2007). Student belonging is also enhanced if they perceive the instructor to be enthusiastic, friendly, prepared, and organised.

The transformative impact was twofold – harnessing the capabilities of the PLD enabled students to feel they were both seen and heard. We established processes within the PLD so that personalised mail messages could be sent to students, with pop-ups on the LMS or taking over their LMS interactions when they were logged into the system. These interactions told them what to do and when to do it, and perhaps more importantly, provided personalised guidance and support just in time (JIT) based on the LMS data. The students were no longer lost when navigating the LMS on their own. For example, with the PLD 'running' the student Moodle interactions, every student was directed to the assessment booklet by the end of week one if they had not already looked at it. This reduced email traffic to the course instructors about simple yet important questions. By directing students' interactions on the LMS, we were able to provide support to those students who lacked educational capital (after Bourdieu, 1986), technical expertise, and/or digital or purposeful curiosity (Andriopoulos, 2022) to use the learning system or navigate the course requirements. Every student was greeted and directed as needed without additional work by the instructor. We could now be certain that every student was informed and track that such activities had been completed. More importantly, the reduction in 'please help me find' emails freed up time and mental load for the course instructors and administrators, providing opportunity to consider other innovations and other areas to unlearn.

The messages and prompts went further than learning environment support, ensuring that when students received feedback on their assessments they had personalised and directive advice on what actions would best support their ongoing academic development and learning. While the LMS could inform us who had read the assessment feedback rather than merely viewing their grade, PLD enabled us to personally email each student a plan to best support their next stages of learning based upon the grade or feedback they had been given. The personalised messages focused on what was achieved or absent from each assessment item, suggesting remedial actions such as writing or language support or a personal consult where appropriate. Our students reported being clear on what to do and what resources were available to them in the remainder of the term, as well as reducing email queries from students. The messages were also seen as valuable by the higher achieving students, with them personally thanking us for the encouragement and acknowledgement of their progress and achievements. Our students overall reported that they had felt supported, seen, and heard throughout the course, despite being dispersed across the globe and lacking the in-person, interpersonal interactions that underpin traditional face-to-face learning experiences.

Harnessing the data and reports generated from the LMS provided other opportunities to nudge our students to act. Those who missed class or had not logged on for a week received messages of care and concern. Messages such as 'we are missing you/we missed you' and 'how can we help you?' encouraged students to reach out and make contact, meaning that we knew what our students were doing and when able to offer assistance (as might happen in a small face-to-face group setting or through personalised tutoring). Despite being located across the globe, we created an environment of belonging.

It appears that most LMSs have such capability (for example, Canvas uses MasteryPaths). Designing the PLD rules of interaction took time, but there was an upside in that once set up, it takes as little as an hour to adjust and deploy these rules for the new cohort each term. Deploying this innovation in subsequent terms reaps approximately 40 plus hours of reduced workload over the term (removing a full week of course administration). The reduction in the administrative burden to faculty during the teaching period was the second transformative outcome of our process of unlearning. Being able to provide personalised learning support to students using technology readily available to us enabled us to reduce the mental load of managing a large course (c. 1,000 students). Further, students improved their ability and confidence to access information and use the learning systems required during their studies, feeling less alienated and more capable, which in turn builds efficacy that they belong here.

It was through exploring how we provided support that we created a space and time to unlearn. Our previous support had been offered physically and JIT, in response to direct questions by students in class rather than hard data as we are now able to work with. Thus, previous support, while planned, was also responsive to what students asked or the class pulse. When the class is in front of you it is easier to 'read the pulse' of the room. With the move online, we lost this vital visual piece of information about our students' learning journey, and it was concerning that those with less educational capital (Bourdieu, 1986) may not ask and as a result may remain lost behind a blank screen. While we found that the emails and 'drop in' sessions provided a consistent view of their needs, the previous way of supporting students was a 'customer driven', JIT, or as-needed response. This way of working needed to be unlearned to take a more directive and corrective approach, something we had previously avoided based on adult learning principles of self-direction. We had to unlearn our expectations of the students that could be relied upon in a face-to-face situation but were perhaps less reliable in a fully online environment.

We also found that long-held administrative practices were challenged in a positive way. Incorporating PLD enabled a more proactive but personalised approach to student needs. There was now a third party in the learning relationship, the instructor, the student, and a type of digital assistant that knew what the student did and when and 'spoke' to the student JIT as a personal tutor or assistant in the learning process. The transformative impact as an instructor was removing the administration at the most burdensome points of the course, freeing up mental load and time at the heaviest points of the teaching load both physically and emotionally.

Transferable Aspect

There are two important transferable aspects to this innovation. Personalisation through the use of technology enabled a sense of belonging to be developed and sought to protect the individual student's self-esteem by providing support and building efficacy regardless of the large numbers taught. It also reduced isolation by ensuring the right resources were deployed when and as needed through predictive data. It also freed up valuable time for the instructors. While this change was instigated to support remote learning during the COVID-19 pandemic, we have continued to implement these tools upon our return to face-to-face learning. The individualised support they provide to students to master their learning environment and the administrative efficiencies they bring irrespective of student numbers means that they are now a regular feature in the course. In leading such a large course that continues to expand (currently operating at approximately 1,350 students per term), the administrative burden remains high. In addition, as universities broaden their student cohorts to include those who may have previously been excluded (directly or indirectly), such as those from low socioeconomic status backgrounds, the need to ensure every student is seen and heard will become more pressing. Technology enhancements, such as those we introduced during the pandemic, thus provide considerable support to students.

As academics, the process of unlearning remains valuable. Consciously choosing to stop certain ways of operating, rather than just adding more things to do in a course, is important for academic and student wellbeing. Unlearning for both students and instructors remains a way to unburden the process of both teaching and learning. Recognising what is no longer needed or appropriate becomes the trigger to unlearn. As a result, rather than changes or technology always becoming an 'and activity', deliberately seeking to unlearn and relearn means that outdated and perhaps more labour-intensive methods can be replaced.

Most importantly, the reduction of course administrative burden of operating such a large course has enabled the opportunity to undertake other processes of unlearning and tackle new challenges. As generative AI (GenAI) fundamentally changed the landscape of teaching and learning from November 2022, we have been able to spend the time on other pressing issues for student learning, such as redesigning assessment items and learning about the possibilities and challenges that GenAI will bring to learning environments.

Conclusion

We have access to many tools in the technology we currently use that are hidden in plain sight. As educators, our role is to discover them and the capability they have to support student belonging. When faced with large class teaching it is important not to lose the personal connection that can be provided in smaller classes such as those with only 25 students. Connecting personally supports students in creating a sense of belonging in terms of navigating the academic environment. It can also build personal connection with the teaching staff. As for students, connecting with each other for now remains in the hands of each student, but technology can support instructors to create belonging for students. Further, it can remove the unnecessary 'noise' of administration, creating space to explore other teaching and learning matters.

References

Andriopoulos, C. (2022) *Purposeful curiosity*. London: Hachette Books.

Bandura, A. (1977) *Social learning theory*. Englewood Cliffs, NJ: Prentice Hall.

Brunton, R., MacDonald, J., Sugden, N. and Hicks, B. (2022) '"Discussion forums are they a misnomer?" Examining lurkers, engagement, and academic achievement', *Australasian Journal of Educational Technology*, 38(5). https://doi.org/10.14742/ajet.7627

Bourdieu, P. (1986) 'The forms of capital', in J. E. Richardson (ed.), *Handbook of theory of research of the sociology of education* (pp. 241–258). Westport: Greenword Press.

Delahunty, J., Verenikina, I. and Jones, P. (2014) 'Socio-emotional connections: identity, belonging and learning in online interactions. A literature review', *Technology, Pedagogy and Education*, 23(2), pp. 243–265.

Dennen, V. P. (2008) 'Pedagogical lurking: student engagement in non-posting discussion behavior', *Computers in Human Behavior*, 24(4), pp. 1624–1633. https://doi.org/10.1016/j.chb.2007.06.003

Freeman, T. M., Anderman, L. H. and Jensen, J. M. (2007) 'Sense of belonging in college freshmen at the classroom and campus levels', *The Journal of Experimental Education*, 75(3), pp. 203–220. https://www.jstor.org/stable/20157456

Gribble, L. and Wardrop, J. (2021) 'Learning by engaging: connecting with our students to keep them active and attentive in online classes, A compendium of the Learning Development community's responses to the Covid-19 pandemic', *Journal of Learning Development in Higher Education*, 22. https://doi.org/10.47408/jldhe.vi22.701

Hislop, D., Bosley, S., Coombs, C. R. and Holland, J. (2013) 'The process of individual unlearning: a neglected topic in an under researched field', *Management Learning*, 45(5), pp. 540–560. https://doi.org/10.1177/1350507613486423

Thaler, R. H. and Sunstein, T. R. (2008) *Nudge. Improving decisions about health, wealth and happiness*. London: Penguin Books.

Chapter 10

What Shared Learning Spaces Taught Me About Student Belonging

Lucinda Becker

Introduction

The COVID-19 pandemic created an urgent need to deal with the mechanics of teaching and learning: When would students be able to come to campus? How could we introduce adequate technology to deliver learning at a distance? This pivotal moment was met by university communities with an impressive response: Within weeks, educators needed to teach online and students needed to develop learning techniques to meet this mode of delivery – and we did it. However, questions remained: How is a community nurtured if not on campus? How can students feel that they belong within a community that manifests itself only through their computer screens? If we must focus on meeting a curriculum online, what might we be losing, almost without noticing?

This chapter therefore addresses some of these issues through an exploration of teaching and learning spaces, student ownership of learning material, the central importance of belonging and mattering, and how the 'casual curriculum' plays a role.

Building Teaching and Learning Spaces

In English literature at my university, we teach in lectures and through seminars of around 15 students. These seminars are intended to give space to students trying out new ideas and closely analysing literature. This sounds simple, but for most students it is not: They are unused to the freewheeling nature of seminar discussion. This can lead to students preferring the comfort of silence to the challenge of responding to discussion points offered by the seminar leader. In a teaching room full of body language and with a careful seating arrangement, using a combination of open discussion and pair or group activity, this can be overcome swiftly.

However, when delivered online, these seminars can become spaces in which many students are silent, passive learners. This is nothing to do with the intelligence of the students; it rests with the space within which they are working. As elsewhere, my university provided formally timetabled online seminars during lockdown, and like others, I urged students to use the 'chat' function and tried interactive online tools and breakout rooms, all with some success but not enough. The material was covered, but the development of learning skills suffered, so I also set up a new and more creative student-centred online space.

I took the opportunity to bring together the whole Shakespeare module group (around 60 students in their second year of university) in weekly online, recorded play readings. There were three student volunteers reading from a play in each session, taking turns to read the speeches, with other students listening live or later. Attendance at the sessions was voluntary, and they were set up online via Blackboard Collaborate. The benefit of using this method was that it appeared in students' timetables and was a familiar online learning space for them. It also allowed me to record the sessions and embed them in a Blackboard module site easily and swiftly.

My aim was to achieve three learning development goals:

1 To ensure that students had read the play before the relevant seminar
2 To help them feel more confident in seminars, as they would know the play
3 To create an informal, enjoyable learning community throughout lockdown

I believe we achieved these goals, with students giving positive feedback on this aspect of the module. The learning community was even better than I had expected: Around a quarter of the students had performed in or directed Shakespeare plays and so brought that perspective to the group. This gave us the chance to recognise their previous learning development and feed that into their new learning.

For those students with an auditory (aural) learning preference, this was clearly going to be an especially beneficial experience, and I shared the text on screen to aid visual learners. I noticed that some of the readers were walking around as they read the text, showing a kinaesthetic preference perhaps. Kolb's work over nearly four decades, developing the idea of learning preferences and the importance of experiential learning, sets up a framework within which this type of activity sits well (Kolb, 2015).

As a profession, we are less wedded to the idea of individual learning preferences or styles than we were in the past. This is to the good, allowing us to see our students in a more nuanced, authentic way, but it can still be useful from time to time to reflect on these potential preferences. Students who walk around during a play reading are not simply kinaesthetic learners but are demonstrating one way in which they like to work, a way that is not likely to be available to them during a standard lecture or seminar on campus.

Students Taking Ownership of the Learning Material

I also learned two things about myself. As we read the plays together, I noticed elements in the plays that I had never spotted before. By being open and sharing this with students, they could recognise that the learning was genuinely shared – I was leading, but that did not mean that I was not learning beside them.

I also found that I am not very good at reading plays aloud. Having assumed that I would always be leading, I soon recognised that the students were better readers than I was, and I turned the reading over to them entirely. This made a significant change in our relationship. They were developing learning skills, such as gaining an ear for the language and immersing themselves in a text, in a situation in which they had largely taken over the learning space – I was the assistant who scrolled through the play text on screen.

The students recognised that they were investing more effort than they were used to, as they were taking the lead, and this energised the group. They seemed more ready to proffer their views in our seminars following the play readings, and this reflects Tinto's assertion that 'the more students invest in learning activities … the higher their level of effort, the more students learn' (1997, p. 600). Students were enriching their curriculum in this online space.

Belonging and Mattering

I then adopted Brookfield's (2009) method to reflect on whether this learning experiment had any value beyond the pandemic. My Shakespeare students no longer had to bluff their way through a text, so I could be bolder in my learning expectations; their learning confidence also increased because of this experiment. Kahu's (2013) work recognises that 'satisfaction' and 'wellbeing' are two social factors that promote student engagement and learning, and online reading groups can achieve this – it is the act of sharing a text that seemed to make the difference to these students, who gain a greater sense of belonging by working with their peers in this way.

In reality, the experiment failed post pandemic. I had made a semi-social learning space that the students had then taken over, but the return to campus hugely reduced the student appetite for this space. It took up two to three hours of their week in what was now a busy on-campus life, with little need for that extra online connection. I also suspect that many of the students just wanted to move on and forget their pandemic learning experience.

I had found the experience transformative, though, and I had seen what a difference semi-social online spaces could make to students. Their feedback had been positive, but I needed to find a way to adapt the situation to make it relevant on a post-pandemic campus. This has led to a productive expansion of the experiment, turning it into a more embedded, long-term part of my students' learning.

I first examined why it had been a transformative experience. I was reminded again of the research carried out by Tinto, which was some time ago, yet his assertion that 'the classroom is the crossroads where the social and the academic meet' (1997, p. 599) is still relevant. On reflection I could see that three factors had been at play:

- Students recognised that they mattered, because an academic was offering them extra contact time outside their formal timetable.
- The activity fostered a sense of belonging, as they came to see (indeed, we all came to see) that they could take ownership of the space.
- Important learning outside the formal curriculum had taken place. This was not planned or prepared; it involved the casual co-creation of an enhanced learning space, and this is a vital, but often overlooked, aspect of teaching and learning.

Offering additional contact hours in a module by sharing, in this case, online play readings was a way to demonstrate that we value students and their learning. Of course, educators have regularly taken this approach and offered their time for activities outside the timetable. What made this experiment different was that it was student-led and that our material was co-created. Although the play to be read was dictated by the module timetable, the way it was read, the pauses for reflection during that reading, and the time for discussion after the reading were all led by the students.

The principles of the activity – sharing space and responding in the moment to create new material – are clearly transferable, if the temptation to take over is avoided. I now include guided screening of films in my teaching, making sure that students take the lead. Although I set up a series of prompt questions for them to consider at each break in our viewing (around every 20 minutes), I would no longer consider leading these discussion breaks. Instead, the students between them choose which, if any, of my prompt questions to answer; those they create for themselves regularly lead to more interesting discussions than I had anticipated. Despite the rising sense of failure (why did I not think of that question for them?), I remind myself of the positive outcomes of offering them the chance to take over the play readings. It is not about who thought of the best question: There is an intrinsic value in students taking over. They learn the art of creating research questions and come to recognise the knowledge and skill set that they possess as a group.

The Casual Curriculum Explored

Demonstrating to students that they matter links to helping them feel that they belong. Even that sentence is full of distancing, deficit-model thinking. If we are 'helping' them to belong, then presumably we know what it is to belong, because we all belong, and they, by implication, must strive to be 'like us'. If we are to help them 'feel that they belong', does that suggest that they will never truly belong, but only feel as if they do?

The pandemic sparked an increasing interest in the links between emotion and the ability to learn (Cleveland-Innes and Campbell, 2012). Although some of this research relates to the challenges of online learning set out earlier in this chapter, my play reading experiment caused me to consider potential barriers to the sense of belonging that I so wish to foster in my students. This is a complex area, with many potential barriers, so I am focusing here on just one: the sense of embarrassment that causes students to disengage instantly, and sometimes permanently.

This sense of embarrassment can often be centred around what might seem to an educator to be very simple, obvious tasks, such as reading a set of instructions for an assignment. It was only during the pandemic that a conversation with students led me to recall just how often I repeat or clarify instructions on the way to and from lectures and seminars. In the pandemic, with the loss of that 'accidental' time, I noticed student anxiety in this area increasing. Even very simple instructions (or those that seem simple to me) can be confusing if you are anxious and not able to ask the meaning of a term in the questions or have clarification on the word count.

These apparently incidental conversations are far more than just a moment taken to clarify some aspect of the system or to reiterate a point from a seminar. They foster, inevitably, a greater sense of belonging. No longer is the educator only visualised in a seminar room; instead, students can 'walk and talk' through a problem in spontaneous, one-on-one conversations that are focused solely on their needs. That conversation demonstrates that the student has every right to ask the question (however minor the query) and that the educator is keen to help. The online play readings replicated this sense of 'spontaneous space' because it became an area for casual conversation around the core activity. The casual conversations have revived with the return to campus, but we need not lose the benefits of offering answers to minor queries in the online space, of reassuring students that their questions are valid – and our reassurance is genuine, because they belong and they are valued.

One threat to the students' sense of belonging can be centred around anxiety and is particularly pronounced for those learners who respond best to visual or aural instructions. The answer was simple: I supplement written assignment instructions with short instruction screencasts uploaded to our VLE. Students tell me that they often go to these audiovisual instructions first, to gain an overview and some confidence, before reading the written instructions. As I already give audiofile feedback on all the assignments I mark, the students hear my voice both to start them on the assignment and to give them feedback and feed-forward once it has been marked.

It is online interventions, sometimes thought of as less personal than on-campus activity, that have added a personal element to the process, which has led to fewer students struggling with assignments because they do not understand the instructions or feedback. For some students, this struggle is a short walk away from deciding that they do not really belong in the class at all and maybe not at university either. This activity could easily be achieved on any module, at any level, with positive effects far outreaching the minimal effort it takes to produce the screencasts or audio files.

The Casual Curriculum Extended

I have extended this type of activity to include motivational videos and screencasts to increase post-pandemic classroom attendance. For a study skills module I designed and convene, and on which I lecture, we noticed a downturn in attendance. Student focus groups revealed that the single largest determiner in nonattendance was a failure to see the immediate relevance of the study skills material being covered. This led to an even greater problem: Students would not attend in a week where they perceived the material to be less relevant, with no idea that a few weeks later they would be required to practise those very skills in a series of assessment tasks.

The solution was simple and easily transferable. Two screencasts were produced for each week's activity and uploaded to the VLE. The first of these explains how students can prepare for the seminar/workshop and what they might expect to get out of the lecture. This is designed to dispel anxiety around expectations, promoting a more positive approach. The second screencast encourages students to reflect on their learning and explains how that week's learning can be applied to specific assessment tasks and their wider learning.

If online activity such as this can make learning feel more personal and positive, I reasoned that it might also help to promote the casual curriculum that I had seen developing in the play readings. Work has been carried out over the years on the idea of a 'hidden curriculum' (see, example.g., Portelli, 1993), but this can often have negative connotations and can also be planned and implemented by the educators in a systematic way. What I am terming the 'casual curriculum' are those activities that are not itemised on module descriptions or formally included within a teaching curriculum but that are nevertheless important in promoting engagement with learning development.

This casual curriculum would include the in-passing conversations in corridors where students ask whether there are any exams on a module or want to explore ideas for placements attached to some specific learning. It would also include the conversations that happen when, on the way to a lecture, students take the opportunity to ask for an explanation of one term used in feedback that makes no sense to them. Also, it covers those discussions at the end of a seminar when a few students ask how to use a particular piece of punctuation or want to know if there is any further reading recommended for a particular essay topic.

Now that we have returned to campus these conversations are happening again, but we can still create online space as well as campus opportunities for this casual curriculum to develop. This increases access to conversations for those students who are on campus less regularly, those commuting students who must dash off after lectures, or those who find such casual conversations socially difficult.

To open up the opportunity for this casual curriculum, I have created regular (usually weekly) online study spaces for groups of students. These are sometimes linked to modules, sometimes dedicated to study projects for just a few weeks, but in them all it is the students who are empowered to drive the learning agenda within those spaces. They enter the online spaces as they like, either via Teams or our VLE; they work together on their projects, often silently; and I work in my office but within the same online space as them.

They will ask a question every now and then, and only the minority of those questions relate to the project or even the module. More often the questions are around their wider study experience, their concerns and anxieties, and their plans for the future. This can lead to quick wins pedagogically as I answer simple but important questions, but it also gives me ideas for new sessions and a greater sense of students' needs at that point. That is why it becomes a casual curriculum: unplanned, but substantial, with useful learning that is not easily captured in the more formal curriculum.

Summary

Most of the examples shared in this chapter came about as a result of specific circumstances; some were the result of reflection following initial experiments; all are scalable and transferable to a range of teaching and learning situations. None take up a great deal of additional time; it could be argued that the time saved later in unravelling more complex problems that could have been avoided makes them a time-saving exercise. Most importantly, each one brings students closer to their educator, closer to each other and, crucially, closer into the learning life of a university.

References

Brookfield, S. (2009) 'The concept of critical reflection: promises and contradictions', *European Journal of Social Work*, 12(3), pp. 293–304. Available at https://doi.org/10.1080/13691450902945215 (Accessed 5 October 2021).

Cleveland-Innes, M. and Campbell, P. (2012) Emotional presence, learning, and the online learning environment. *The International Review of Research in Open and Distributed Learning*, 13(4), p. 269. https://doi.org/10.19173/irrodl.v13i4.1234

Kahu, E. R. (2013) 'Framing student engagement in higher education', *Studies in Higher Education*, 38(5), pp. 758–773. Available at https://www.tandfonline.com/doi/pdf/10.1080/03075079.2011.598505 (Accessed 5 October 2021).

Kolb, D. A. (2015) *Experiential learning: experience as the source of learning and development* (2nd ed.). Upper Saddle River, NJ: Pearson Education.

Portelli, J. P. (1993) 'Exposing the hidden curriculum'. *Journal of Curriculum Studies*, 25(4), pp. 343–358. https://doi.org/10.1080/0022027930250404

Tinto, V. (1997) 'Classrooms as communities: exploring the educational character of student persistence', *The Journal of Higher Education*, 68(6), 599–623. Available at https://doi.org/10.2307/2959965 (Accessed 5 October 2021).

Chapter 11

What Podcasting Taught Us About Innovative Pedagogy as Disruption in Higher Education

Julia Bohlmann and Micky Ross

Introduction

In this chapter, we present podcasting as a liberatory yet disruptive pedagogy that can foster inclusivity and accessibility in higher education. Specifically, we seek to show that podcasting breaks with traditional academic conventions and can therefore be seen as a less serious and even disruptive teaching practice. The chapter will address this misconception and make the case for podcasting in teaching and scholarship. Therefore, rather than writing an academic article in the conventional sense, we decided to record a podcast and shape its transcript into a text that we hope embodies the unconventional nature, informality and accessibility of podcasting itself. In the following, we will first introduce the idea of podcasting as innovative practice before discussing its potentially transformative impact and transferability.

Innovative Practice: Podcasting

JB: What would you say were the most important things you learned from the podcast series we ran for international students during COVID-19?

MR: I learned that higher education teaching and learning practice can be significantly enhanced by involving students in a dialogue. I learned that there's richness to that method of teaching. I learned that it is far more interesting than lecturing at people. Doing something like a podcast live, as we did then, where participants could interact with us, was an interesting way to facilitate learning.
   What do you think about that?

JB: Yeah, it was so much fun doing these podcasts. And during the pandemic, when we needed to connect with our students remotely, it was the only space where a dialogue could really happen. Podcasting took away some barriers for them around asking questions.
   We showed a different side of ourselves to the students when we moved from lecturing to podcasting. I remember lots of conversations about us being learners and doing things wrong, and I think the students

DOI: 10.4324/9781003503149-14

really liked that because it changed the dynamic. We also did it to build community. I don't think it replaced the community on campus, but it was important at the time.

MR: The experience of moving from lecturing to a podcast in this dialogic way that we did was influenced by Dewey's (2008) *Democracy in Education* and impactful in that we changed the power dynamic with the students.

JB: Exactly. I think that was key. We decreased the power distance between teacher and student. You know podcasting is fun and, in that way, a little bit subversive. I recently read *Teaching to Transgress* by bell hooks (1994). She had a similar experience in her teaching career all those decades ago when she wrote:

> Excitement in higher education was viewed as potentially disruptive of the atmosphere of seriousness assumed to be essential of the learning process. So, to enter the classroom with the will to share the desire to encourage excitement, was to transgress.
>
> (p. 7)

For me, podcasting was a transformative experience in that I was suddenly able to view teaching as something exciting and a lot of fun.

Transformative Impact

JB: I wonder whether it still rings true that innovative teaching methods are disruptive and that they are viewed with scepticism and maybe even looked down upon by some educators, but also students. hooks in her book also talks about their reluctance to open up to new teaching methods.

MR: Yeah, I think we're challenging a belief system about *how* education should be, how it should be delivered, how serious it should be, how it shouldn't be fun, how it should be the giving of knowledge compared to the constructing of knowledge. I totally agree with you that when we innovate, we disrupt. It's something which I find frustrating. We're supposed to be in this hive of innovation and thinking. However, when you innovate certain things, you can meet a lot of resistance. Innovation can make some people feel uncomfortable. Maybe for good reason, educators need to meet intended learning outcomes and are worried if they are not laid out in a lecture. It is a safety and trust issue for me. That's something that Freire (2000) talks about, a climate of mutual trust. And I think that in the podcast we did, we opened up with the dialogue, we created this trust with the students. They trusted us, we trusted them. Our innovation brought a freshness to practice, which was great.

JB: I find it quite interesting that you talk about intended learning outcomes (ILOs) and that educators might worry about not reaching them. I've moved from student learning development to academic development, where we talk a lot to lecturers about active learning strategies. These new methods or things that promote active learning take time out of your lecture schedule. So yes, there is certainly a concern about: well, if I do this activity as a podcast, I will take time away from covering this ILO. So, I understand that there's always a balance to strike. But it also points towards something that doesn't work in our education system, where we drag students through tons of content and ILOs that can never be met because they are taught passively. Nobody will remember what they have learned two or three years later. Do I remember what I taught three years ago? No. But do I remember the podcast conversations? Yes, because these actually connected with me.

MR: You don't rattle through something you have to tell people, you actually listen and create that dialogue. I'm always fairly cynical about the term active learning, because I think of Dewey's (1986) learning by doing, which is over 100 years old now. For me, these are not new ideas at all, which actually casts a light on the slowness of innovation in our sector.

JB: So if it's not new, how would you say it has transformed your teaching practice and the way you think about teaching?

MR: For me, something transformative is something very impactful. It is different to development. For instance, to develop, you add something on. To transform, you deconstruct and then put it back together a different way. Therefore, I believe that transformative pedagogy needs to be active because it needs to be the students' choice to transform; it needs to be on their terms. We shouldn't transform our students; they should *be* transformed. Being passive in that process is really wrong for me.

JB: Yeah, we can't really transform other people. I think active learning tries to bring students on board with their own learning. Our podcast demonstrated this because students were able to steer the conversation by asking questions in the chat. For me, the transformative impact plays into the idea that the way we teach matters; *how* we teach matters. It is about getting away from the content and thinking more about what shape or form teaching and learning takes. If you want to discuss progressive ideas, you have to be able to embody them. You can't just teach that from the front.

What I find really important about podcasting is that element of dialogue, and how a dialogue between people can model respectful conversation that shows that you can engage with others with different opinions or different backgrounds with respect and with an awareness of the difficulties they went through. For example, *The Pluriversity Podcast* (2024) – the podcast I did after ours – was focused on decolonising the curriculum and antiracism. I remember having very frank conversations with speakers. The feedback I got from speakers was very positive. They felt that conversations were respectful and facilitated with care and honesty. I especially remember one about racism. I didn't have the same experience as my podcast guests as I'm a white person, but I could try to relate to theirs to some extent. I think that is really important in the polarised world we live in right now, where everybody retreats into bubbles of just speaking to people with similar experiences and views.

MR: I think it speaks to Freire's (2000) banking versus problem posing. Here's a problem, and we can come to a better understanding of it with dialogue rather than someone telling us what to do, lowering power distance and countering the polarisation that we talked about by preventing alienation and atomisation. We can start to solve problems by bringing voices together, and by podcasting, we can share them.

JB: Bringing people together to have a dialogue even though it's uncomfortable is important. I certainly felt very nervous in that conversation.

MR: This takes us back to the idea of disruption to teaching practices. It is disruptive to you as the educator or facilitator. I've also thought about my own practices. I've taught groups before that had lots of strong personalities, which was intimidating. However, it was good for me to go through that and to have that experience because it forced me to think about my practice and made me reevaluate it. It stopped me from just going through the motions with students and instead made me think: what am I doing here? How can I navigate these students? These students disrupted my practice and made me develop and even transform it.

JB: It totally makes sense because it returns to the idea that you can't teach progressive ideas without embodying them. You don't connect across divides without feeling discomfort, and you don't develop an understanding of experiences that are unfamiliar to you by staying in your own bubble.

A podcast I listened to before creating *The Pluriversity Podcast* was the *Pedagogies for Social Justice Podcast* (2021–ongoing), a student–staff partnership at the University of Westminster. Kyra Araneta and Fatima Maatwk were guests on one of my episodes as I wanted to learn from their experience. With the *Pedagogies for Social Justice Podcast*, they are trying to centre marginalised voices and create a space for 'ideation and dreaming' (Araneta *et al.*, 2023). I really liked that the podcast and dialogue can be something where you can imagine something that is maybe not yet present in reality.

MR: Podcasting fits perfectly with what we're trying to do at university. It's the gap. To fill it you must first engage your imagination. So, for me, this is where podcast as part of pedagogy makes complete sense because it allows us to open a space to talk, to share ideas that are in our heads which can then germinate in some way – or not! I guess it depends on the idea, but it's the start of the innovation process.

JB: Exactly! There are two things I'm thinking about right now; one is the people from the *Pedagogies for Social Justice Podcast* use podcasting as a particular framework that is supported by critical race theory. One aspect of critical race theory is counter-storytelling. So, it's trying to counteract official, canonical discourses and debates with 'other' stories, i.e., lived experiences of racism or stories of success where all we ever talk about is lack of attainment. And through those counter-stories, the podcast contributes to deconstructing dominant structures and reinstates some human agency (Ladson-Billings, 1998).

    A podcast can also be a non-traditional scholarly output by making episodes citable. That way they are protected by copyright. After all, we are working within this framework of education where publications are highly valued. It was really important to me to protect the ideas of the guests because they shared their knowledge with us. Whether they have careers in academia or are community practitioners, their knowledge counts!

MR: And that knowledge doesn't always have space in academia because it's viewed as too close to personal experience or lacking objectivity. However, citing that knowledge transforms it into capital and gives it value within a discourse community.

JB: Yes. I also use the podcast as a learning tool in my teaching. I wrote and deliver a course called 'Intercultural Learning and Teaching in Higher Education', which is part of the PGCAP (Postgraduate Certificate in Academic Practice) at the University of Glasgow. The discussions informed by the podcast were so valuable. For time poor academics and students, it's often easier to listen to a podcast than reading an academic article where you have to churn through methods, findings and so on. I'm not saying I have no academic reading on the course, I do. But the podcasts are easier to access and mix things up a bit, which helps with engagement. It contributes to a more flexible and multidimensional syllabus.

    I was actually interested to hear more about your podcast, for ELINET (Education Languages and Internationalisation Network).

MR: Yeah, this podcast episode was on teaching practice innovation, particularly on a transcultural communication course, where participating students wrote their own marking rubric to grade themselves. During the podcast, we discussed innovative practices with other interested practitioners, focusing on what it took to challenge traditional assessment practices and getting innovative ideas through a board of studies. What came out if it was that innovative practice can be hard work and that change doesn't come about quickly. However, it is worth doing, even if it's incremental.

JB: The realities of our higher education teaching system, where you have to go through a board of studies, especially when it comes to assessment, can involve conforming. This is despite calls for more innovative or meaningful assessment, for example, video essays or audio files instead of written assessment. However, getting these things through board of studies is hard because it is often not seen as serious enough. This is a form of gatekeeping built into higher education institutions.

Transferable Impact

JB: When you did the podcast for ELINET what did you transfer from the podcasting that we did together during the pandemic? What was your approach? Was it the same?

MR: I took a lot of those practical skills with me. I made an outline to guide it. I wrote down the points that I wanted to cover, and I had an opening and closing kind of spiel. The soft skills for a podcast are having slightly elevated energy to engage the listener. I took those skills with me as well. I recorded it on Zoom, which worked well. It gave me a transcript. I also took the confidence to do it with me.

JB: Zoom is great and absolutely sufficient as a recording platform because most people know how to use it and it's relatively easy to access. Remember, when we started the podcast during COVID19 we thought: let's just have it on Zoom and share the audio files with students afterwards? When I got involved with *The Pluriversity Podcast*, we tried another platform (Zencastr), which gives you a bit better audio quality. But the problem with that was that it does not work on all browsers. We tried this platform a couple of times, and then guests could not log in. And you know the speakers were busy, so it was frustrating for them and us. I found it a bit exclusionary. After the pandemic, pretty much everybody knows how to operate Zoom, so it's more inclusive. And, as you say, it gives you a transcript, which is good for accessibility and the audio quality is fine.

MR: At the beginning it is about getting it off the ground, isn't it? And just doing it with what you have got because producing something is better than not producing anything.

JB: In terms of what I transferred from our podcast I also took a semi-structured approach in that we agreed questions in advance with the speakers. First, we met to build rapport, to have a chat, to see whether we could actually talk to each other in a productive way. Then we agreed on questions which were sent over to the speakers to be sort of signed off, so they knew what they would be asked. This is especially important for sensitive topics.

I am very pleased about the podcast giving me the opportunity to make topics like decolonisation available to a non-academic audience, to open it up to people across the world.

MR: That is another example of how podcasting can be an effective innovation tool for pedagogy in higher education where the majority of students are from non-traditional backgrounds. Podcasting helps our practices become more accessible.

JB: Yes, exactly. We talked to many students over the years who find academic reading hard. I have been in academia for decades, and I still find it hard! But over the years I have also become a bit impatient with writers using jargon when it's not necessary. Many concepts and theories are less complex than they are made out to be, so we shouldn't be afraid to break them down and describe them in simple terms. With podcasting you can break with this type of gatekeeping by using informal language and engaging in critical dialogue about academic concepts and ideas.

MR: We understand complex ideas not by reading necessarily, but by engaging with them and talking about them. We understand the world through dialogue and stories.

JB: I have got a really nice quote to finish off with from *Teaching to Transgress* where bell hooks (1994) speaks to her colleague Ron Scapp, who says:

> Don't confuse informality with lack of seriousness and don't confuse boredom and authoritative methods of teaching with being taught something important.
>
> (p. 146)

In that way, using podcasting does not mean you are doing something that is not important. It is actually an embodiment of an innovative and progressive teaching method.

MR: Yeah, it brings us back to how we may believe things should be. We often don't even question something because it is so familiar.

Conclusion

What podcasting taught us about innovative pedagogy as disruption is that it can be challenging to pursue but also that it's always worthwhile to do so because it can result in more accessible and inclusive teaching practices. We can use podcasting to bring academic ideas and concepts closer to our students, using informal language to make them more relevant and less abstract. Podcasting can be a lot of fun for us as teachers too and at the same time appeal to audiences beyond academia. In that way, podcasting offers a unique opportunity to make the academy more inclusive by embodying dialogue and inviting in non-traditional students and audiences.

References

Araneta, K., Fraser, J. and F. Maatwk (2023). 'Podcasting for social justice', Advance HE Equality, Diversity and Inclusion Conference 2023: The Shoulders of giants: listening, learning and improving our practice, Hull, UK, 15–16 March 2023.

Dewey, J. (2008). Democracy and education 1916. *Schools (Chicago, Ill.)*, 5(1–2), 87–95. https://doi.org/10.1086/591813

Dewey, J. (1986). Experience and education. *The Educational Forum (West Lafayette, Ind.)*, 50(3), 241–252. https://doi.org/10.1080/00131728609335764

Freire, P. (2000). *Pedagogy of the oppressed* (30th anniversary). Continuum.

hooks, b. (1994). *Teaching to transgress: Education as the practice of freedom.* Routledge. https://doi.org/10.4324/9780203700280

Ladson-Billings, G. (1998). 'Just what is critical race theory and what's it doing in a nice field like education?', *International Journal of Qualitative Studies in Education*, 11, 7–24.

The Pedagogies for Social Justice Podcast. (2021–2023). https://open.spotify.com/show/1BhrbuKdFOIBmlzGYAZyui (Accessed 29 February 2024).

The Pluriversity Podcast. https://open.spotify.com/show/27S7VhmKSH9LIRtbUkkcSO (Accessed 29 February 2024).

Chapter 12

What Podcasting Taught Me About Writing

Revelations from Behind the Mic

Alicja Syska

Strange things happen when the world challenges us to think differently. During the pandemic of 2020, unable to do things as they have always been done, like every educator across global higher education (HE) I scrambled to find new ways of not only teaching but also connecting with students. What I sought to create was a supportive but not laboured, academic but also intimate, space for students to stay connected to the university while also providing opportunities to explore aspects of their academic work. When other colleagues were opening wonderfully innovative online spaces including fikas, wellbeing sessions, open Zoom rooms, and virtual teas, I settled on a podcast. It became an exciting and enjoyable way to speak to students (and, as it turned out later, also to colleagues) about all the things that there was simply no time to cover in teaching sessions and impossible to casually explore in the temporarily defunct informal, non-monitored spaces of university corridors, cafes, lifts, queues, not to mention field trips or the proverbial water cooler moments. Revival of such spaces was the promise of the podcast, and to some extent it succeeded (Syska and Mesley, 2021).

What I did not expect was that podcasting would teach me lessons about a much better-established academic preoccupation – writing. Some of these revelations were fairly obvious, others slightly surprising, and a couple downright controversial. There is wisdom to be gleaned from doing more unusual things (like podcasting) that is useful when performing seemingly more familiar and well explored things (like writing). Despite being an ostensibly opposite type of activity – talking and writing engage different cognitive processes and require different skills – podcasting makes certain truths about writing difficult to ignore.

The Obvious Revelations

Revelation 1: Writing Is Conversational

The model of podcasting I chose – inviting a speaker to have a conversation with – was based on the premise that we learn and grow best when exchanging ideas with others, often those ideas we are least prepared to articulate effectively, so we can grapple with them together. The purpose of a podcast conversation is not to present (by the host) or extract (from the guest) a definitive point on the matter, but rather to generate a discussion, invite novel perspectives, and promote a dialogic exchange of ideas so the conversation can continue beyond its immediate setting (McHugh, 2022). When we talk to people, their ideas instantly shape our ideas as we respond to their reactions and change the direction of our words depending on the interpellation. We talk to learn from and about each other.

The same conditions can, and perhaps more emphatically *should*, be recreated in writing. Richardson's words, 'I write because I want to find something out. ... to learn something that I didn't know before I wrote it' (1997, p. 87), had chimed in my ear for a long time, but podcasting was the first experience that allowed me to properly understand them. Podcast conversations – with their occasional chaos and inability to predetermine what the guest will say or where the conversation will go – made me appreciate the value of, first, talking to think, and then writing to think. This is in marked contrast to how I used to write – only after I completed a long slog of research and made sure I read everything I could possibly read before putting my own words down. It may have been because my writing used to be a solitary pursuit, and the sense of conversation did not become real until I began to write collaboratively. Writing together provides an excellent starting point to the scholarly dialogue, with 'co-writing tensions' reminding us that there is not one way to write or say things (Dunlap, 2007, p. 84) and meanings are negotiated.

Both conversations with others and writing itself deepen our thinking and consequently improve our writing. A written piece should not be an exposition of a conclusive standpoint or a final statement on any matter. Of course, most writers acknowledge their intellectual debt and make links with the existing knowledge base, but this can turn into an occasional 'game of who cites whom' (Murray, 2020, p. 79) with that sense of conversation – intellectual curiosity even – sorely absent from the piece of writing. Seeing all writing – whether academic or fictional – as a response to previous writing or an invitation to future writing (Elbow, 2000, p. 158) creates conditions that let it develop in a non-predetermined direction and leave some loose ends for another writer to step in to pick up the discourse.

Revelation 2: Editing Is a Gift

Podcasting made me appreciate the value of rewriting. Once a conversation is recorded, there is only so much that can be done about the content – should they become too distracting, 'ums' and 'errs' can vanish with a click of the mouse; editing can cut out a digression or add an explanation. But even the best editing, bar digital manipulation, cannot rearrange or reshape words to achieve more precision of expression.

Only when editing my first podcast episode did I realise how unclear, imprecise, and inexact my phrasing was (I did not pass judgment on my guests – they always seemed perfect) and how much I wished I could change the way I said things. Words uttered and recorded are 'irreversible' and 'cannot be *retracted*' (Barthes, 1977, p. 190) in the same way as in writing – seamlessly, without leaving a shadow of that absence or affecting adjacent words and meaning. Revising would effectively require re-recording a podcast, already knowing where it was going and how it could be refined. The inability to do so forces us to accept that the final product is as good as it can be.

The same cannot be said about writing, however. As if to mock a podcaster, Germano (2021) compares revising to reading with your ears; one must be able to really listen to the work, even read it out loud, in order to see it through the eyes of the reader. Zinsser calls rewriting 'the essence of writing well' (2006, p. 83), touting its pleasures in words that speak to my writerly soul: 'With every small refinement I feel that I'm coming nearer to where I would like to arrive, and when I finally get there I know it was the rewriting, not the writing, that won the game' (p. 87). In rewriting, however, cutting out words, adding, or refining them is only a small part of what editing is about. Effective rewriting involves rethinking ideas so they can be presented to the world in their most precise form. Rewriting is particularly enjoyable for those who consider themselves better listeners than speakers; what podcasting affirmed in me is that good listeners are also great rewriters. That last opportunity to rewrite our words before the world sees them – a luxury not afforded to most verbal communicators – is the greatest gift a writer has in the writing process.

The Surprising Revelations

Revelation 3: Perfection Lies in Imperfection

No podcast episode is ever perfect, but this is just a reminder that writing too – even after multiple rewrites and endless editing – is always imperfect work. I can rarely bring myself to relisten to a podcast I recorded or reread a piece of writing I published because once it is out in the world, it cannot be perfected anymore. Yet I keep writing and publishing because, as Keneth Atchity reminds us, 'The product is what readers value. But writers love the work' (1995, p. xvii).

The unpredictability of podcast conversations affirms the value of letting thoughts travel in their own, not predetermined direction. While on the podcast I always tried to be as accurate as possible, I also found it liberating to share 'facts' that might still need checking and to rely on anecdotes and personal experience just to retain the flow of conversation. I began to do that in my writing too – instead of stopping to check ideas or find good references, I learnt to leave blank spaces and insert citations later. Instead of trying to find that one perfect word, I go with handy approximations to protect the writing flow (Ricchiuto, 2023). Podcasting taught me the value of relinquishing control.

Elbow calls trying to 'get it right' the first time 'the dangerous method' (1998, p. 39) and recommends freewriting as an alternative. Podcasts are essentially 'mad drafts' (Dunlap, 2007, p. 69) or 'shitty first drafts' (Lamott, 1995) that writing can revise while podcasting retains the 'madness'. When in throes of a vivid discussion, it can be easy to touch a nerve or broach a sensitive topic in an insensitive way, and perfectionist podcasters will shun controversy by diverting more difficult discussions or self-censoring to protect themselves and guests; others will embrace the chaos and consider the imperfections a blessing that comes with the format. Writing freely, as if conducting a conversation (sometimes with ourselves) helps to reduce the (often self-) silencing (Dunlap, 2007) or autocorrecting of our ideas that comes with perfectionism. For good thinking to develop, it is helpful to take risks with ideas or to get things wrong (Elbow, 1998). Frantic drafting liberates the voice so it can articulate everything that can possibly be said on the topic before letting ideas incubate and percolate in the mind. Those imperfect deliberations, even if ultimately expunged, may open up new ways of thinking.

Knowing that perfection lies in imperfection is a useful reminder that it is permissible to do what can be done in the moment and not put things off in pursuit of perfection. Even if we produce something that is not perfect (can anything ever be?), we are not going to get ostracised for it or made to feel like a failure. One podcast episode or published article will be more successful than another, but it will have been published, and there will still be value in that perfectly imperfect work.

Revelation 4: Authenticity Is the Secret Ingredient

Podcasting forces you to accept who you are. This is something that can be hidden in writing, but only to the writer's detriment. What every writer sells is 'not the subject being written about, but who he or she is' (Zinsser, 2006, p. 5). Good writers know and accept who they are, with their talents and limitations, and use that self-awareness to develop an authentic voice that resonates with readers.

Speaking on air can be a humbling and humiliating experience, especially for a speaker of English as a second language. In my experience, quick thoughts often joust with slow neural connections impeding access to the wider vocabulary, and two languages compete for primacy, attention, and authority. The asymmetry of the intellect processing the information on one plane of existence and the tongue rolling out yet another word that seems to follow logically but does not always make sense or contribute to the sharpness of the argument can be a source of considerable anxiety. When recording a podcast episode, I often found myself either cornered by imprecisely formulated ideas or trying to build congruence on a yet unprocessed inner dialogue. And then there is the accent: a signifier that marks me as the 'other'. Had I spent too much time thinking and obsessing about it, I would have never produced a podcast. Instead, I had to embrace it and come to believe that there would be listeners who appreciate the diversity in the texture of voices, rhythms, and tonalities that reveal the humanity of speakers more easily than writing can.

When writing for publication, we often put ourselves in the straitjacket of a particular format to satisfy publishers and achieve our professional goals, but it is often to the detriment of our writing style. According to Elbow, 'the best writing has voice: the life and rhythms of speech' (2000, p. 159), although we rarely teach our students to hone it or are encouraged by academic publishers to develop it. Richardson laments the state of academic writing that 'requires writers to silence their own voices' and 'ignores the role of writing as a dynamic, creative process' (1997, p. 88). Many academic authors have been found to resist this silencing, even if making writing lively may come with the cost of editors and reviewers' disapproval (Buckley *et al.*, 2024).

I always valued writing for its ability to hide my accent; for this exact reason I even considered writing my superpower. What readers' responses to my writing made me realise, however, is that it still *has* kind of an accent. That accent is a particular style of expression, a certain confidence to own my strengths and weaknesses, a distinct personality shaped by my lived experience and the obsessions with writers I wanted to emulate. What podcasting taught me is that instead of putting my energy into not embracing who I am, it might be better spent being and writing *like me*.

The Controversial Revelations

Revelation 5: Your Audience Is Not (Necessarily) Who You Think

Most advice on writing says something along the lines of 'know your audience'. There is a lot of wisdom in that. After all, we do need to know who we want to speak to when producing something, as it requires decisions regarding where to publish and how to write.

While I dispensed this advice in the past (Syska and Buckley, 2022, 2023), when positioned in the context of my experience with podcasting, I felt forced to reconsider it. When recording podcasts, I often found myself paralysed by the thought of who would be listening; I worried about what they might think, how they would interpret the words and ideas uttered, how I could please invisible 'them'. Audiences can be 'tricky' (Dunlap, 2007, p. 81) and even 'dangerous' (Elbow, 1998, p. 185) to consider as every reader or listener will bring different social and cultural characteristics with them, not to mention stylistic preferences and mood at the time, so we never know who will ultimately consume our ideas. Knowing one's audience is never truly possible, so putting too much energy into finding out who is looking over our shoulder may not be as productive as advised. Indeed, if we worry too much about what our audience might want, we might bend ourselves and contort our message in ways that might satisfy no one, especially not ourselves as authors. This has nothing to do with clarity – clarity is paramount, and it will be guided by the audience as we write differently for an academic or popular reader, advanced or novice, familiar with our vernacular or not. But there should be limits to which we will go to adjust what we want to say to that anticipated audience.

Audiences will come if they find value in what we do, even if the contribution is modest (Murray, 2020, p. 21). The podcast was never about me but about the guests and their voices, and me trying to extract the best out of them. And this is what needs to happen in writing – the best things must be extracted out of the writer so they can find a reader who appreciates what they have to say. This does not mean to ignore who the potential readers are, but rather to draw a Venn diagram of our goals, interests, and passions, and those of our potential readers, so we can meet them halfway and take them on a journey with us. In writing, it might be best to leave the audience concerns for the rewriting stage, so they don't constrain the writing itself. While always striving to improve their craft, good writers find their groove and their audience by staying steadfastly, unapologetically themselves on the page. To the question of audience, Zinsser gives a simple answer: 'You are writing for yourself' (Zinsser, 2006, p. 24).

Revelation 6: Writing Calls for a Love Affair with Time

One of the central truths that podcasting revealed to me about writing was simply that to get it done, I actually had to *do* it. Recording a podcast requires certain conditions for it to happen – time needs to be secured, guests invited, regular episodes released, platform set up, perhaps a co-host tempted to join in. The same with writing – it will not get produced unless time is set aside, a few words put down, and the commitment is made to see it through despite obstacles and inner resistance (Pressfield, 2002).

Finding the time to write is difficult, and the lack-of-time excuse is used so ubiquitously that Silvia has facetiously nominated it 'for academia's hall of fame' (Silvia, 2007, p. 12). There is plenty of advice on how to secure time, including scheduling writing, writing with others, and experimenting with different processes until we find one that works (Atchity, 1995). But my experience with podcasting – the activity I came to love and pursue despite the evident lack of time – makes me put forward a more controversial proposition. I came to the conclusion that in order to write, we must *steal* away time. Snatch it from the grips of mundane tasks that dominate our daily lives and willingly hand it over to writing. Writing must become a priority we give ourselves to with joy and great anticipation.

In pursuit of controversy, I will even follow Susan Sontag's (1963) lead and postulate that we must take on writing like one takes on a lover. That lover will take second place to our daily husbandry, but they will be there, always on call, making our writing exciting, risky, deliciously promiscuous, and irresistible. That lover will belong to no one but you – heck, give them a name! They will whisper sweet words and put you in the bliss of timeless flow that can only be reached in self-abandonment to writing. A love affair with time will make writing feel like the highest expression of your creative potential.

Transformative Crossovers Between Podcasting and Writing

My pandemic experience with podcasting taught me many lessons about writing, bringing into sharp relief the similarities between the two ways of engaging ideas. The moment of enunciation in speaking is the moment of negotiation in writing – when interpellated to respond to a call in a conversation, it is not uncommon to feel a bit of panic, resistance, or blankness of the brain – feelings familiar in the context of writing. In both genres, good work emerges not in miraculous bursts but through the gruelling labour of consistently pushing forward. The confrontation with words that do not work and the imprecision of language discoverable in every utterance often show us how unprepared we are to articulate our ideas, how clumsy and lacking in knowledge and ability we present at the keyboard or in front of the microphone. It becomes even more complex and unpredictable once we start adding the external pressures of audience or demands of scholarship. Like podcasting, writing becomes an outcome of the combination of this inner and outer conversation.

Podcasting sits somewhere between the ephemeral reality and writing – you cannot rewind the movie of your life the same way you can rewrite its story – but the permanence of the podcast is what moves it away from standard, transient speech and closer to writing. I continue podcasting because it continues teaching me things. It allows me to connect with people, explore ideas, challenge my world of knowledge. And it strengthens my relationship with writing. It transformed the way I think about writing, the way I teach it, and the way I think of myself as a producer of knowledge. The obvious, surprising, and downright controversial lessons and revelations I took from podcasting are daily reminders that the journey of creative expression requires courage to keep showing up, a willingness to learn from missteps, and an unwavering commitment to the craft itself.

References

Atchity, K. J. (1995) *A writer's time: making the time to write*. Norton & Company.

Barthes, R. (1977) *Writers, intellectuals, teachers: image music text*. Trans. S. Heath. London: Fontana Press.

Buckley, C., Syska, A. and Heggie, L. (2024) Grounded in liquidity: writing and identity in third space. *London Review of Education*, 22(1), pp. 26–38.

Dunlap, L. (2007) *Undoing the silence: six tools for social change writing.* New Village Press.

Germano, W. (2021) *On revision: the only writing that counts.* University of Chicago Press.

Elbow, P. (2000) *Everyone can write: essays toward a hopeful theory of writing and teaching writing.* Oxford University Press.

Elbow, P. (1998) *Writing with power: techniques for mastering the writing process.* Oxford University Press.

Lamott, A. (1995) *Bird by bird: some instructions on writing and life.* Anchor Books.

McHugh, S. (2022) *The power of podcasting: telling stories through sound.* Columbia University Press.

Murray, R. (2020) *Writing for academic journals* (4th ed.). London: Open University Press, McGraw-Hill Education.

Pressfield, S. (2002) *The war of art: break through the blocks and win your inner creative battles.* Black Irish Entertainment.

Richardson, L. (1997) *Fields of play: constructing an academic life.* Rutgers University Press.

Ricchiuto, J. (2023) *Words in flow: Zen and the art of writing.* Cleveland: Nuance Works.

Silvia, P. J. (2007) *How to write a lot: a practical guide to productive academic writing.* American Psychological Association.

Sontag, S. (1963) 'The ideal husband'. *The New York Review*, September 26.

Syska, A. and Buckley, C. (2022) 'Writing as liberatory practice: unlocking knowledge to locate an academic field', *Teaching in Higher Education*, 28(2), pp. 439–454. https://doi.org/10.1080/13562517.2022.2114337

Syska, A. and Buckley, C. (2023) Learning Developers as writers: the four tendencies framework to get writing, In A. Syska and C. Buckley (eds.), *How to be a Learning Developer in higher education: critical perspectives, community and practice.* Routledge.

Syska, A. and Mesley, M. (2021) Keep learning in a pandemic: podcasts for learning development conversations and informal learning, *Journal of Learning Development in Higher Education*, Special Edition: Compendium of Innovative Practice, 22, pp. 1–5.

Zinsser, W. (2006) *On writing well: the classic guide to writing nonfiction.* Harper Perennial.

Section 3

Crossing Boundaries
Individual and Institutional Impact in Higher Education

Gita Sedghi

Educators need to be proactive and adaptable to be successful in today's rapidly evolving landscape of higher education (HE). One effective approach involves the willingness to cross boundaries when necessary, driving change and making a positive impact both for staff and students. Instances of crossing boundaries abound and include sustained interdisciplinary education within the competing institutional and academic agendas of the university (Hannon *et al.*, 2018), leadership for a fractured world (Williams, 2015), a complex network of personal connections (Buckley, 2023), and cross-boundary collaborations for the creation of new courses (Vartiainen *et al.*, 2022). This cross-boundary work has been captured by the concept of 'Third Space', which has unique implications for individuals and institutions (Whitchurch, 2012). At the same time, the growing number of Third Space professionals spanning academic positions, professional services, and administration has identified several challenges, such as uncertainty around one's professional identity, place in the institutional culture and infrastructure, entitlement to continuous professional development (CPD), leadership, and career progression trajectory (Kukhareva and Buckley, 2023). This section explores transformative practices in which educators have leveraged boundary crossing to address complex, real-world challenges in contemporary higher education.

In Chapter 13, Nicola Grayson reflects on her authentic leadership journey within Third Space as she pushes boundaries to become a leader without formal authority. Her journey started with advocating for equity and encouraging a sense of community during the pandemic. Grayson continued her journey as an editor to practise experience-based leadership where she pushed boundaries to create powerful writers and communicators (Arao and Clemens, 2013). Her journey successfully ended with leading the institutional enhancement of teaching practice. This chapter navigates from safe to brave spaces, challenging dominant narratives and boundaries to become an authentic leader.

Navigating challenges in an ever-changing environment requires effective mechanisms for change, such as collaboration and reflection on practices (Akkerman and Bakker, 2011). However, Chandler (2013) adds certain factors in educational settings that are commonly experienced by staff as key triggers for resistance to change, including the faculty culture, a sense of territory, friction between functional divisions, resource allocation, traditions, leadership, communication, the power of unions, and individual idiosyncrasies. It has also been found that HE institutions are more inclined to resist change management; this resistance is particularly evident in the context of online and blended learning environments. Dumford and Miller (2018) show the inverse correlation between the number of online courses and effective teaching practices. While online environments might have several advantages, they may also lack interaction, which can undermine their effectiveness. Vuojärvi *et al.* (2022) demonstrate the boundary-crossing processes students encountered during an online multidisciplinary course focused on generic skills through collaborative learning, providing insights into the pedagogical principles in HE online learning settings. Enhancing blended learning with technology has the potential to shift the essence of learning, often leading to a transformative journey where learning has no boundaries (Ilyas and Malik, 2024).

In Chapter 14, Sandra Abegglen, Tom Burns, John Desire, Janet Gordon, Fabian Neuhaus, and Sandra Sinfield explain how groups and individual educational professionals worked together to provide support, foster exchange, and amplify the voices of those at the forefront of new, emerging practices and research. Consequently, TALON, the Teaching and Learning Online Network, was created as a hub for the different initiatives and activities to support educational online practice. The authors argue that our educational activities should be designed to transform educational practice, a paradigm shift where we collectively shake up traditional notions of what university is and what it can become.

An example of successful digital transformation is demonstrated by Darina Slattery (Chapter 15), who crossed boundaries to embark on a substantial project to acquire a new learning management system (LMS) at the institutional level. A change management project of this scale is usually difficult to implement. Nevertheless, a shift in organisational digital culture was even more challenging. In line with the institution's strategic plan to enhance digital education, Slattery applied the relevant practices and guidance from the JISC framework (JISC, 2023) to support knowledge development and enhance the organisational digital culture and digital infrastructure. Collaboration and development within creative social environments, such as when co-designing and implementing large-scale digital change, are powerful examples of transformative practices in accomplishing mutual goals in higher education, leading to innovative and adaptive educational experiences. However, the challenges of co-design are undeniable, as it requires people to understand each other and develop trust (Calvo and Sclater, 2021). DiSalvo (2016) demonstrates co-design practice as a method used to scaffold the design experience, increasing participants' reflection on their own knowledge and accounting for their previous knowledge. Mutual learning between the participants in co-design processes plays an important role in the success of projects (Chandler, 2013).

Bringing together students from different disciplinary backgrounds, in Chapter 16, Zoe Enstone demonstrates the value of co-creation with students while helping them navigate not only institutional boundaries but also those existing between the physical and the digital learning spaces. This approach allowed her to facilitate the integration of skills required to work with physical primary sources and those needed for digital research. This was not a passive process but a practical, focused opportunity for developing individual skills and wider disciplinary engagement. Ultimately, skills-based content enriched the online provision, encouraging critical engagement with digital materials.

In Chapter 17, Sandris Zeivots, Dewa Wardak, Andrew Cram, and Joanne Nash introduce their interdisciplinary unit, which has embraced the co-design approach as a cornerstone of educational transformation. The chapter introduces and examines a three-year program, offering a unique perspective on transformative practice and academic development in a co-design context. As the authors reflect on their experience, three key lessons stand out: intentional flexibility, capacity building, and the value of customisable resources for sharing. The authors challenge educators to share, implement, and tailor resources to meet diverse needs. They highlight that fostering a culture of open dialogue and collaboration amplifies the impact of successes and catalyses transformative changes across institutions.

The final chapter by Andrea Todd offers an insight into co-designing a new undergraduate module in partnership with students who receive academic credit for their contribution to it. The module learning outcomes, content, delivery and assessment methods are all devised by students, following the principles of direct democracy, which place control 'in the hands of the people themselves' (Dalton *et al.*, 2001). Todd argues that we need to redefine what it means to be a module leader; if we want to give students agency, truly being a module leader does not mean being simply a module creator or taking responsibility for design and delivery. It means placing power in students' hands, facilitating their work as module creators and liberating them to design and deliver a module that meets their needs.

Boundary-crossing learning opportunities that help generate valuable ideas and interventions could open up connect, or co-design with professional communities, employers, and institutions' learning activities and resources (Nerantzi, 2019). The collaborative open learning experience of academic staff and learners in cross-institutional environments provides insights for academic developers and course designers about the benefits of crossing boundaries. It promotes the engagement of academic staff in novel approaches to learning, teaching, and developing as practitioners.

References

Akkerman, S. F. and Bakker, A. (2011) 'Boundary crossing and boundary objects', *Review of Educational Research*, 81(2), pp. 132–169, https://doi.org/10.3102/0034654311404435

Arao, B. and Clemens, K., (2013) 'From safe spaces to brave spaces: a new way to frame dialogue around diversity and social justice'. Available at https://www.anselm.edu/sites/default/files/Documents/Center%20for%20Teaching%20Excellence/From%20Safe%20Sp (Accessed 1 August 2024).

Buckley, C., (2023) 'Leadership in Learning Development', pp. 211–219, in A. Syska and C. Buckley (eds.), *How to be a Learning Developer in higher education*. Routledge.

Calvo, M. and Sclater, M., (2021) 'Creating spaces for collaboration in community co-design', *International Journal of Art and Design Education*, 40(1), pp. 232–250. https://doi.org/10.1111/jade.12349

Chandler, N. (2013) 'Braced for turbulence: understanding and managing resistance to change in the higher education sector', *Management*, 3(5), pp. 243–251. https://doi.org/10.5923/j.mm.20130305.01

Dalton, R. J., Burklin, W. and Drummond, A. (2001) 'Public opinion and direct democracy', *Journal of Democracy*, 12(4), pp. 141–153.

DiSalvo, B., (2016) 'Participatory design through a learning science lens', *CHI '16: Proceedings of the 2016 CHI Conference on Human Factors in Computing Systems*, Association for Computing Machinery, New York, NY, USA, pp. 4459–4463. https://doi.org/10.1145/2858036.28584

Dumford, A. D. and Miller, A.L., (2018) 'Online learning in higher education: exploring advantages and disadvantages for engagement', *Journal of Computing in Higher Education*, 30, pp. 452–465.

Hannon, J., Hocking, C., Legge, K. and Lugg, A. (2018) 'Sustaining interdisciplinary education: developing boundary crossing governance', *Higher Education Research and Development*, 37(7), pp. 1424–1438. https://doi.org/10.1080/07294360.2018.1484706

Ilyas, M. and Malik, A. (2024) 'Beyond boundaries: enhancing learning through blended education', pp. 132–144, in S. Saluja and M. Hamid (eds.), *The Future of Academia: Transforming Learning*. Walnut Publication.

JISC. (2023) 'Framework for digital transformation in higher education'. Available at https://repository.jisc.ac.uk/9056/1/framework-for-digital-transformation-in-higher-education.pdf (Accessed 15 August 2024).

Kukhareva, M. and Buckley C. (2023) 'Why and how you matter: learning development as everyday leadership', [special issue] *Journal of Learning Development in Higher Education*, 29. https://doi.org/10.47408/jldhe.vi29.1079

Nerantzi, C. (2019) 'The role of crossing boundaries in collaborative open learning in cross-institutional academic development', *Research in Learning Technology*, 27. http://doi.org/10.25304/rlt.v27.2111

Vartiainen, H., Vuojärvi, H., Saramäki, K., Eriksson, M., Ratinen, I., Torssonen, P., Vanninen, P. and Pöllänen, S. (2022) 'Cross-boundary collaboration and knowledge creation in an online higher education course', *British Journal of Educational Technology*, 53(5), pp. 1304–1320. https://doi.org/10.1111/bjet.13186

Vuojärvi, H., Vartiainen, H., Eriksson, M., Ratinen, I., Saramäki, K., Torssonen, P., Vanninen, P. and Pöllänen, S. (2022) 'Boundaries and boundary crossing in a multidisciplinary online higher education course on forest bioeconomy'. *Teaching in Higher Education*, 29(5), pp. 1197–1214. https://doi.org/10.1080/13562517.2022.2122791

Whitchurch, C. (2012) *Reconstructing identities in higher education: the rise of 'Third Space' professionals*. London: Routledge.

Williams, D. (2015) *Leadership for a fractured world: how to cross boundaries, build bridges, and lead change*. Oakland: Berrett-Koehler.

Chapter 13

What Advocating for My Expertise Taught Me About Authentic Leadership

Nicola Grayson

Introduction

In this chapter I reflect upon what advocating for my expertise (Grayson and Theis, 2021) taught me about leadership. I refer to three case studies: completion of an umbrella project, editing the work of others, and leading the institutional enhancement of teaching as programme leader of a Postgraduate Certificate in Higher Education (PGCAP). The case studies present the trajectory of my leadership journey and have generalisable value in supporting HE professionals working in fields that may dictate leading without what Blanchard terms 'position power' (Blanchard, 2007, p. 109).

I will draw out how advocating for my expertise contributed to the development of a resilient, authentic, and iterative approach to leadership that is responsive and harnesses the unique power of vulnerability. I have intertwined the words of others with my own reflections to present a marriage of internal and external experiences. My intention is to contribute a holistic insight into how Third Space roles (Whitchurch, 2013) may necessitate leadership styles that transgress traditional position-power bounds in favour of 'distributed' and community-focused approaches (Bolden *et al.*, 2009). In doing so, using writing as a form of liberatory practice (Syska and Buckley, 2022), I seek to write my own existence as a leader into actuality.

I will begin by outlining how my experience of advocating for the specific needs of researchers throughout the early stages of the COVID-19 pandemic taught me that equity (the principle of treating people in a fair and just way so they might fulfil their potential) matters in the provision of support. I will then reflect on how my role as an editor for the *Journal of Learning Development in Higher Education* (JLDHE) allowed me to mentor and cultivate others to develop their authentic voice, drawing out their latent potential as writers. Finally, I will gather the threads of my emergent leadership to demonstrate how, in a more explicit leadership role as programme leader of the PGCAP, I sought to develop and enhance the teaching of others, drawing on my lived experience, expertise, and invaluable community connections.

DOI: 10.4324/9781003503149-17

Equity must be considered and addressed if people are to have hope of being treated equally; it concerns the application of the principle of fairness and equality is the outcome of taking a considered (or equitable) approach. Advocacy combines *vocare* 'to call, name, or invoke' with *ad* 'on behalf of, or in favour of'. Advocacy leadership thereby involves taking action to address concerns on behalf of others; it is the capacity to direct actions and recognise opportunities to *shift* and inspire, to solve problems together. I will argue that, as with teaching practice, the development of leadership should always be *iterative* and to develop an authentic approach one must continually adapt, respond, and redefine – continually encountering 'brave spaces' in which vulnerability might be transposed into power (Arao and Clemens, 2013).

Advocating for Equity in the Provision of Support

Looking back at the original innovation published in the *Compendium of Innovative Practice* (Grayson and Theis, 2021), I sought to advocate for postgraduate researchers and staff in respect to the provision of tailored support during the pandemic. The My Research Essentials (MRE) support programme that I led was designed to promote and encourage a sense of community (Grayson and Napthine-Hodgkinson, 2020, pp. 4–5). Our first problem concerned how to maintain the community focus in a virtual space; the second was related to pressure to align with an asynchronous approach devised with the largest student cohort in mind (undergraduates). The combined challenge became how to provide support, which gave researchers access to their community while also striving to ensure inclusivity.

I worked with the MRE team to pilot synchronous support using Shut up and Write (SUAW) sessions as a case study. Pilot trialling of synchronous support meant data could be gathered and reviewed, formative feedback could be sought, and the offer could be refined in line with an informed and agreed approach. To provide further context, I was working as a Learning Developer (LDer) at the time, and from October 2019 to October 2020, I led a large umbrella project to successfully move MRE from project to service capacity. The MRE Review Project encompassed a series of smaller project groups, which worked on the following areas:

- Quality assurance
- Impact and feedback
- Content, creation, and pedagogy
- Marketing and engagement
- Programme management

To facilitate this work, I chaired monthly MRE Operational Group meetings to gather updates and steer the project teams. I also attended monthly MRE Board meetings with senior managers to report on overall progress.

I led the umbrella project from an LD role without line management or 'position power'. Buckley fittingly argues that leadership in LD might be understood as 'a network of relations between equals, distributed through personal connections and reinforced by actions and outputs' (Buckley, 2023, p. 212). This encapsulates the way I led MRE, and the leadership approach I began to develop helped me to build confidence in myself and gain respect from the team and senior managers. It afforded me insight into the value of participatory decision making and in granting space for others to input into iterative support. The projects were inevitably steered by me but collaboratively enhanced and co-created in a way that ensured different perspectives were taken into account.

Buckley writes of the LD leader as one who must *leverage* 'the value of their knowledge, abilities, position, relationships, and personal qualities' towards achieving their aim 'whilst helping others develop in a similar way' (Buckley, 2023, p. 212). I had to leverage and draw upon the trust I'd developed through the MRE project work in order to steer the piloting of the synchronous support. As Buckley describes, in leading I also sought to support the development of others – both the researchers and my colleagues – and I believe this is captured through the collaborative publications (Grayson and Theis, 2021; Grayson and Napthine-Hodgkinson, 2020). Although I undoubtedly took on a lead role, for me the publications symbolise the solidification of partnership, co-creation, and mutual support.

In summary, the MRE review project gave me a platform from which I could advocate for my expertise in respect to supporting researchers during the pandemic (Grayson and Theis, 2021). The seeds for my emergent 'distributed' leadership style (Bolden *et al.*, 2009) were sown from my LD work from a position without explicit power, using principles of community – and in documenting this work through publications, I began to write myself as a leader into existence.

Cultivating Emergent Voices

Supporting and mentoring writers in respect to publishing their educational research has become a valued part of my practice. I joined the JLDHE editorial board in December 2021 and worked with three experienced editors to produce the *Compendium of Innovative Practice* (Syska, 2021).

I conceptualise editing as mentoring, or experience-based leadership in relation to publication processes and procedures. However, it also involves recognising and drawing out latent potential from writers in order to reflect and nurture their authenticity. In this way, editors can curate the development of a writer's emergent voice. It is *responsive* work, but not in the same way that the aforementioned distributed leadership of project work is responsive. With editing, the 'leveraging' aspect Buckley identifies is not at the forefront; rather, the 'helping others develop' part plays a dominant role (Buckley, 2023, p. 212).

Editing involves *careful listening* to what a writer wants to say but has not quite said. It necessitates a 'switching' of roles as one moves from *editor* to *reader* and even to *writer* to communicate changes and enhancements from a combined perspective (for more on 'switching' in respect to roles and hybridity, see Grayson and Syska, 2023).

For me, editing is a role that holds privilege. As an editor you are the first, privileged reader of an author's work and you work with them to shape and harness potential that might increase the works' clarity, power, and reception. You work with writers at their most vulnerable as they enter a 'brave space' subject to acceptance, revision, or rejection, and you must seek to lead them through it (Arao and Clemens, 2013).

In the *Compendium* I supported two doctoral researchers to share their experience of writing and researching during the pandemic (Grayson, 2021), and I want to share a quote from Dr Abdelhafid Jabri, who was a postgraduate researcher at the time but has since successfully defended his thesis:

> Publishing in the Compendium was invaluable for me. It was a psychological relief to express the challenges I was facing during my doctoral journey and an intellectual workout during the stressful confinement period. This could not be possible without the unconditional support of Dr Nicola Grayson ... When reading her pertinent remarks and encouraging words related to my piece, *I felt as if an inner voice was guiding me.*
>
> (My emphasis added)

Jabri beautifully captures how editing the work of others is a reciprocal dialogue of inner voices. It requires you to listen to the inner voice of the writer and to guide them using yours, and through this process the writer becomes attuned as their voice sharpens and is cultivated. In order to anticipate the impact of potential changes, an editor must attune to a writer's implicit intentions behind their explicit text. We must connect *beyond* the sphere of explicit meaning to draw on the implicit receptions of our words and meanings, projecting forward to grasp how words might land in the minds of others based on how you are experiencing them yourself.

Editing is also about being mindful of how feedback and revisions might be received by one who occupies that vulnerable, 'brave' space that is the humble domain of partially completed writing (Arao and Clemens, 2013). An editor offers mentorship and leads without position power; the leadership is not distributed – though there are elements of this at play in the wider project of scholarship. Instead, editing involves experience-based leadership in respect to faith in dialogue and the fruitful attunement of a shared goal: to further knowledge and scholarship for the wider community. In Third Space, and in Learning Development specifically, there is a lot at stake for the community as we write our field into existence (Syska and Buckley, 2022).

Leading the Institutional Enhancement of Teaching Practice

Becoming the programme leader of the PGCAP at the University of Salford was my first experience of being in a more explicit leadership role. It brought me the opportunity to influence teaching practice across the institution at a time when Advance HE's Professional Standards Framework (PSF) had been revised, with the changes having a great impact across the sector (Advance HE, 2023). In a new role, institution, and field (academic development), I needed to design a new programme in line with the new PSF. I led the PGCAP team in respect to the design (in part a redesign) to gain internal validation, and then I led our application to Advance HE for accreditation of the new programme under the new PSF. The following effectively shows an outsider's perspective of my experience from my line manager:

> Nicola stepped into a leadership role in an environment of change and had to quickly find her authentic brand of leadership ... This was challenging in a setting when there's pressure to demonstrate that you are leading by example whilst also immersed in your own learning journey.
> (Davina Whitnall, EDI lead and Academic Development Manager, University of Salford)

To gain the internal validation, I led the team to complete the required documentation, which was subject to scrutiny and subsequent approval by a panel of internal senior staff, students, and an external advisor. In addition to the requirements of the revised PSF, we updated the resources and theoretical underpinnings of the core module and, in consultation with Advance HE, sought to combine the two optional modules into an additional core module. I took this decision to ensure all participants would complete the PGCAP armed with insight into both inclusive curriculum design *and* assessment and feedback as opposed to only one of these areas. I worked with transparency to keep all stakeholders informed, and this helped me to build trust. I worked in partnership with quality management and equity, diversity, and inclusion (EDI) and gained external input. Once the programme was successfully validated, the paperwork was held as exemplary within the institution and by the external advisor, particularly in relation to EDI.

I believe that the transparency helped to demonstrate and cultivate trust with my peers and in my new institution. In addition, advocating for the PGCAP participants in working hard to ensure inclusive practice was embedded throughout the programme made it easy for my proposed changes to be accepted. I hope the words of my valued colleague who played a crucial role in both the MRE review project and the PGCAP validation will show what worked well for us:

I have worked with Nicola in two different institutions, across three different projects and areas of work. Although the challenges of these projects are distinct, with different stakeholders, aims and time-pressures, I have seen, and experienced, how Nicola's leadership has developed over-time, whilst also remaining consistent in terms of approach, *with delegation, trust and advocacy at the core of how she manages people and projects.*

(Dr Craig Morley, academic developer, University of Salford. My emphasis)

Once the redesigned PGCAP programme was validated, I led the work on the programme's accreditation. Careful preparation of extensive, newly drafted paperwork was required, and I made the unpopular decision to pause the programme in order to complete this on time and up to the required standard. It was difficult to manage the challenges that came with this decision and with navigating new territory, and it exposed my vulnerabilities. However, my earlier experiences working with a distributed leadership style served me well as I sought to maximise and harness the strengths, connections, collateral, and insights of my colleagues. The value I have always placed on participatory design and decision making and collaborative enhancement meant we worked *together*, in a respectful community, with a clear shared vision and values. The new programme was successfully awarded accreditation in May 2024, two days before I left Salford for a new role as a Senior Lecturer in Academic Development at Manchester Metropolitan University.

The programme leader role drew upon the distributed leadership and mentoring but had a higher degree of position power with wider institutional responsibility for shaping, influencing, and supporting the enhancement of teaching. In order to embrace this role, I used my combined experience as an academic, a Third Space professional, and a hybrid practitioner. I gained an informed perspective in a holistic way that transcends arbitrary boundaries that could limit the perspective of what it means to be an HE educator. Being new to a role, field, and institution brings its own vulnerabilities, but these can correspondingly be transposed into areas of strength when colleagues witness you navigating the 'brave space' of new territory within your own sphere. I tried to be transparent about this within and outside of my institution (on social media) to draw in support and advice wherever possible in order to strengthen my drive and resolve. My previous line manager provides her perspective on this:

There is a misconception that allowing your vulnerability to be seen is showing that you are weak ... Nicola, was able to utilise her vulnerability despite its discomfort through drawing on her lived experience ... *I clearly hear her voice, the voices of those that she supported and their lived experience in the programme and outputs she developed.*

(Davina Whitnall, EDI lead and Academic Development Manager, University of Salford; my emphasis)

The newly designed PGCAP programme makes greater space for inclusivity throughout and for partnerships with students and with other areas of the university. There is a renewed focus on equity, equality, diversity, and inclusion across the programme and the paperwork, and it was particularly important to push for change in this area, as at Salford the PGCAP not only supports academic staff, but also those in professional and public services such as Greater Manchester Police.

I want to end with reference to the importance and strength of the authentic connections we build along our learning and leadership journeys. Just as the joint publications mentioned earlier are symbols of my attempts to support the development of others, my working relationships have been an invaluable source of support for me. At times of doubt and crisis, my relationships gave me a mirror through which I could see a trusted reflection of myself that reaffirmed my own strength and celebrated the value of my connections as friendships:

> In a leadership position without traditional 'authority' or line-management responsibility, Nicola challenged, motivated and empowered me to make individual decisions and actions in my own areas of work. She did this through *advocating and celebrating the expertise and value I could bring* to wider projects, both internally within the project team and externally to a variety of audiences and stakeholders.
> (Dr Craig Morley, academic developer, University of Salford; my emphasis)

Some Transferable Features of My Journey

My experience of advocating for my audience proved an early catalyst for my development as an authentic leader, and in documenting it, I began the process of writing myself as a leader into existence. In the hope that my experiences might be useful to others, I will end by drawing together some transferable features:

- In advocating for my expertise, I had to *push against the dominant narrative*, but I did this armed with expertise, insight, trust, and a willingness to refine my approach in partnership with respected peers. In documenting my work, I could *participate in the wider conversation*, support others, and begin the ongoing task of writing my leadership into existence.
- In leading others through editing, I learnt to *listen and attune to implicit goals in light of explicit needs*; guiding others to publish helped me to reaffirm my position and value to myself.
- Working with *transparency served to build trust*; it enabled me to ask for support and make connections, and it demonstrated my progress. Sharing with openness helped me to actualise myself as a leader, just as writing about this journey brings further actualisation and affirmation.

- Finally, in *recognising and valuing supportive professional relationships* I saw myself reflected well in the eyes and words of my colleagues, and for me, this is reward in itself as I no longer solely advocate for others but have people who will also advocate for me.

References

Advance HE. (2023) 'Professional standards framework for teaching and supporting learning in higher education.' Available at https://advance-he.ac.uk/knowledge-hub/professional-standards-framework-teaching-and-supporting-learning-higher-education-0 (Accessed 19 Mar 2024).

Arao, B. and Clemens, K. (2013). 'From safe spaces to brave spaces: a new way to frame dialogue around diversity and social justice.' Available at https://www.anselm.edu/sites/default/files/Documents/Center%20for%20Teaching%20Excellence/From%20Safe%20Sp

Blanchard, K. (2007) *Leading at a higher level: Blanchard on leadership and creating high performance organisations.* Harlow: Financial Times Prentice Hall.

Bolden, R., Petrov, G. and Gosling, J. (2009) 'Distributed leadership in higher education: rhetoric and reality'. *Educational Management Administration & Leadership*, 37(2), pp. 257–327. https://doi.org/10.1177/1741143208100301

Buckley, C. (2023) 'Leadership in Learning Development', in A. Syska and C. Buckley (eds.), *How to be a Learning Developer in higher education* (pp. 211–219). Taylor and Francis.

Grayson, N. (2021). 'Section editorial: responding to the needs of doctoral researchers', *Journal of Learning Development in Higher Education*, 22. https://doi.org/10.47408/jldhe.vi22.851

Grayson, N. J. and Syska, A. (2023) Hybrid Learning Developers: between the discipline and the Third Space, in A. Syska and C. Buckley (eds.), *How to be a Learning Developer in higher education* (pp. 43–50), Taylor and Francis.

Grayson, N. J. and Theis, A (2021) 'Adapting community-focused writing support for researchers to synchronous online delivery', *Journal of Learning Development in Higher Education*, Plymouth, UK, 0(22). https://doi.org/10.47408/jldhe.vi22.758

Grayson, N. J. and Napthine-Hodgkinson, J. (2020) 'Enhancing public speaking skills using improvisation techniques', *Journal of Learning Development in Higher Education*, 19.

Syska, A. (2021) 'Compendium of Innovative practice: Learning Development in a time of disruption', *Journal of Learning Development in Higher Education*, 22. https://doi.org/10.47408/jldhe.vi22.850

Syska, A. and Buckley, C. (2022) 'Writing as liberatory practice: unlocking knowledge to locate an academic field', *Teaching in Higher Education*, pp. 1–16. https://doi.org/10.1080/13562517.2022.2114337

Whitchurch, C. (2013) *Reconstructing identities in higher education.* London: Routledge.

Chapter 14

What Floating in Pandemic Hyper Space Taught Us About Grounding Creative Academic Practice in the Here and Now

Sandra Abegglen, Tom Burns, John Desire, Janet Gordon, Fabian Neuhaus, and Sandra Sinfield

Introduction

> The playful experimenters full of curiosity who are not afraid to break the rules, invent new ones and explore new territories, are stepping into the limelight.
> (Nerantzi, 2019, p. 318)

COVID-19 in early 2020 forced a global reset of education (Robinson, 2020). Specifically, the shift to emergency remote teaching left a lasting and transformative impact on our practice. Based on two case study examples, we discuss the lessons learned from that period. Whilst acknowledging the challenges involved, we celebrate the positives of this explosion of informal practice-based research. For us, there was hope and opportunity: the bringing together of an international, interdisciplinary team involved in design education and hybrid pedagogy, and practitioners involved in learning and staff development, online praxis, and action research. In many ways we were primed for online connectivity: we had worked together in 'real' life in different forms and combinations – and continued working together when some of us relocated to Canada. We had lived the potential of collaborative researching, teaching, and writing online before the emergency reset. When the pivot came, we were ready to embrace the opportunities and develop – and support the development of – the creative, embodied, and collaborative virtual classrooms we imagined, in granular and strategic ways.

At the micro level, we consider a postgraduate certificate (PGCert) Learning and Teaching in Higher Education (LTHE) module that we moved online whilst still embracing and developing its collaborative, research- and arts-based, and ludic praxis (see Huizinga, 2002 – *Homo ludens*, the playful human). At the macro level, we consider the Teaching and Learning Online Network (TALON), an initiative designed to bring the online 'alive' for practitioners by the sharing of practices and experiences, tools and approaches internationally across the HE sector. At the meso level, practitioners in the UK-based PGCert module worked with the TALON community – contributing to podcasts and books, sharing ideas and practices – thus producing a virtuous circle of innovative collaboration where what was happening in real virtual classrooms was investigated and disseminated as it emerged. This research in action illustrates what we can develop when we are open and when we inhabit educational spaces together. A cautionary note, however: after this explosion of creative activity, by how much and how far would practitioners remain free to experiment and develop their innovative practice once the emergency was over?

Case Study 1: PGCert Apron Challenge

The 'apron challenge' invited participants in our PGCert module in a UK inner-city widening participation university to experience a Learning Development–inspired LTHE module (ALDinHE, 2021) in light of the shift to online instruction. The module was designed to be a face-to-face (F2F) and highly creative, ludic module (Sinfield et al., 2019) that 'de-schooled' (Illich, 1970) and 'unschooled' (Holt 1977, 1981) participants, helping to disrupt normative expectations of education, teaching, learning, and assessment. With COVID-19 and the move to remote teaching, the 'normal' was already disrupted – and not in a good way (Jandrić et al., 2020). For many lecturers – and ours were new to teaching or new to teaching in the UK – the 'architecture' of the online classroom appeared best suited to a more single-voiced, monoglossic, transmissive, and didactic practice, that is, a sage-on-the-stage approach where the knowledgeable expert tells the novice learner what they need to know and do. Our challenge was to lead our participants into a creative, embodied, and playful experience online – when they may not yet have conceived of that as a possibility in the F2F classroom. The module, as with the others on the PGCert course, was therefore designed to be a support system, standing alongside staff unfamiliar with teaching, learning, and assessing online whilst modelling the sort of liberatory practice that was possible in virtual space. We wanted to design, and for participants to experience, that learning itself is not just a cognitive process but is experiential, emotional, social, interpersonal, and embodied.

We wrestled with how to build bonding and belonging (Leathwood and O'Connell, 2003) and an embodied sense of the module learning process itself without 'meeting' the students in-person and having immediate access to the usual, varied physical resources we would normally use in the classroom. We undertook a complete overhaul and redesign of the module, opening ourselves up to different ways of conceptualising the curriculum online. Where previously each F2F session would harness play, collage making, drawing, blackout poetry, textscrolls, role play, free writing, and other forms of emergent and playful practice, we worked out how to recreate and reimagine these experiences in 'class' via our virtual learning environment. The challenge was how to prepare our potential students for the 'difference', the creative pedagogy, that was to come.

Previously, our colleague Simone Maier (2020) had developed a 'jeans to study apron' activity in which the making process allowed her to 'physically' think about preparing herself for study. We decided to adopt this creative and embodied activity as an induction challenge for our online learners, with alternatives available that would allow everybody to participate and succeed: so, our students could make an apron, design a study space for themselves, or share a 'study object' that was important for their own learning, and then share an image of that in the class Padlet. Our goal was to help students bring their whole human selves on this academic journey: the ontological route into the epistemological community.

Once we decided to take the leap and include a diverse range of hands-on activities in our online classroom, we discovered that so much was possible. The apron challenge was not just a throwaway one-off icebreaker but a metonym or synecdoche (the part that stands for or represents the whole) for the module itself: playful, collaborative, supportive, embodied, and online. We found that it provoked curiosity and engagement before the staff-as-students arrived in the online class. It helped disrupt normative expectations of education, teaching, learning, and assessment and positioned the participants to accept the creative, haptic, multimodal experiences that followed – and to embrace the uncertainty everyone was facing at the time. By 'being with' (Nancy, 2000) in creative and embodied ways, students experienced that it is possible online to develop impactful, collective, reflective, and dialogic experiences.

Since then, we have continued to deliver the whole PGCert, including this first module, online. Not only does it make it more flexible and accessible to participants who are themselves teaching across campuses or working from home, it continues to model what is possible when your courses are born digital – but engaged with experientially. Thus, our staff continue to make, do, play, read, and write together online – and then adapt those activities in their F2F or online practices, for example, seeding student writing by free writing and collage work, scaffolding academic reading by blackout poetry and textscrolls, and playing with alternative formats like blogs and Padlets for reflective practices. Our staff creatively integrate learning development as part of knowledge-making; further they find that they have the self-confidence to set their students alternative assignments – patchwork texts, video essays, podcasts, and Vlogs – because they had the space to play with these strategies as part of their own teaching, learning, and assessment journeys.

Case Study 2: The Teaching and Learning Network

Despite the opportunities we found and have created with the pivot to emergency online teaching, many staff were and continue to be challenged. Thus, it is impossible to overstate the extent of the challenges posed by COVID-19 (Abegglen *et al.*, 2022). In HE, beyond the sociopolitical, these challenges were far ranging for teaching and learning: from access to technology and the

Internet to developing effective and engaging methods and methodologies for remote delivery, and the struggle to overcome structural bias built into university processes, software, and applications. The virtual classroom, often praised as the 'future', proved to be far from unproblematic. Yes, as with Case Study 1, there were many instances where innovative and transformative practice happened; but overall there was a sense of being overwhelmed and under-supported – and that was where TALON stepped in.

TALON, the Teaching and Learning Online Network, was born in the early days of COVID-19, aiming to bring educational professionals together to provide support, foster exchange, and amplify the voices of those at the forefront of new, emerging practices and research. The TALON (2023a) website acted and acts as the hub for the different initiatives and activities – as a point of contact, reference, and connection, with the aim of fostering a sustainable ecology of online education through an active exchange between all those involved in HE. For example, the website contains an A-to-Z guide that showcases free and open-access software and tools for learning and teaching that education professionals find useful. As the academic world stood lonely and puzzled, TALON also produced a podcast series – interviewing everybody from digital experts to the 'also confused' – a companion space to stand alongside and in support of the many who were not receiving that support from their own institutions.

Through this activity, what has emerged is an active network that showcases educational technology, highlights lecturer and student voices, spotlights classroom practice and experiences, and aids development of resources and materials. This has led to the creation of a manifesto (TALON, 2023b) for transformative educational online practice: inclusive and equitable online education; open and positive learning environments; interactive and engaging pedagogy; transformative and imaginative design curricula; empowering virtual classrooms; collaborative learning and design teaching; software and tools enabling meaningful learning experiences; respect and care for all students and instructors.

TALON continues to promote the exchange of ideas, cultivating a 'community of practice' (Lave and Wenger, 1991; Kimble *et al.*, 2001) around new, emerging practices in online HE because it regards reflection and continued research as an essential part of teaching and learning. At the same time, connection and discussion are still much needed in these uncertain times (Abegglen *et al.*, 2020; Hall, 2021) to develop more creative and inclusive models and methods – to nourish, sustain, and support us – to keep us connected and to keep the conversations going.

A Cautionary Note

After the lockdowns, many immediately found their institutions insisting on a complete and immediate return to campus and traditional F2F teaching that was very frustrating for some. And all of us, even those who were frustrated by the digital revolution, acknowledged the potential benefit of a wholesale collective reflective moment: to value and appreciate all that we did, to recognise all the labour we put in, to surface the lessons learned and all the questions we asked and continue to ask: What does it take to teach well online? How and what should we teach online? What is the benefit of using technology in education? Who profits from online learning and how? How can we best support students online? What can and did we learn from the online experiment that we could take back into our F2F practice? Thus, TALON remains a live moment in radical educational practice – and a record of what was achieved when it was needed.

Take-away Culture: Lessons Learned

> dialogue must be understood as something taking part in the very historical nature of human beings. It is part of our historical progress in becoming human beings. That is, dialogue is a kind of necessary posture to the extent that humans have become more and more critically communicative beings. Dialogue is a moment where humans meet to reflect on their reality as they make and remake it.
>
> (Shor and Freire, 1987, p. 98)

Our philosophy as educators is to facilitate learning that works in partnership with students, colleagues, and external partners, to make transparent the contested forms and processes of academia and to develop empowering strategies that promote higher learning (Angelo, 1993), online and F2F. In the PGCert module, lecturers-as-students collaborate to experience creative processes that enable them to participate actively, powerfully and with agency in their own learning – and to facilitate that agency and ownership in their students. With TALON, diverse educators, internationally, are connected with each other to share their practice and reflect on teaching and learning – and envision a different, more inclusive online education. What emerges is a new ecology of collaborative practice (Abegglen *et al.*, 2023): urgent, emergent, and experimental. In this way, we argue that our educational activities are designed to transform education and educational practice, a paradigm shift where we collectively shake up traditional notions of what university is and what it can become.

References

Abegglen, S., Burns, T. and Sinfield, S. (Eds.) (2023) *Higher education collaboration: A new ecology of practice*. Bloomsbury.

Abegglen, S., Burns, T., Maier, S. and Sinfield, S. (2020) 'Supercomplexity: acknowledging students' lives in the 21st century university', *Innovative Practice in Higher Education*, 4(1), pp. 20–38. https://journals.staffs.ac.uk/index.php/ipihe/article/view/195

Abegglen, S., Neuhaus, F. and Wilson, K. (Eds.) (2022) *Voices from the digital classroom: 25 interviews about teaching and learning in the face of a global pandemic*. University of Calgary Press.

ALDinHE. (2021) *Association of Learning Development in higher education*. https://aldinhe.ac.uk/

Angelo, T. A. (1993) 'A teacher's dozen: fourteen general, research-based principles for improving higher learning in our classrooms', *AAHE Bulletin*, 45(8), pp. 3–7. https://www.researchgate.net/publication/237489105_A_Teacher's_Dozen-Fourteen_General_Research-Based_Principles_for_Improving_Higher_Learning

Hall, R. (2021) *The hopeless university: intellectual work at the end of the end of history.* May Fly.

Holt, J. (1977) Growing without schooling. GWS, 1, August/Summer. https://johnholtgws.squarespace.com/growing-without-schooling-issue-archive

Holt, J. (1981) *Teach your own: a hopeful path for education.* Delacorte Press/Seymour Lawrence.

Huizinga, J. (2002) *Homo ludens: a study of the play-element in culture.* Routledge.

Illich, I. (1970) *De-schooling society.* NHarper and Row.

Jandrić, P., Hayes, D., Truelove, I., Levinson, P., Mayo, P., Ryberg, T., Monzó, L. D., Allen, Q., Stewart, P. A., Carr, P. R., Jackson, L., Bridges, S., Escaño, C., Grauslund, D., Mañero, J., Lukoko, H. O., Bryant, P., Fuentes Martinez, A., Gibbons, A., ... Hayes, S. (2020) 'Teaching in the age of Covid-19', *Postdigital Science and Education*, 2, pp. 1069–1230. https://doi.org/10.1007/s42438-020-00169-6

Kimble, C., Hildreth, P. and Wright, P. (2001) Communities of practice: going virtual. In Y. Malhotra (Ed.), *Knowledge management and business model innovation* (pp. 216–230), Idea Group.

Lave, J. and Wenger, E. (1991) *Situated learning: legitimate peripheral participation.* Cambridge University Press.

Leathwood, C. and O'Connell, P. (2003) '"It's a struggle": The construction of "new student" in higher education', *Journal of Education Policy*, 18(6), pp. 597–615. https://doi.org/10.1080/0268093032000145863

Maier, S. (2020, June 11) Jeans to apron. *YouTube.* https://www.youtube.com/watch?v=ty_ztNPoEp4

Nancy, J. (2000) *Being singular plural.* Stanford University Press.

Nerantzi, C. (2019) The playground model revisited: a proposition for playfulness to boost creativity in academic development. In A. James & C. Nerantzi (Eds.), *The power of play in higher education: creativity in tertiary learning* (pp. 317–332). Palgrave Macmillan.

Robinson, K. (2020) A global reset of education. *Prospects*, 49, pp. 7–9.

Shor, I. and Freire, P. (1987) *A pedagogy for liberation: Dialogues on transforming education.* Bergin and Garvey.

Sinfield, S., Burns, T. and Abegglen, S. (2019) Becoming playful: The power of a ludic module. In A. James & C. Nerantzi (Eds.), *The power of play in higher education: Creativity in tertiary learning* (pp. 23–31). Palgrave Macmillan.

TALON. (2023a) Home. https://taloncloud.ca/

TALON. (2023b) Manifesto & glossary. https://taloncloud.ca/Manifesto-Glossary

Chapter 15

What a New LMS Adoption Taught Us About the Nature and Range of Supports Needed for Academic Stakeholders

Darina M. Slattery

Introduction

In early 2021, our institution embarked on a substantial project to acquire a new learning management system (or LMS). Planning for the LMS project had actually commenced in 2019, when the institution applied for substantial funding to facilitate a strategic academic and digital transformation project—that funding was awarded in late 2020, a few months into the COVID-19 pandemic. The primary goal of the transformation project was to invest in a new LMS to support the development of more flexible and professional programmes, facilitate greater access, and deliver improved functionality, reliability, scalability, and security in blended and fully online teaching environments.

As an enhanced digital teaching and learning experience should be at the core of any higher education (HE) digital transformation plan (JISC, 2023), it was also at the core of our institution's strategic plan (University of Limerick, 2019). The remainder of this chapter uses relevant practices and guidance from the JISC framework for digital transformation in higher education (JISC, 2023) to explain the rationale behind the decisions made and supports provided during this transformation project, particularly to support knowledge development but also to enhance the organisational digital culture and digital infrastructure (see Figure 15.1).

While the majority of the campus had been using the same LMS (Sakai) for well over a decade, small pockets of the institution had been using Moodle, so the decision was made to procure one new LMS for the entire institution. While the pandemic brought with it many challenges for HE (Cutri *et al.*, 2020; Trust and Whalen, 2020), the institution decided to capitalise on the skills that were developed during the sudden move to emergency remote teaching (ERT) (Hodges *et al.*, 2020) by introducing the new LMS within two to three years, thereby facilitating the digital transformation (JISC, 2023).

A change management project of this scale would have been challenging at the best of times, given the inevitable resistance that comes with change (Oreg, 2003), but a shift in organisational digital culture (JISC, 2023) was even more challenging immediately after a global pandemic. While many staff members

DOI: 10.4324/9781003503149-19

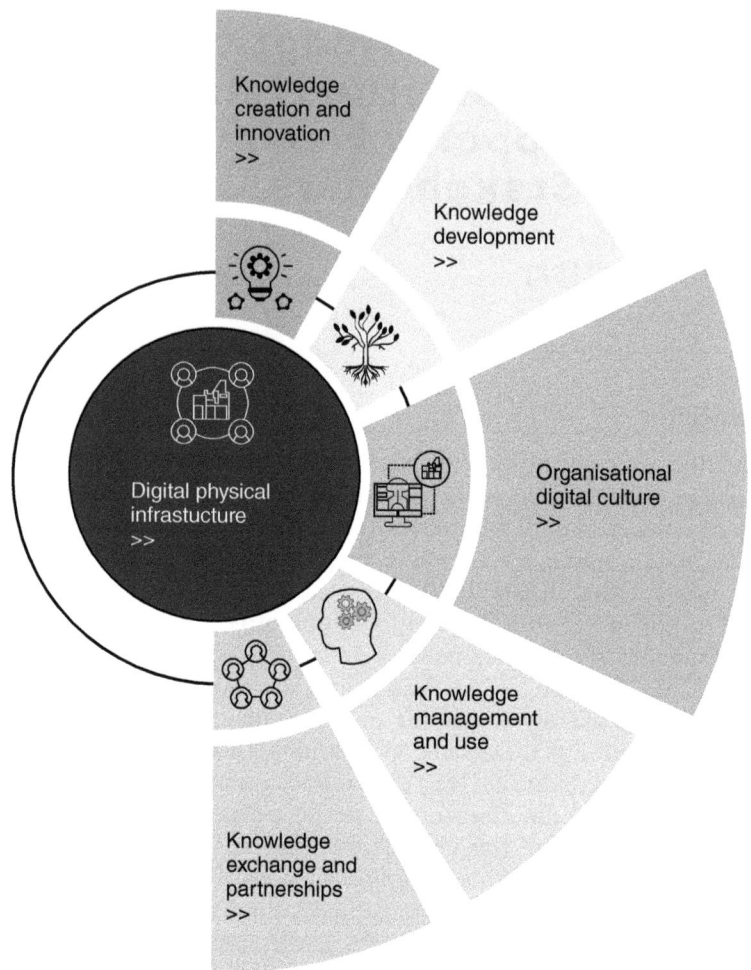

Figure 15.1 The JISC Framework for Digital Transformation in Higher Education (JISC, 2023).

were enthusiastic about the affordances that technology-enhanced learning can provide, and some had been early adopters, many questioned the need for a new LMS just as they were getting familiar with the existing platform—unfortunately, some staff had used the previous LMS on a limited basis before the pandemic. Others saw the introduction of the new LMS as *yet another institutional challenge* that would discommode them, and many worried about the time it would take to learn the new platform and redevelop their content. Others worried that there would be extra work involved but not necessarily substantial improvements in functionality. To encourage more forward thinking in our organisational digital culture, we had to raise awareness early on of *why* we were changing LMS platform and what advantages this change would bring—this was achieved through a dedicated website and email campaign. We also asked our LMS Steering Group, which comprised senior leadership from key divisions, to explain in their own words how the new LMS platform would facilitate the planned academic and digital transformation, and we shared that recording on our website.

Horizon scanning and stakeholder engagement are critical for a successful digital transformation (JISC, 2023). While the *previous* LMS had been chosen by a handful of staff, we consulted widely with all the relevant stakeholders (teaching staff, students, and support staff), reviewed industry trends, and benchmarked with other institutions that had changed LMS in recent years, in line with best practice (JISC, 2023). As five LMSs were originally under consideration, we also engaged with the LMS vendors and service providers and gave them opportunities to demonstrate their platforms, and then our team of learning technologists and instructional designers asked them technical questions about the platforms to really 'dig deep'. All these consultations resulted in an extensive list of LMS requirements, which was later used to shortlist the LMS platforms. In the end, this active consultation process enabled us to choose D2L Brightspace as our new LMS, as it was deemed the most appropriate platform for *our* staff and student requirements.

Using the New LMS as a Conduit to Transforming Teaching and Learning in a Predominately On-Campus Institution

Before we moved everyone to the new LMS, we undertook two small-scale pilots in the academic year 2022/23 to ensure we would identify any issues that might arise during the campus-wide transition from one LMS to another and to inform the range of supports that would be needed for the rest of the campus. It is not enough to provide new digital infrastructure – appropriate digital support is also needed to ensure staff develop appropriate digital competencies (JISC, 2023, 2024; Redecker, 2017). As everyone on the team was new to the platform, we first had to 'train the trainer', thereby building capacity. Fortunately, the chosen LMS has a dedicated online community of users, and a variety of 'how to' resources were available online, so the team used those resources to upskill. Another early task was to decide on the look and feel of the interface; to that end, the team engaged in extensive consultations about the naming and categorisation of LMS menu items and finally settled on a 'skin' and layout that would make sense to our users while also adhering to institutional branding.

Early on, the LMS team decided it would take advantage of this 'fresh start' in a new LMS by embedding good practice into the design of course sites. Accessibility, universal design for learning (UDL) and inclusion were central to these considerations (Bracken and Novak, 2019; CAST, 2024; JISC, 2023). During the phase 1 consultations, students had frequently requested more consistency in the presentation of course sites – they reported that some teaching staff used the LMS extensively whereas others used it solely as a file repository, resulting in fragmented learning experiences. While the members of the LMS team had extensive experience in designing blended and fully online courses, and they were brimming with ideas, the decision was made to implement a universal course template, which would support curriculum development (JISC, 2023) without being overly prescriptive. We knew from the phase 1 consultations that staff wanted to have control over how they teach and how they present content, so we designed a template that would serve as a baseline to ensure some consistency, but staff would still have the option to hide or customise features if required. That universal course template comprised a course overview area, with some prompts to remind teaching staff of the kinds of guidance they might want to provide at the start of the course (e.g., objectives, details of assessments, reading lists, and so on), followed by a structure that enabled staff to drag and drop content into weekly folders. These folders could also be renamed, if staff preferred a themed structure over a weekly structure, for example. The creation of a campus-wide template was a departure from the previous arrangements and signified a strategic commitment to improving the digital teaching and learning experience for staff and students (JISC, 2023).

Once the team got to grips with the key features of the LMS and the interface was agreed on, the team started working on localised resources for an online knowledge base, which would become a permanent digital support (JISC, 2023). While the initial plan was to make use of the generic resources provided by the LMS provider, we had customised our interface and functionality, so it was necessary to recreate many of the resources to ensure the interface matched what our users would see. The knowledge base was later split into two sections – one for staff and one for students. As our in-house knowledge base of 'how to' resources began to grow, that content was then used to inform the development of a Brightspace 101 course, which was developed *within* the LMS platform to teach our users how to use the key functionality. As some staff members had never received formal instruction on how to design blended or fully online courses (or even how to teach!), we grasped that opportunity to introduce some key concepts relating to curriculum design and UDL. We also signposted related supports that were already available, such as curriculum development workshops and the like. The Brightspace 101 course then honed in on practical LMS considerations, such as how to create and edit content, how to use the communication and collaboration tools, and how to use the assessment and feedback tools, and then it briefly introduced some of the platform's more advanced features. All course instructors had automatic access to this course when they logged into the platform, and they were encouraged to work through the course in their own time, while experimenting with the sandbox (practice area) we also provided, before attending the formal training sessions.

When it came to designing the formal training sessions, we went through a few iterations. The team considered various options, but as many staff were still working remotely a few days every week, and staff had previously expressed a preference for training in a variety of formats, we decided to develop live, online training sessions that would be recorded, so attendees could consult them later if required. We also decided to keep each of the three sessions short (one hour each) to ensure as many people as possible would be encouraged to attend. During those live sessions, a learning technologist (LT) demonstrated key functionality, while other LTs responded to questions and posted links to resources in the chat area, so the session could flow uninterrupted. From March to July 2023, before the campus-wide launch in September, we offered those live training sessions to staff on a reservation-only basis to ensure the numbers attending were manageable. Whenever we noticed a sudden increase in registrations, we scheduled additional sessions to accommodate those people. Meanwhile, a targeted communications campaign (using email predominantly but also dissemination via faculty committees and on our website) was used to promote the training and to remind staff of the impending move to a new platform. While often we felt that we were repeating ourselves, we also encouraged the members of our LMS Academic Advisory Group and LMS Stakeholder Forums to disseminate relevant updates to their own faculties. Knowledge exchange and partnerships are critical for a successful digital transformation (JISC, 2023).

Once the formal training sessions ended, we made the recordings available to the entire campus community to facilitate people who may have just started working at the institution or were unable to attend the sessions earlier in the year due to sabbatical or parental leave, for example. Those recordings were later embedded in the Brightspace 101 course, so they were permanently available as a digital support (JISC, 2023).

In addition to the Brightspace 101 course for staff, the team also developed an Introduction to Brightspace course for students, which was automatically available to students once they logged on to the platform. That course provided an overview of the main features while also familiarising students with the interface while *in* the platform itself, thereby facilitating the development of LMS competencies (Redecker, 2017).

We knew from our phase 1 consultations that staff expected a variety of flexible, digital supports. As a result, in addition to the knowledge base, online training sessions, and promotional campaigns, we also procured 24/7 support from the LMS vendor, which was available to all staff and students. We promoted the chat support over phone or email because the response time was quicker. We also ran additional training sessions the first two weeks of the autumn semester to ensure we offered support to new hires, staff returning from leave/sabbatical, and hourly paid staff and students.

Towards the latter half of 2023, we encouraged the early adopters from the pilots to participate in a 'Show and TEL' (TEL for technology-enhanced learning) campaign to create some momentum, promote the platform, and highlight and recognise good practice and innovation (JISC, 2023). The Show and TEL sessions were publicised across the campus and recorded for later viewing.

Another consideration as we approached the campus-wide launch in September 2023 was whether we would migrate content from the old LMSs to the new one, or if we should promote a 'start from scratch' approach. While some institutions had advised the latter approach, and we could see the benefits, the LMS team felt that staff had been through enough change in recent years and would need the extra support. In the end, we migrated the previous year's content for all Sakai users (the majority of the campus), and the learning technologists rebuilt the Moodle content in the new LMS to reduce the workload for teaching staff.

For the first few weeks of the autumn semester, we offered short Introduction to Brightspace drop-in workshops for students. These in-person sessions provided students with an overview of the interface while also pointing students to the range of other digital supports that were available to them (e.g., the Introduction to Brightspace course, 24/7 support, and the online knowledge base). We also publicised the Brightspace student supports through the social media campaigns of our Centre for Transformative Learning and undergraduate and postgraduate students' unions.

As we approached the end of the first year of the campus-wide rollout, we held an on-campus event to showcase the platform and generate enthusiasm for future developments. The purpose of the event was to enhance the digital culture and mindset (JISC, 2023) by letting attendees hear about the experiences of other institutions that use the same platform, see demos of new third party tools that would soon be available, and hear about the experiences of colleagues at our own institution. We also invited five shortlisted Show and TEL participants to give presentations to showcase their digital innovations and the competencies they had already developed (JISC, 2023; Redecker, 2017).

Moving Beyond the LMS Project to the Next Academic Transformation

In the three years before the launch of the new LMS campus-wide (2020–2023), our staff went from mostly on-campus teaching, to emergency remote teaching, and back to classroom teaching with some blended delivery. In that time, the needs and expectations of staff and students changed significantly. If staff were going to invest so much time in learning a new platform (having just become really familiar with the previous one), they expected to receive a lot of support and to see improvements in functionality.

It is evident from the previous section that we provided extensive support to staff and students as they transitioned from one LMS to another. This level of support was transformative and far more extensive than what we had provided previously, but it was necessary as the new LMS was more advanced and staff were likely to use it more extensively in the post-pandemic period. At the time of writing this chapter, staff have just finished their first academic year on the new LMS, and there were very few issues, which is evidenced by the relatively stable number of support calls being logged. Furthermore, students seem to have adapted to the platform very quickly. This evidence suggests that we are providing enough support and that staff have adapted well to the change (JISC, 2023).

In terms of functionality, the new LMS provides various improvements, including more functionality for group work and grading, but some limitations have been identified. Some new third party tools were recently acquired, including a tool to facilitate the creation of accessible content, an interaction and polling tool, and a tool for peer review. More recently, some staff in STEM disciplines have found that the tests and quizzes functionality does not meet all their needs; likewise, the blogging and e-portfolio tools might need to be replaced with new integrations to ensure staff can continue to incorporate those kinds of activities into their courses. Ongoing investment in digital infrastructure will be needed to ensure staff and students can continue to work and learn in a robust and enhanced learning environment (JISC, 2023). Having consulted with other institutions and with the literature more broadly, we know that we need to remind staff that no LMS can do everything, and it is just one tool in the teaching and learning ecosystem (Sridharan *et al.*, 2010). An LMS should *support* other technologies and practices at the institution.

At the time of writing this chapter (May 2024), we have just finished working on post-project governance and handover tasks, as the LMS project has ended. Nonetheless, our knowledge base will still need ongoing maintenance as new updates are applied to the LMS every month. Training sessions will also need to be offered at appropriate times to cater not only to any new third party tools we acquire but also to provide training on the LMS itself, which will continue to evolve. The new project governance will also need to be able to handle requests for new functionality – requests will first need to be investigated for use cases, tested, procured, and then implemented. Furthermore, whenever bugs or issues are identified in the platform, we will need to make sure that the relevant stakeholders are notified quickly, with solutions proposed. This digital transformation project will continue to have wide repercussions for the institution for the foreseeable future.

As mentioned at the start of this chapter, the LMS project is just one step in a wider academic and digital transformation at the institution. In the next two years, the institution will embark on another significant project to transform curricula. While the new LMS will facilitate that project, the next project will also require the ongoing cooperation of staff from across the institution — academic stakeholders (staff and students), IT support staff, instructional designers, learning technologists, staff working in accessibility and the library division, and other support services. While the competing needs will be challenging to satisfy, the LMS project has taught us that the organisational digital culture and digital infrastructure can be enhanced when a team frequently consults with stakeholders and develops innovative solutions and supports that are tailored to their needs (JISC, 2023).

References

Bracken, S. and Novak, K. (eds.). (2019) *Transforming higher education through universal design for learning*. Oxon UK/ New York: Routledge.

CAST, Inc. (2024) 'About universal design for learning'. Available at https://www.cast.org/impact/universal-design-for-learning-udl (Accessed 15 May 2024).

Cutri, R. M., Mena, J. and Feinauer Whiting, E. (2020) 'Faculty readiness for online crisis teaching: transitioning to online teaching during the COVID-19 pandemic', *European Journal of Teacher Education*, 43(4), pp. 523–541. DOI: 10.1080/02619768.2020.1815702

Hodges, C., Moore, S., Lockee, B., Trust, T. and Bond, A. (2020) 'The difference between emergency remote teaching and online learning'. Available at https://er.educause.edu/articles/2020/3/the-difference-between-emer.ency-remote-teaching-and-online-learning (Accessed 15 May 2024).

JISC. (2023) 'Framework for digital transformation in higher education'. Available at https://repository.jisc.ac.uk/9056/1/framework-for-digital-transformation-in-higher-education.pdf (Accessed: 15 May 2024).

JISC. (2024) 'Building digital capabilities framework: the six elements defined'. Available at https://repository.jisc.ac.uk/8846/1/2022_Jisc_BDC_Individual_Framework.pdf (Accessed 15 May 2024).

Oreg, S. (2003) 'Resistance to change: developing an individual differences measure', *Journal of Applied Psychology*, 88(4), pp. 680–693. DOI: 10.1037/0021-9010.88.4.680

Redecker, C. (2017) 'European framework for the digital competence of educators: DigCompEdu'. Y. Punie (ed.), EUR 28775 EN. Publications Office of the European Union, Luxembourg. DOI: 10.2760/159770 (online), JRC107466.

Sridharan, B., Deng, H. and Corbitt, B. J. (2010) 'Critical success factors in e-learning ecosystems: a qualitative study', *Journal of Systems and Information Technology*, 12(4), pp. 263–288, DOI: 10.1108/13287261011095798

Trust, T. and Whalen, J. (2020) 'Should teachers be trained in emergency remote teaching: lessons learned from the COVID-19 pandemic', *Journal of Technology and Teacher Education*, 28(2), pp. 189–199.

University of Limerick (2019) 'UL@50 Strategic Plan 2019-2024'. Available at https://www.ul.ie/media/23444/download?inline (Accessed 15 May 2024).

Chapter 16

What Blended Learning Taught Me About the Strengths of Collaboration for Interdisciplinarity

Zoë Enstone

Introduction

During the COVID-19 pandemic's constraints on in-person teaching, I redesigned a skills development thread on working with primary sources for an interdisciplinary liberal arts foundation year programme in the UK. Foundation years are generally an additional year at the start of a degree programme and are designed to support the transition into higher education. This thread was part of an initial module and ran alongside introductory skills sessions and the delivery of content. It had traditionally consisted of a series of workshops, independent activities, and an archival visit but moved to a blended learning design. This redevelopment retained some in-person workshops and the trip, but also included a new blended learning aspect with the integrated online component incorporating collaborative resources and co-creation opportunities (Enstone, 2023). This redevelopment work was subject to particular challenges as a skills thread that was intended to support both students' critical and practical engagement with primary sources (Enstone, 2021). Consideration of the skills thread was particularly important, as it formed part of the initial content in the students' transition to higher education (HE), which as Chivers (2019) has noted is often a period of complexities. Moreover, it constituted a fundamental component of the provision for supporting the development of the skills necessary for students' current and ongoing studies. Beyond the pandemic, it was necessary to reconsider the approach in the light of ongoing pedagogic considerations regarding blended or online learning as both 'the new normal' (Megahed and Ghoneim, 2022, p. 1) but also as a nuanced development for student experience and the higher education sector at the programme, institutional, and national level (cf. Hill and Smith, 2023; Tomej et al., 2022; Watermeyer et al., 2021).

Despite this context, the nature of this programme and the nature of the changes meant that transforming these components for a blended delivery model led to a transformational moment in pedagogic approach. Blended learning offered significant opportunities that were not afforded by the original format, particularly in integrating input from diverse contributors within

DOI: 10.4324/9781003503149-20

and outside the academic institution. These benefits led to the continued use and refinement of this approach beyond the easing of the pandemic restrictions. The blended learning design facilitated a shift in focus for the in-person elements, but it was the online content and its incorporation into the module that drove innovation in integrating varied subject disciplines, fostered student-led resource generation, and enabled challenging disciplinary boundaries in the analysis of primary resources. Moreover, this approach facilitated the integration of skills beyond working with physical primary sources and extended to navigating online spaces and digital research. This approach has wider implications for other programmes facing similar challenges around integrating interdisciplinarity into skills delivery and, more broadly, for programmes developing flexible approaches or resources for a range of subject disciplines.

Development and Redevelopment: The Transformation

The complex context of the skills thread meant that there were key considerations in reconfiguring it as a blended learning opportunity in its initial reworking, but also in retaining the blend post-COVID-19. It was positioned in the initial introductory module of an interdisciplinary foundation year programme, where students only study interdisciplinary content for a year before progressing onto more traditional single or joint honours degree programmes. This foundation year, therefore, needs to provide skills pertinent to various progression routes but also allow students the opportunity to establish or challenge the perceived boundaries of their disciplinary area both for their foundation year-level studies and also as a strategy for advancing their disciplinary engagement longer-term. The blended learning development therefore involved navigating the complexities of interdisciplinary provision (Brewer, 1999; Hollmén, 2015), addressing pedagogic challenges of developing skills in working with sources (Anderson *et al.*, 2006; Garcia *et al.*, 2019), and considering the nature of provision at foundation year level and with widening participation factors (Sanders and Daly, 2013; Warren, 2002; Webber, 2023). In particular, this was focused on students being able to navigate a range of considerations related to the complexities of diverse source types, contexts, and applications. The initial version of the skills thread comprised in-class sessions concentrating on working with different kinds of primary resources. These sessions served as an introduction, supporting students from differing disciplinary backgrounds in engaging with unfamiliar primary sources, and were also an opportunity for students to establish the significance of these sources within their respective disciplinary areas. The final activity of this phase was a visit to an archive, where students worked with a diverse range of sources to consider the varied contexts, influences, and analytical approaches that might be used in a critical analysis.

The transition to a blended delivery model and, in its initial iteration, the removal of the archive visit due to COVID-19 restrictions necessitated a comprehensive redesign. The skills thread was initially reconceived as a series of classroom sessions that still mapped onto the distinct source types but that were integrated with online resources that addressed some of the complexities inherent to varied disciplinary areas' use of different sources. This modification allowed for a broader range of staff contributions and culminated in a virtual archive visit, facilitated by archive staff providing digital versions of materials and contextual commentary. The shift to a partially online delivery encouraged students to access resources that initially explained and defined different source types, exploring disciplinary applications, challenging preconceived notions of disciplinary relevance, and addressing specific issues related to finding and using these sources. These ideas were explored further in in-class sessions focused on examining various (sometimes overlapping) source types, such as textual, visual, historical, statistics and data, and maps. The online aspects situated these practical sessions within a discourse on disciplinary significance and ongoing relevance to future studies that were reiterated through the integration of disciplinary experts as well as interdisciplinary staff.

The online component of this skills thread was not intended to merely replicate missing elements but to harness the full potential of the blended methodology for more ambitious and comprehensive learning experiences. This approach facilitated participation from academic staff across disciplines, who each contributed short videos and resources identifying the primary sources that were integral to their disciplinary area. This was especially valuable in challenging students' preconceived notions about the disciplinary relevance of source types. Students were able to benefit from academics' insights into the sources they would encounter in their studies, which were often more expansive than what they had covered in their previous studies. For instance, the film studies video discussed the centrality of film as a primary source but also looked at direct alternative sources, like film posters, reviews, and novels in relation to adaptation as well as drawing attention to the subject's interplay with other disciplinary areas and the range of sources central to those areas, for example, philosophy, sociology, history, cultural studies, gender studies, literature, music, politics, ethics, religion, and geography, flagging the need to engage with the kinds of primary sources used in each of these areas (Enstone, 2023). The videos utilised the authority and expertise of discipline-specific experts who were able to contextualise and give examples to support their assertions about the significance of the content. Students appreciated this insight and brought elements of this new approach to the in-class discussion and the final activities on the thread. Beyond subject-specific insights, the provision also included professional and skills-based content, such as a video featuring an archivist discussing the complexities of working with archival sources. This offered an opportunity for students to scrutinise their use of these resources and contemplate their continued use beyond the foundation year. The blended learning approach also ensured active student engagement with online activities as well as reading or viewing materials. For instance, one activity used online archives pertinent to students' subject disciplines. This activity, which was completed online but integrated into class sessions through discussion and feedback, prompted critical evaluations of the archives' inclusivity, accessibility, and significance. Thus, further to what was possible in the classroom, students also began to navigate the digital spaces that would enable them to discover and explore these significant sources for their area of study, moving beyond a consideration of the physicality of these works to consider their ongoing digital preservation and integration.

Although the in-person trip to the archives resumed once the COVID-19 restrictions had been lifted, the skills thread retained aspects of the online element of this visit. This allowed students to engage with resources before the visit, contemplate the distinctions between virtual and in-person access, and reference key details and context in subsequent activities. This provision fostered a more independent approach to academic skills development, as students were able to establish their understanding of their work with these primary sources within their own specific contexts and interests. The thread had previously concluded with an in-person discussion about the materials at the archives, but the revised model involved consolidating learning through online student collaboration to co-create a final resource reflecting on the different archival materials. Although the co-created resources were not part of a formal assessment, this was integrated into a module where the skills were a key element of the formal summative assessment point, and this also gave staff an opportunity to establish where students were in need of further support and development or where there were particular strengths. This post-COVID transformation maintained the strengths of blended learning while reintegrating valuable in-person teaching elements, and meant that the ongoing structure of this provision enhanced skills and approaches in a way that significantly exceeded the original delivery.

This innovation had a transformative impact on the foundation year programme by introducing a new approach to academic development provision. Much as the students benefitted from the impact of the co-created resource opportunity that was the reflection of the skills they had developed across the thread, the resource and pedagogic approach benefitted from the expertise and collaboration of a wide range of academics and professionals. This meant that resources were accessible through a subject-specific customised pathway, which would imply a multidisciplinary resource that was split, but in fact reiterated the interplay of different disciplines, the blurring of perceived boundaries, and the significance of the development of working with different sources to all arts and humanities disciplines. Blended learning retained and developed the benefits of in-person provision while being supported by online content. Although originally designed in response to specific circumstances, its effectiveness led to its adoption as a long-term strategy for the module beyond the pandemic restrictions. On a practical level, this redevelopment provided room for a broader range of contributions not feasible in person, addressing some of the multidisciplinary and interdisciplinary aspects of the provision, but the asynchronous aspects also meant that students could work through some online components at their own pace. This, in combination with the high level of support offered by the in-person sessions mean that students were receiving more support with the development of their skills than they had been before the redesign.

Wider Application and Next Steps

This revised approach instigated a more comprehensive reflection on the Liberal Arts Foundation Year programme, prompting the incorporation of further asynchronous blended learning activities and resources. There was also an exploration of ways to add more co-creation opportunities for students, both in online and offline formats. The specific tools used for this resource (Wix, Wakelet, Padlet, and Mentimeter for the creation of resources) proved instrumental in different aspects of the development of the project and gave rise to different ongoing enhancements across the programme. Although used effectively in combination for this project, they generally had more distinct and varied advantages in supporting a blended learning approach to learning and teaching. Specifically, Padlet emerged as a versatile resource that has been integrated into other aspects of delivery in the programme, including an online poster exhibition where the comment function facilitated synchronous or asynchronous interactions among students regarding their respective posters. Additionally, Padlet played a crucial role in the development of an interactive critical textual interrogation project both within and beyond in-person classroom sessions. The breakdown and consideration of the distinct tools of the project underscored the significant use and value derived from the various resources employed.

Although there is a wide range of pre-existing resources available online, the blended approach here meant that students were never expected to work through the complexities of content completely independently but rather were given the opportunity to integrate some independent work and development with provision and support in class. This has particular significance for transitional provision and complicated skills development activities, perhaps around 'threshold concepts', which are 'key to transforming the way students understand a whole subject' (Olaniyi, 2020) and also for the ongoing development of information literacy, which is now so significant in academic skills development (Jarosz and Kutay, 2017; Johnston and Webber, 2003; Wang 2007).

Having taken the opportunity to rethink methodologies and pedagogies as a result of the shift to a mostly online and then more of a blended approach, there were also substantial advantages to careful blending as a potential strategy for inter- or multidisciplinary subject provision due to the flexibility of the content and the potential it offers for student-led approaches and exploration.

This is especially important in delivering programmes that require students to navigate the permeable boundaries between academic disciplines and come to their own realisation about the kinds of skills and approaches that they will need for their future studies. But most significantly for an interdisciplinary programme, this format also allowed for disciplinary experts to be involved in the navigation of skills for their particular discipline, but also to ensure that students were able to structure these activities and discussions around the crossover of disciplinary areas. This is, of course, particularly relevant in the humanities where there is a substantial crossover between disciplinary areas and it is important for students not to limit themselves by thinking of disciplines as siloed. An approach like this would allow experts with different disciplinary fields to provide a range of content for academic skills development, but also for staff with expertise and knowledge of the students' requirements to construct approaches that support students to navigate some of these complexities and work towards their own understanding of different kinds of resource. The complexity of interdisciplinary provision is often making the transition from multidisciplinarity to interdisciplinarity, especially in a programme that works at a transitional point within the two (cf. Klein, 2010). The establishment of disciplinary areas as permeable begins this process of redefining and problematising the disciplinary divide but also draws on the significance of the expertise of the staff from different areas to reinforce this concept.

Conclusion

As a programme with a complex set of contexts, the liberal arts foundation year's blended approach to the redesign of the skills development thread in response to the challenges posed by the restrictions of COVID-19 allowed for a transformation of approach that extended beyond the limitations of the pandemic. In particular, the reconfiguration of the skills thread addressed the complexities of interdisciplinary provision. The most significant feature was the ability to integrate materials produced by disciplinary experts that reinforced the skills and approaches that were central to the interdisciplinary provision of the programme.

In particular, subject experts contributed valuable insights, challenging students' preconceptions and enhancing their understanding of the disciplinary relevance of source types. This would not have been possible in a traditional classroom setting; thus the blended learning approach provided substantial additional benefits in terms of content. The blended delivery also allowed students to navigate their own way through the material and activities and to come to terms with the ideas and strategies of their own disciplinary area in combination with other related fields through the optionality offered by the website design. This was reinforced by the co-creation opportunity; this was not a passive process but a practical and focused opportunity for the development of individual skills and wider disciplinary engagement. Skills-based content that included input from professionals further enriched the online provision, offering students insights into working with archival sources and encouraging critical engagement with digital materials. The retention of the blended approach post-COVID reinforced the independent and reflective nature of academic skills development on the programme, with substantial potential beyond the programme for application to other developmental provisions. The transformation of this skills development thread serves as a model for the effective integration of blended learning, providing valuable insights for ongoing programme development and the value of a collaborative approach in allowing the continuation of the exploration and ongoing challenge to disciplinary boundaries.

References

Anderson, C., Day, K., Michie, R. and Rollason, D. (2006) 'Engaging with historical source work: practices, pedagogy, dialogue' *Arts and Humanities in Higher Education* 5(3), pp. 243–263. https://doi.org/10.1177/1474022206067623

Brewer, G. D. (1999) 'The challenges of interdisciplinarity', *Policy Sciences*, 32, pp. 327–337. https://doi.org/10.1023/A:1004706019826

Chivers, E. (2019) 'The trials and tribulations of transition into foundation year study' *Journal of the Foundation Year Network*, 2, pp. 69–78.

Enstone, Z. (2021) 'Blended learning opportunities: skills for working with primary sources' *Journal of Learning Development in Higher Education*, 22. https://doi.org/10.47408/jldhe.vi22.668

Enstone, Z. (2023) Working with primary sources. Available at https://zenstone9.wixsite.com/primarysources

Garcia, P., Lueck, J. and Yakel, E. (2019) 'The pedagogical promise of primary sources: research trends, persistent gaps, and new directions', *The Journal of Academic Librarianship* 45(2), pp. 94–101. https://doi.org/10.1016/j.acalib.2019.01.004

Hill, J. and Smith, K. (2023) 'Visions of blended learning: identifying the challenges and opportunities in shaping institutional approaches to blended learning in higher education', *Technology, Pedagogy and Education* 32(3), pp. 289–303. https://doi.org/10.1080/1475939X.2023.2176916

Hollmén, S. (2015) 'The pedagogical challenge of interdisciplinary university programs', *Research in Arts and Education*, 2015(2), pp. 1–14. https://doi.org/10.54916/rae.118808

Jarosz, E. E. and Kutay, S. (2017) 'Guided resource inquiries: integrating archives into course learning and information literacy objectives', *Communications in Information Literacy*, 11(1), pp. 204–220. https://doi.org/10.15760/comminfolit.2017.11.1.42

Johnston, B. and Webber, S. (2003) 'Information literacy in higher education: a review and case study', *Studies in Higher Education*, 28(3), pp. 335–352. https://doi.org/10.1080/03075070309295

Klein, J. T. (2010) 'A taxonomy of interdisciplinarity', in R. Frodeman *et al.*, *The Oxford handbook of interdisciplinarity*. Oxford, Oxford University Press, pp. 15–30.

Megahed, N. and Ghoneim, E. (2022) 'Blended learning: the new normal for post-COVID-19 pedagogy', *International Journal of Mobile and Blended Learning* 14(1), pp. 1–15. http://doi.org/10.4018/IJMBL.291980

Olaniyi, N. E. E. (2020) 'Threshold concepts: designing a format for the flipped classroom as an active learning technique for crossing the threshold', *Research and Practice in Technology Enhanced Learning* 15(2). https://doi.org/10.1186/s41039-020-0122-3

Sanders, L. and Daly, A. P. (2013) 'Building a successful foundation? The role of foundation year courses in preparing students for their degree', *Widening Participation and Lifelong Learning* 14, pp. 42–56. https://doi.org/10.5456/WPLL.14.S.42

Tomej, K., Liburd, J., Blichfeldt, B. S. and Hjalager, A.-M. (2022) 'Blended and (not so) splendid teaching and learning: higher education insights from university teachers during the COVID-19 pandemic', *International Journal of Educational Research Open* 3, 100144, pp. 1–6. https://doi.org/10.1016/j.ijedro.2022.100144

Wang, L. (2007) 'Sociocultural learning theories and information literacy teaching activities in higher education', *Reference & User Services Quarterly*, 47(2), pp. 149–158. https://doi.org/10.5860/rusq.47n2.149

Warren, D. (2002) 'Curriculum design in a context of widening participation in higher education', *Arts and Humanities in Higher Education*, 1(1), pp. 85–99. https://doi.org/10.1177/1474022202001001007

Watermeyer, R., Crick, T., Knight, C. and Goodall, J. (2021) 'COVID-19 and digital disruption in UK universities: afflictions and affordances of emergency online migration' *Higher Education* 81, pp. 623–641. https://doi.org/10.1007/s10734-020-00561-y

Webber, L. (2023) 'Using capital, habitus and field to explore foundation year students' higher education experiences', *Journal of Further and Higher Education*, 48(1), pp. 110–124. https://doi.org/10.1080/0309877X.2023.2277418

Chapter 17

What Co-Design Has Taught Us About Transformative Practice and Academic Development

Sandris Zeivots, Dewa Wardak, Andrew Cram, and Joanne Nash

Introduction

In the rapidly evolving landscape of higher education, universities face unprecedented challenges. These range from integrating technology and artificial intelligence in learning and teaching (Crompton and Burke, 2023; Tay *et al.*, 2023) to catering to diverse student and educator needs (Núñez-Canal *et al.*, 2022; Stentiford and Koutsouris, 2021), necessitating greater flexibility, critical thinking, and tailored course design. Conventional approaches often fall short in addressing these multifaceted and complex issues, calling for more collective and relational problem-solving strategies (Bovill, 2020).

Among these emerging strategies is co-design, which we define as a purposeful, participatory, and collaborative design process that involves multiple stakeholders (Vargas *et al.*, 2022). As an emergent field in higher education (Örnekoğlu-Selçuk *et al.*, 2023), co-design has shown promising results in fostering the design of more engaged and effective teaching and learning environments (Ahmadi, 2023). Our interdisciplinary unit called Business Co-design has embraced the co-design approach as a cornerstone of educational transformation. This chapter introduces and examines three years of the Light Touch Program (2020–2023), offering a unique perspective on transformative practice and academic development in a co-design context.

Light Touch Program

The Light Touch Program is part of the Connected Learning at Scale (CLaS) initiative by the University of Sydney Business School in Australia (Bryant, 2022; Wilson *et al.*, 2021), which commenced in 2019 aiming to enhance student learning experiences in large courses of up to 2,000 students. Initially, several core courses were selected for 18-month Deep Touch co-designed transformations. However, the onset of the pandemic and associated adoption of online learning in 2020 required adaptation. A new 8-week Light Touch Program was designed to provide swift and flexible support for a broader range of courses.

DOI: 10.4324/9781003503149-21

The Light Touch Program is a targeted, tailored, short-term initiative focusing on transformative course design. The program is driven by a co-design approach involving educational developers, course coordinators, learning designers, media specialists, and evaluators, bringing together different perspectives to refine and enhance course quality. It is designed to be agile and responsive, providing quick yet effective interventions that align with educational leadership's priorities and the needs of academics. The support includes one-on-one consultations between course coordinators and educational developers, and tailored workshops aligned with CLaS priorities: embedding active engagement with content, fostering connected student participation, and designing relevant and authentic assessments and feedback (Bryant, 2022).

The program invites course coordinators to nominate courses needing design and development support, which varies from active learning enhancements to multimedia interventions. In its inaugural semester in 2020, the program supported 27 courses across five business disciplines, which showcases the high demand and relevance of such a program (Wardak *et al.*, 2021).

The co-design teams are led by educational developers who specialise in curriculum design. After an initial meeting with the coordinator to scope priorities and needs, the educational developers tailor how the co-design teams meet and communicate with academic partners and respond to their needs and preferred meeting settings (Zeivots *et al.*, 2023). For example, whilst the majority of courses engaged in one-on-one consultations and workshops, some coordinators preferred email correspondence. Depending on the coordinators' needs, the co-design process can involve a learning designer (who oversees the learning management system, interactive tools, and design solutions), an educational technologist (who consults on tools and software), or a media specialist (who manages multimedia solutions, including professional recording and editing).

Although brief (approximately 8 weeks), the program has made a significant impact on the Business School's teaching and learning ecosystem (Wardak *et al.*, 2021). The success of the program has led to it being run annually or biannually. From 2020 to 2023, there have been five cycles of the Light Touch Program, which have supported 70 courses, including 201 one-on-one consultations and 50 tailored workshops (see Table 17.1). The University's Human Ethics Research Committee granted permission [protocol number: 2019/892] to collect stakeholders' data.

In the first cycle, coordinators were nominated by their heads of discipline, and seven coordinators opted not to engage. In later cycles, staff coordinating a course were able to request assistance in curriculum development through an expression of interest (EOI) process.

Drawing from our experience as educational developers in the Light Touch Program, this chapter engages in practitioner inquiry (Wall, 2018) to explore co-design and its transformational role on stakeholders. More specifically, we collectively inquire about what co-design has taught us about transformative practice and academic development. We aim to illuminate how co-design assists us and

What Co-Design Has Taught Us About Transformative Practice

Table 17.1 Light Touch Program cycles: Participation metrics

Cycle	Expressions of interest/Confirmed courses for support	Number of one-on-one consultations	Number of offered tailored workshops	Total attendances at workshops
2020 Light Touch in response to Covid: Aug–Nov	34/27	92[a]	34[b]	99
2021 Jun–Jul	22/15	28	5	30
Dec 2021–Feb 2022	20/11	29	6	14
Dec 2022–Feb 2023	14/11	32	5	39
2023 Jun–Jul	7/6	20	0[c]	0
Total	**97/77**	**201**	**50**	**182**

[a] Some consultations were held as group consultations where educators from the same discipline shared similar requirements.
[b] Six types of workshops were offered, all delivered five or six times tailoring the needs of a particular business discipline.
[c] Workshops were not delivered due to a smaller cohort of courses. Most needs were addressed during one-on-one consultations.

other stakeholders to produce transformative practice and academic professional learning and development. To achieve this, we have reflected collaboratively on the transformative lessons derived from co-design's role in the Light Touch Program and thus aim to enhance practice and professional development.

Transformative Lessons

The Light Touch Program, whilst developed in response to the pandemic, helped create and embed co-design processes that accelerated the transformation of courses. By providing course coordinators with access to education and design expertise, it played a crucial role in enhancing student experience and professional development, as well as in implementing innovations underpinned by collaborative planning, design, and evaluation. As one course coordinator stated about substantial assessment changes:

> These are things that we couldn't have done on our own, or only with huge effort … It's not so much a question of whether the school can provide a seminar or website or something to tell you, there's far too much involved, and far too much detail and fine-tuning … That's where your short time personal advisor is indispensable.

In this section, we unpack three transformative lessons about what co-design has taught us about transformative practice and academic development. These transformative lessons discuss the role of flexibility, benefits of co-design approaches, and the use of customisable resources that accelerate transformation.

Transformative Lesson 1: Intentional Flexibility Is Required to Meet Academics' Diverse Needs

The program took a highly flexible approach to adapting each course to the goals, interests, availability, and capabilities of the coordinators, with great diversity across the courses. Academics new to the institution were often making small course refinements while learning institutional processes and systems. Others had more ambitious goals, including revising content and online class space design; introducing new synchronous and/or asynchronous strategies and techniques for active learning, collaboration, engagement, and participation; or revising assessments with increased authenticity and relevance. Some academics were located overseas or had restricted availability during the program period. After the first program cycle, in which several course coordinators opted not to engage after nomination by their discipline leader, an EOI process was introduced for coordinators to self-nominate their courses. This gave course coordinators greater agency over their needs and pedagogical priorities while also aligning the stated goals of the coordinators with the objectives and scope of the Light Touch Program. This reduced the extent to which the program adopted a 'top-down' approach, in which change is imposed by more senior management but may be resisted by individual coordinators (Honkimäki *et al.*, 2022). Instead, the focus shifted towards additional capability development and support to motivated coordinators, aligning more with a 'middle-out' approach (Bryant, 2021) that seeds change that germinates throughout the university.

In light of this diversity, our co-design approaches required tailoring of roles, goals, design focus, and schedule to fit the particular situation of each course and coordinator. This aligns with contemporary project management approaches that cater for subjectivity, emergence, and collaborative practices (Lippe and vom Brocke, 2016; Huff, 2016), and perspectives that emphasise the process of 'becoming' through which the project stakeholders and practices can change and evolve (Gherardi, 2012).

To achieve this, we encouraged 'design' and 'learning' mindsets (Zeivots *et al.*, 2023), which assisted stakeholders' acknowledgement that our understanding of each educational innovation project would develop as it unfolded. A flexible toolkit of co-design resources was iteratively developed that could be rapidly customised to fit most of the situations encountered within the program. These resources included induction documents (e.g., describing 'standard' roles and design processes) and educational design templates and examples (e.g., a course Welcome Module). Additionally, projects were occasionally rolled up into a larger project (e.g., 'Medium Touch') with increased resources and timeframe to achieve even more ambitious course design modifications.

Our approach to supporting flexibility was incrementally developed over several cycles of the program and involved iterative improvement and consolidation. Introducing the EOI process was pivotal in ensuring all coordinators were motivated and engaged; however, this did not reduce the variance in coordinator goals, capabilities, and schedules. Our ability to flexibly and rapidly cater for each course was underpinned by the set of customisable resources, which was developed in conjunction with the academics and continuously extended and refined. Transferring this approach to other institutions and teams should similarly be expected to require sustained effort to iteratively develop customisable resources to meet what is needed and valued by each coordinator.

Transformative Lesson 2: Co-design Facilitates Capacity Building

Co-design facilitates knowledge-sharing within collaborative teams, a crucial aspect of capacity building, as it enables individuals and groups to benefit from the collective intelligence of the diverse stakeholders involved (Steen *et al.*, 2011). Our co-design approach facilitated the incorporation of diverse perspectives and experiences from stakeholders including course coordinators, educators, students, alumni, and industry partners to design solutions for large courses (Wardak *et al.*, 2024). This ensured that all stakeholders' voices were valued and considered, breaking down traditional hierarchies and facilitating a more inclusive decision-making process. Targeted consultations tailored to stakeholder needs facilitated the generation of innovative ideas and unconventional solutions to complex problems of teaching and learning. The co-design process also strengthened informal relationships between the course coordinators and industry partners. Both learned appreciation for better alignment of curriculum, teaching methods and workplace practices to equip students with life-long learning skills.

One benefit of co-design is the facilitation of long-term learning and development for and from stakeholders (Blomkamp, 2018). We observed that course coordinators involved in the co-design developed more holistic perspectives on students' learning rather than being mostly concerned with the content. Through their direct interaction with students and alumni, coordinators gained fresh insights and awareness that led to more inclusive teaching practices that resonate with the diverse student population.

One strategy for supporting stakeholders in sustained learning and development was to develop tailored resources as part of the handover process for future teaching teams. The resources were housed on the learning management system (LMS) for each course, accessible to the teaching team but hidden from students. These included information on LMS tools and plug-ins as well as assessment, marking guides for tutors, and support channels.

Our transformative approach aligns academic practices with the dynamic demands of a changing world, ensuring an ever-evolving culture of learning and innovation. When transferring this approach to other institutions, we recommend embracing a collaborative ethos with co-design principles, fostering adaptability and collective intelligence. Co-design drives continuous learning by engaging diverse stakeholders, which can lead to valuable insights. Co-design encourages stakeholder involvement throughout the process to instill a sense of co-ownership and adaptability. For example, learning designers can provide their expertise on tools and know-how for video captions and accessible text alternatives, which other stakeholders may not have previously been exposed to. Similarly, educational developers can propose a tailored set of strategies to the co-design team to improve the quality of student engagement with content. The exposure and attunement to these ideas can facilitate the incorporation of diverse perspectives and expertise from stakeholders to design more inclusive solutions. This helps foster innovation and cultivate a sustained learning culture with accessible resources to promote ongoing development within your institution or context.

Transformative Lesson 3: Customisable Resources Accelerate Sharing and Adoption

Within higher education, educators, educational developers, and learning designers rarely use repositories to share teaching and learning materials, which reflects a broader trend where interprofessional sharing remains similarly scarce (Maloney *et al.*, 2013). This can extend to standardised templates, which have been recognised for their effectiveness for quality online learning. Faculty adherence to standardised templates is a related and persistent issue (Judge and Murray, 2017). Further, when universities focus on curriculum resource development (Aitchison *et al.*, 2020) then coordinators may feel diminished autonomy. Accordingly, a challenge is to facilitate sharing of resources whilst ensuring their acceptance and long-term use by coordinators. One solution is highly customisable shareable resources/templates that are adapted to the coordinator's needs. These can be stored in an organised repository, then shared and customised by educational developers or learning designers during workshops and consultations with coordinators. This process of sharing then becomes one mechanism underpinning a 'middle-out' approach (Byrant, 2021).

An example of a customisable resource is our five-page Welcome Module, which is added to a course within the LMS. This is introduced to coordinators in a workshop with a focus on how individual academics can use and adapt the module to suit their level of technical expertise and teaching preferences. This positioned coordinators as co-designers (Viberg *et al.*, 2019) and helped them gain ownership of the modules, which facilitated adoption (Treasure-Jones and Joynes, 2018).

The Welcome Module summarised crucial information for students, including how to study the course, assessments, teaching team, course timetable, and where to find help. As part of the co-design process, the module was evaluated by surveying students and coordinators, then refined. The evaluation revealed that 90% of staff agreed the module was useful. Furthermore, 74% of students found the module easy to navigate. Students indicated the Assessment page and the How to Study this Course page as the most useful (Wardak *et al.*, 2021).

When transferring this approach to other institutions, we invite educators and developers to consider the mechanisms through which resources can be shared and tailored to meet diverse needs. Creating adaptable resources and designing systematic approaches to sharing, implementing, and refining them is a persistent challenge. By fostering a culture of open dialogue and collaboration, we can amplify the impact of our successes and catalyse transformative changes across institutions.

Wrapping Up

Our journey with the Light Touch Program has provided valuable insights into the transformative potential of co-design in academic development. As we reflect on our experience, three key lessons stand out: intentional flexibility, capacity building, and the value of customisable resources for sharing.

Intentional flexibility emerged as a crucial element. By adapting our processes and systems to meet the diverse needs of course coordinators, we ensured our interventions were tailored and effective. This lesson underscores the importance of agile, responsive strategies in addressing the complex challenges of educational development. Another significant element of our co-design journey was the facilitation of capacity building. Through collaborative design processes, we created opportunities for knowledge sharing and innovation, empowering stakeholders to develop more holistic perspectives on student learning. This also fostered a sense of co-ownership and accountability, leading to more inclusive teaching practices. Finally, our experience highlighted the transformative potential of customisable resources for sharing. We facilitated the uptake of innovative teaching practices through adaptable templates and tools, leading to widespread adoption and adaptation of transformative innovations.

In our co-design team, we are committed to active sharing and collaboration. Building on the lessons learned from the Light Touch Program as well as the broader CLaS initiative, we continuously share our transformative lessons through publications (Wardak *et al.*, 2024; Zeivots *et al.*, 2023; Wilson *et al.*, 2021), Design Patterns (https://clasdesignpatterns.com), and learning and teaching blog posts (https://diberg.blog).

As we look to the future, we invite further exploration and research on co-design in higher education. While our experience with the Light Touch Program has provided valuable insights, there remains much to learn about the complexities of co-design. By sharing our lessons and experiences, we aim to contribute to a growing body of knowledge on transformative practice and academic development.

References

Aitchison, C., Harper, R., Mirriahi, N. and Guerin, C. (2020) 'Tensions for educational developers in the digital university: developing the person, developing the product', *Higher Education Research and Development*, 39(2), pp. 171–184. https://doi.org/10.1080/07294360.2019.1663155

Ahmadi, R. (2023) 'Student voice, culture, and teacher power in curriculum co-design within higher education: an action-based research study', *International Journal for Academic Development*, 28(2), pp. 177–189. https://doi.org/10.1080/1360144X.2021.1923502

Blomkamp, E. (2018) 'The promise of co-design for public policy', *Australian Journal of Public Administration*, 77(4), pp. 729–743. https://doi.org/10.1111/1467-8500.12310

Bovill, C. (2020) *Co-creating learning and teaching: towards relational pedagogy in higher education*. St Albans: Critical Publishing.

Bryant, P. (2021) 'Innovations to improve the student experience: HigherEd showcase', *EduGrowth*, 2 July. Available at https://edugrowth.org.au/2021/07/02/innovations-to-improve-the-student-experience-highered-showcase

Bryant, P. (2022) 'Transforming business education through connected learning—Part 3', *Disruptive Innovations in Business Education Research Group*, 2 March. Available at https://diberg.blog/2022/03/03/transforming-business-education-through-connected-learning-part-3

Crompton, H. and Burke, D. (2023) 'Artificial intelligence in higher education: the state of the field', *International Journal of Educational Technology in Higher Education*, 20(1), pp. 1–22. https://doi.org/10.1186/s41239-023-00392-8

Gherardi, S. (2012) 'Why do practices change and why do they persist? Models of explanations', in P. Hager, A. Lee and A. Reich (eds.), *Practice, learning and change*. Dordrecht: Springer, pp. 217–231.

Honkimäki, S., Jääskelä, P., Kratochvil, J. and Tynjälä, P. (2022) 'University-wide, top-down curriculum reform at a Finnish university: perceptions of the academic staff', *European Journal of Higher Education*, 12(2), pp. 153–170. https://doi.org/10.1080/21568235.2021.1906727

Huff, A. S. (2016) 'Project innovation: Evidence-informed, open, effectual, and subjective', *Project Management Journal*, 47(2), pp. 8–25. https://doi.org/10.1002/pmj.21576

Judge, D. S. and Murray, B. (2017) 'Student and faculty transition to a new online learning management system', *Teaching and Learning in Nursing*, 12(4), pp. 277–280. https://doi.org/10.1016/j.teln.2017.06.010

Lippe, S. and vom Brocke, J. (2016) 'Situational project management for collaborative research projects', *Project Management Journal*, 47(1), pp. 76–96. https://doi.org/10.1002/pmj.21561

Maloney, S., Moss, A., Keating, J., Kotsanas, G. and Morgan, P. (2013) 'Sharing teaching and learning resources: perceptions of a university's faculty members', *Medical Education*, 47(8), pp. 811–819. https://doi.org/10.1111/medu.12225

Núñez-Canal, M., de Obesso, M. D. L. M. and Pérez-Rivero, C. A. (2022) 'New challenges in higher education: a study of the digital competence of educators in Covid times', *Technological Forecasting and Social Change*, 174, 121270. https://doi.org/10.1016/j.techfore.2021.121270

Örnekoğlu-Selçuk, M., Emmanouil, M., Hasirci, D., Grizioti, M. and Van Langenhove, L. (2023) 'A systematic literature review on co-design education and preparing future designers for their role in co-design', *CoDesign*, pp. 1–16. https://doi.org/10.1080/15710882.2023.2242840

Stentiford, L. and Koutsouris, G. (2021) 'What are inclusive pedagogies in higher education? A systematic scoping review', *Studies in Higher Education*, 46(11), pp. 2245–2261. https://doi.org/10.1080/03075079.2020.1716322

Steen, M., Manschot, M. and De Koning, N. (2011) 'Benefits of co-design in service design projects', *International Journal of Design*, 5(2), pp. 53–60.

Tay, A. Z., Huijser, H., Dart, S. and Cathcart, A. (2023) 'Learning technology as contested terrain: Insights from teaching academics and learning designers in Australian higher education', *Australasian Journal of Educational Technology*, 39(1), pp. 56–70. https://doi.org/10.14742/ajet.8179

Treasure-Jones, T. and Joynes, V. (2018) 'Co-design of technology-enhanced learning resources', *The Clinical Teacher*, 15(4), pp. 281–286. https://doi.org/10.1111/tct.12733

Vargas, C., Whelan, J., Brimblecombe, J. and Allender, S. (2022) 'Co-creation, co-design, co-production for public health: a perspective on definition and distinctions', *Public Health Research & Practice*, 32(2). https://doi.org/10.17061/phrp3222211

Viberg, O., Bälter, O., Hedin, B., Riese, E. and Mavroudi, A. (2019) 'Faculty pedagogical developers as enablers of technology enhanced learning', *British Journal of Educational Technology*, 50(5), pp. 2637–2650. https://doi.org/10.1111/bjet.12710

Wall, K. (2018) 'Building a bridge between pedagogy and methodology: emergent thinking on notions of quality in practitioner enquiry', *Scottish Educational Review*, 50(2), pp. 3–22. https://doi.org/10.1163/27730840-05002002

Wardak, D., Wilson, S. and Zeivots, S. (2024) 'Co-design as a networked approach to designing educational futures', *Postdigital Science & Education*, 6, pp. 194–210. https://doi.org/10.1007/s42438-023-00425-5

Wardak, D., Zeivots, S. and Cram, A. (2021) 'CLaS light touch project: scaling up educational co-design process', *Journal of Learning Development in Higher Education*, 22. https://doi.org/10.47408/jldhe.vi22.692

Wilson, S., Huber, E. and Bryant, P. (2021) 'Using co-design processes to support strategic pedagogical change in business education', in T. U. Thomsen, A. Lindgreen, A. Kjaergaard, E. Rosier and A. Tuncdogan (eds.), *Handbook of teaching and learning at business schools: a practice-based approach*. Cheltenham: Edward Elgar Publishing, pp. 20–35.

Zeivots, S., Cram, A. and Wardak, D. (2023) 'Developing project management principles by examining codesign practices in innovative contexts', *Project Management Journal*, 54(6), pp. 651–664. https://doi.org/10.1177/87569728231176924

Chapter 18

What Democracy in Action Taught Me About Student Empowerment

Andrea Todd

Introduction

Students often lack agency and voice (Mann, 2008) in decision-making around teaching and learning at university, not least because academic staff can underestimate the meaningful contribution that students can make (Bovill, 2014). Despite literature supporting the notion that co-creation of learning and teaching can be a positive experience for both staff and students (e.g., Lubicz-Nawrocka and Bovill, 2023), the idea of opening up to co-creation with students, even at teaching-intensive providers, can be a challenge as it requires both staff and students to move 'beyond and across traditional roles' (Bovill *et al.*, 2016, p. 196).

In 2022 I facilitated a group of law students in devising the pilot iteration of Law in Action, a new undergraduate module for third year (final year) undergraduates designed to provide students with academic credit for participating in pro bono activities. Acknowledging students as 'holders and creators of knowledge' (Delgado-Bernal, 2002, p. 106), and placing my trust in them as experts both at being a student (Cook-Sather, 2014) and in knowing what they need from their learning experiences, this is a module whose learning outcomes, module content, delivery, and assessment methods were all devised by students, following the principles of direct democracy that place control 'in the hands of the people themselves' (Dalton *et al.*, 2001, p. 142).

The precursor to this project was an intervention I devised in 2020 which was grounded in the basic principle that, despite being forced to pivot online during lockdown and deal with a change in delivery method, students should still be given the opportunity to exercise some agency in how their modules were delivered. Students thus voted on delivery patterns and content, and I made changes in response, in real time, within the boundaries of pre-existing modular and institutional constraints. This gave students a taste of empowerment within the context of an existing module descriptor, with preset learning outcomes and assessment methods. The positive student response to this intervention – born of a crisis – encouraged me to think more deeply about what could happen if I passed students the reins to create an entire module from a blank piece of paper, with me acting as a genuine facilitator, rather than leader, of the design and delivery process. This thought process culminated in a student-built, student-delivered social justice and employability module delivered for the first time in 2022–2023, which empowered students to be the 'authors of their own destiny' (Gravett et al., 2020, p. 2584).

Process

Bryson (2014) describes collaboration between student and teacher as a democratic relationship where the teacher becomes a facilitator and co-learner. The process adopted for the Law in Action module (Figure 18.1) empowered final year undergraduate law students at one UK university to 'make wise decisions [through] direct means' (Dalton et al., 2001, p. 142) and to be 'active collaborators' (Dunne and Zandstra, 2011, p. 4). This required a repositioning of me, as the module leader, from expert to facilitator (Bovill et al., 2016).

Delivery for this module was due to start in November 2022, with the module running from November 2022 to April 2023. Planning for the November 2022 rollout started in February 2022 with the creation of a module code (via a module shell) so that students wishing to participate in the new, as yet unwritten, module could select this choice via the university's Online Module Selection process in March 2022.

Six students (the Law in Action students) selected to create, and then study, this module for the 2022–2023 academic year. Little and Williams (2010, p. 117) note that 'in co-production, power is seen to be shared, which might be too challenging for students'. To minimise the risk of overwhelm, in June 2022 the Law in Action students attended an ethically approved focus group with me to elicit 'insights that would be less accessible without the interaction found in a group' (Morgan, 1997, p. 2). Once the Law in Action students had agreed the rules for focus group discussions (focusing on mutual respect and an open mind), and mindful that co-creation 'does not mean that all standards are up for debate' (Bovill et al., 2016, p. 201), we moved on to a discussion of the standards set for third year undergraduate (Level 6) students by sector-wide level descriptors in the UK. I also provided examples to illustrate how

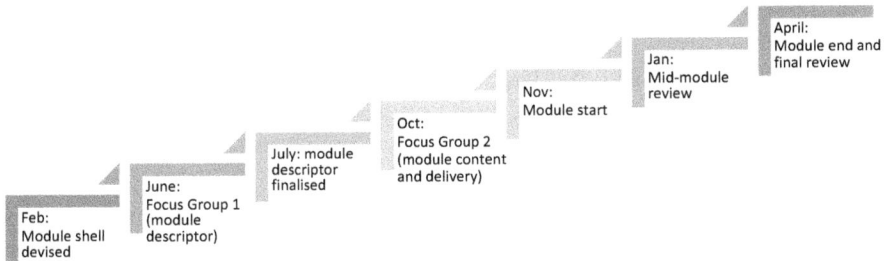

Figure 18.1 Module creation process.

module descriptors are devised and how learning outcomes are drafted. The Law in Action students could then devise the learning outcomes, general module content, module aims, and assessment methods for the module.

In response to the question 'in an ideal world, what would this module do for you?' the message from the Law in Action students was very clear: They wished to engage in a module that helped them understand and prepare for life post-graduation. During the focus group they noted '[it's] important to know where it [the need for pro bono services] all comes from ...' (P1, FG1). They felt that it was important to 'understand and evaluate the real-world practicalities of life in practice' (P2, FG1) and wanted to both 'understand how to do well in interview' (P4, FG1) and have the opportunity to 'self-reflect and take what you already know about yourself and translate that onto paper' (P3, FG1). In terms of preferred assessment method, the consensus from the group was resounding: the Law in Action students wanted to be assessed in 'any way that isn't an essay' (P4, FG1), 'using something that's actually going to help inform my practice' (P3, FG1).

Via these discussions, the Law in Action students created a module aimed at enabling them to better understand the modern legal landscape and identify and confidently articulate their skills for work.

I translated the discussions from the first focus group into 'module descriptor language' before presenting the draft descriptor to the Law in Action students for approval and then sending it to the external examiner for comment (his comments were shared with the students and agreed by them), and then to the university committee responsible for approving the same. The committee accepted the module descriptors without amendment. The agreed learning outcomes were as follows:

1 Critically evaluate the role of pro bono initiatives in today's legal landscape by applying a wide range of evidence to develop well-argued critiques and present valid conclusions;
2 Deploy techniques of analysis and enquiry to identify and analyse the key skills required for successful participation in pro bono initiatives ('pro bono skills') and for life as a practising lawyer;
3 Analyse, synthesise, and critically reflect on how their pro bono skills have developed through engagement with the module and involvement in pro bono initiatives;
4 Critically examine and clearly articulate how the pro bono skills developed through engagement with the module and involvement in pro bono initiatives translate to the work of junior lawyers in practice.

Focus group two was held in October 2022 and focused on the Law in Action students agreeing on detailed module content, and delivery, from week to week. They decided to split the module into two sections:

- Part 1, which discusses the place of pro bono legal provision within the wider legal landscape and leads to the first assessment (30%), a presentation to a university's senior management team or to a law firm's executive board explaining why they should invest in pro bono and how the institution's pro bono offering could be structured; and
- Part 2, which is focused on the students identifying the skills that law firms require from graduates and articulating how they can demonstrate to future employers that they have these skills. The second assessment (70%) was a job interview.

The Law in Action students led every workshop session during the module. They prepared PowerPoint presentations and detailed notes for their colleagues, uploading them to the module's Teams site prior to the workshops. They then presented during class, engaging with peer and module leader feedback on their presentation style and content. In doing so, they became 'active participants in the learning process, constructing understanding and resources' (Bovill *et al.*, 2016, p. 197), and evaluated their learning by way of peer feedback in a manner that was 'personally meaningful' (Cecchinato and Fosschi, 2017, p. 3).

The Law in Action students made some further fundamental decisions as the module was running. For example, they decided during term one that they would welcome a choice of recording or live delivery for their presentation assessment. Both options were thus provided. The students also kept a Skills & Experience Portfolio during the module, but they decided, as the module was closing, that they did not wish for this to be part of the formal assessment, choosing instead to focus on their preparations for the interview assessment rather than formatting their portfolio. The portfolio was not therefore formally assessed. The Law in Action students have since reported that the portfolios have been useful as a point of reference when preparing for job applications and interviews, and therefore remain a useful resource even post-graduation.

Impact

During this project, the Law in Action students controlled the decision making and had substantial influence over the design, delivery, and assessment of the module. This placed them at the top of Arnstein's (1969) citizen participation ladder and of Bovill and Bulley's (2011) model of active student participation.

Feedback from the Law in Action students, collated via ethically approved surveys during and following the module, demonstrates that active involvement in curriculum creation gave these students an increased sense of belonging and importance, as envisaged by Cook-Sather and Agu (2013):

> I feel extremely proud to have co-created [the] module [and] assessment with the other participating students. (Mid-module feedback, R1)
>
> It is great to have an opportunity to create a module ... a professional collaborative experience in a safe setting. It is good to be able to put ideas out there and have them heard. (End-module feedback, R4)
>
> I'm excited that I've had a chance to work collaboratively on such an impressive module. It has been a privilege to be able to be a part of co creating a module that [has] allowed me to feel like I was able to give back. (End-module feedback, R2)

This feedback reflects Bovill *et al.*'s (2016, p. 196–197) findings that working with students in this way represents a 'democratisation of the educational process', shifting them from 'passive recipients or consumers to being active agents' with authentic responsibility for the educational process.

Further, comments from the Law in Action students also chimed with Cook-Sather's (2011) assertion that a shift in power relations enhances students' confidence and capacity and Murphy *et al.*'s (2017, p. 68) contention that involving students in module creation 'can facilitate the design of curricula that are engaging and empowering':

> I feel great when I speak about the module. We selected assessment types that challenged us and we all still achieved great things, despite pushing ourselves out of our comfort zones. (End-module feedback, R2)
>
> It made me feel more positive and confident ... it made me feel as though my opinions and thoughts were valid and welcomed [and] this module felt really fresh because it made me feel like a young professional, rather than an inexperienced student. (End-module feedback, R3)
>
> It made me feel engaged and confident. (End-module feedback, R1)
>
> It has made me feel like I am tailoring my own learning to my own personal development. (End-module feedback, R3)

It was also clear that the experience had created a sense of community between the Law in Action students, who designed and delivered the module, and the module leader, chiming with Deeley and Bovill's (2017) assertion that co-creation can help to foster the development of a learning community and Bovill's (2020) argument that co-creation leads to strengthened positive relationships:

> Any ideas we have are welcomed with open arms. It's lovely that we are made to feel like equals. (Mid-module feedback, R2)
>
> We all listen to each other and are very supportive. (Mid-module feedback, R4)
>
> It always felt like a safe space to share thoughts and opinions. (End-module feedback, R2)

The environment was collaborative and supportive [and] allowed me to grow immense confidence within myself and my learning. (Mid-module feedback, R1)

Conclusions

It is important that collaboration is a meaningful exercise and not simply an empty promise (Cook-Sather *et al.*, 2014). When a genuine attempt at trusting students to take control is made, great things can happen. For the Law in Action module, it resulted in engaged students producing excellent quality work, being assessed in innovative ways.

Projects of this nature challenge the power dynamics that underpin the traditional relationships between staff and students in higher education. As Murphy *et al.* (2017) note, practical guidance for academic staff around engaging students in the process of designing and developing curriculum is scarce. Here are my top three reflections on engaging in a democratic process of module creation with students.

1 *Trust is imperative*: Students need to trust their module leader (particularly where the module is as yet unwritten and where the module is 'high stakes', as is the case for final year undergraduate modules); the university's quality team must trust in the module leader to permit the generation of a module code without an indication of the module content, outcomes, or assessment methods; and, crucially, the module leader must trust the students to know what they want from the module and to lead on delivery of the sessions.
2 *Laying the ground rules is essential*: Rules around how to behave in focus groups need to be developed between students and the module leader before substantive discussions around the module can commence. It is also vital that students understand the fundamental principles around what learning outcomes can achieve and the need to align them with level descriptors, which necessarily means talking students through examples of learning outcomes from other modules at the same level prior to asking them to devise their own.
3 *Adaptability is key*: Module leaders need to be agile and willing to adapt to what will be delivered week by week, given that the workshop material is produced and presented by students. This involves setting time aside to check the content uploaded to Teams by students prior to the workshop sessions to know how best to facilitate student contributions in the classroom. This is the case both in the first iteration of the module and in subsequent iterations, as the module descriptor should be drafted sufficiently loosely to allow students room for co-creation even within the constraints of a module descriptor that has been designed by previous students.

Reconceptualising students as active agents in module creation necessitates a rethinking of assumptions about teaching, learning, power, and knowledge (King and Felten, 2012). This rethinking can help us redefine what it means to be a module leader: If we want to truly give students agency, being a module leader does not mean being a module creator, taking responsibility for design and delivery. At its best, it means placing power in students' hands, facilitating them in their own work as module creators and liberating them to design and deliver a module that meets their needs.

References

Arnstein, S. R. (1969) 'A ladder of citizen participation', *Journal of the American Institute of Planners*, 35(4), pp. 216–224.

Bovill, C. (2014) 'An investigation of co-created curricula within higher education in the UK, Ireland and the USA', *Innovations in Education and Teaching International*, 51(1), pp. 15–25.

Bovill, C. (2020) 'Co-creation in learning and teaching: the case for a whole-class approach in higher education', *Higher Education* 79, pp. 1023–1037.

Bovill, C. and Bulley, C. J. (2011) *A model of active student participation in curriculum design: exploring desirability and possibility*, n C. Rust (ed.), *Improving student learning 18: global theories and local practices: institutional, disciplinary and cultural variations*. Series: improving student learning (18) (pp. 176–188). Oxford: Brookes University, Oxford Centre for Staff and Learning Development.

Bovill, C., Cook-Sather, A. Felten, P., Millard, L. and Moore-Cherry, N. (2016) 'Addressing potential challenges in co-creating learning and teaching: overcoming resistance, navigating institutional norms, and ensuring inclusivity in student-staff partnerships', *Higher Education*, 71(2), 195–208.

Bryson, C. (Ed.). (2014) *Understanding and developing student engagement* (1st ed.). London: Routledge.

Cecchinato, G. and Fosschi, L. C. (2017) 'Flipping the roles: analysis of a university course where students become cocreators of curricula', *Teaching and Learning Together in Higher Education*, 22, https://repository.brynmawr.edu/tlthe/vol1/iss22/5

Cook-Sather, A. (2011) 'Layered learning: student consultants deepening classroom and life lessons', *Educational Action Research*, 9(1), pp. 41–57.

Cook-Sather, A. (2014) 'Student-faculty partnership in explorations of pedagogical practice: a threshold concept in academic development', *International Journal for Academic Development*, 19(3), pp. 186–198.

Cook-Sather, A. and Agu, P. (2013) Students of color and faculty members working together toward culturally sustaining pedagogy. in J. E. Groccia and L. Cruz (eds.), *To improve the academy: Resources for faculty, instructional, and organizational development* (Vol. 32, pp. 271–285). San Francisco, CA: Jossey-Bass.

Cook-Sather, A., Bovill, C. and Felten, P.(2014) *Engaging students as partners in learning and teaching*. San Francisco, CA: Jossey Bass.

Dalton, R. J., Burklin, W. and Drummond, A. (2001) Public opinion and direct democracy. *Journal of Democracy*, 12(4), 141–153.

Deeley, S. J. and Bovill, C. (2017) 'Staff student partnership in assessment: enhancing assessment literacy through democratic practices', *Assessment and Evaluation in Higher Education*, 42(3), 463–477.

Delgado-Bernal, D. (2002) 'Critical race theory, Latino critical theory, and critical raced-gendered epistemologies: recognizing students of color as holders and creators of knowledge' *Qualitative Inquiry*, 8(1), pp. 105–126.

Dunne, E. and Zandstra, R. (2011) *Students as change agents - new ways of engaging with learning and teaching in higher education*. Bristol: A joint University of Exeter/ESCalate/Higher Education Academy Publication. Available at http://escalate.ac.uk/8064 (Accessed 22 April 2024).

Gravett, K., Kinchin, K. and Winstone, N. E. (2020) 'More than customers': conceptions of students as partners held by students, staff, and institutional leaders', *Studies in Higher Education*, 45(12), pp. 2574–2587.

King, C. and Felten, P. (2012) 'Threshold concepts in educational development: an introduction', *The Journal of Faculty Development*, 26(3), 5.

Little, B. and Williams, R. (2010) 'Students' roles in maintaining quality and in enhancing learning—is there a tension?', *Quality in Higher Education*, 16(2), pp. 115–127.

Lubicz-Nawrocka, T. and Bovill, C. (2023) 'Do students experience transformation through co-creating curriculum in higher education?', *Teaching in Higher Education*, 28(7), pp. 1744–1760.

Mann, S. J. (2008) *Study, power and the university: the institution and its effects on learning*. Berkshire: Open University Press.

Morgan, D. L. (1997) *Focus groups as qualitative research*. Newbury Park, CA: Sage Publications.

Murphy, R., Nixon, S., Brooman, S. and Fearon, D. (2017) '"I am wary of giving too much power to students:" Addressing the "but" in the principle of staff-student partnership', *International Journal for Students as Partners*, 1(1), pp. 67–82.

Section 4

Homo ex Machina

Transforming Practice to Keep Sight of Our Humanity

Carina Buckley

In the film *The Terminator* (1984), writer-director James Cameron presented a dystopian vision in which humans fought for their survival in a post-apocalyptic world dominated by a hostile artificial intelligence, Skynet. Having achieved consciousness, Skynet unleashed the full and violent potential of technology onto the people who had created it, with devastating results. Although the film's Judgement Day (29 August 1997) passed without these fears being realised (as did the revised Judgement Days of the various sequels), we live in the long shadow of the film's insistent question: How can humanity continue to survive and thrive in the face of the relentless march of technology? Our fascination (and concern) with this question, and the lack of a satisfactory answer, is perhaps evident in the multiple sequels spawned by this initial Hollywood production – six films and two TV series to date – and the ongoing negotiation of our relationship with technology. The leaps made by various generative AI platforms since 2022, introduced because they were possible rather than necessary, have brought disruption to higher education (HE) in their wake, and now these heightened capabilities must somehow be managed, if not tamed. Although we cherish the illusion of harnessing the technologies we have created, their release into the world and the speed of their change has taken them far beyond our control.

How, then, can we hope to contain this Pandora's box? After all, there is much that technology gifts us. During the most dire moments of the pandemic lockdowns, we used technology to bring people together to create, nurture, strengthen, and extend personal connections. It allowed us to leave our homes even as we were confined to them, and it opened up new possibilities for education that would help us to break down barriers to access and to belonging, seek new routes to supporting student achievement, and reconsider what we believed learning and teaching could be. The surge in popularity of blended learning provoked a panoply of vibrant, innovative, and agential approaches, many of which have since been evaluated (OfS, 2023), championed (Anderson, 2022), celebrated (*JLDHE*, 2021), and integrated into a reimagined HE (Snelling, 2021). Yet despite this boon, technology does not think (artificial intelligence is neither artificial nor intelligent; Xiang, 2022), nor does it care. Technology is not in itself adaptable or flexible. But humans

DOI: 10.4324/9781003503149-23

think, humans care, and humans can adapt, flex, and reimagine the tools they have available. To privilege the technology over the human, then, would be a loss for humanity as a whole and for the individuals elided by automation.

Our goal, as educators as well as simply humans, should therefore be to release the human from the machine and liberate human thinking from the wild novelty of these technological constraints. For Haraway, this creates space for the emergence of the cyborg, her attempt to resolve 'the tension of holding incompatible things together because both or all are necessary and true' (2004, p. 7). In this case, it is the demands of the lived and social realities of those who populate 'worlds ambiguously natural and crafted' (p. 8) that require the rupturing of boundaries between organism and machine, the material and the imaginative. The explosion of generative AI blurs those boundaries even further, with humans writing in partnership with a predictive algorithm, voice and code blending in calculable yet unforeseeable ways.

The current preoccupation with AI obscures the ancient relationship humans have had with technology. More than just the development and usage of tools, stretching back over 2.8 million years to the earliest worked cobbles of Olduvai Gorge, we enter into relation with them so that their affordances become part of our social reality. Aristotle, writing in his *Politics* (Book 1) over 2,000 years ago, imagined a world in which 'the shuttle would weave and the plectrum touch the lyre without a hand to guide them'. The current capabilities of AI place it in a human-like position, able to pass the Turing test and induce us to treat software as if it were a person. We seek the human element within the machine. In an extension of Aristotle's simple framing, our use of technology, particularly in HE, is oriented towards finding ways to connect with others and build relationships. The chapters in this section explore this from five key perspectives, all of them central to helping us understand our relationship with technology and with each other.

As a form of socially situated material culture, technology operates within power structures, and empowerment through confidence-building is the theme of the opening chapter of this section. Rachel Bancroft and her colleagues at Nottingham Trent University – Rachel Challen, Amanda Neylon, and Bethany Witham – identified an important distinction between digital capabilities and digital confidence. We are not passive consumers of technology, allowing it to happen to us, but instead we are active agents in its use, driven by curiosity, partnership, and a sense of ownership. It is our duty as educators to support our students and colleagues in developing this empowering confidence for themselves, as someone who is confident with technology has access to not just *doing* more but *being* more.

When we are able to access the online space, we can find each other there. Debbie Holley, Anne Quinney, and John Moran use Chapter 20 to explore the vital importance of developing an authentic presence in an asynchronous environment, ensuring that the space is inclusive of everyone. If the classroom is the crossroads where the social and the academic meet, its digital variant is the junction where ideas and action merge, as long as we allow ourselves to be creative in its use. A tool does not have to simply be functional; it can be communal, messy, fluid, open, and amorphous. Our task is only to claim the space and hold the space without feeling the need to define and constrain it, so that we can connect to others there.

Sometimes it is not possible to define a space that is itself a hybrid, a cyborg that unites the incompatible and holds multiple perspectives and voices in tension. Blending methods for interactivity and engagement, in Chapter 21 Daniel Tinnion, Thomas Simpson, and Mitchell Finlay explore the significance of self-determination theory in education. Our psychological needs, as people and as learners, are for feeling that we have some control, that we are competent, and that we are included in a community of others. These authors blend space and place to support students in a range of sensemaking and confidence-building activities that construct knowledge within learning networks. Technology can mediate connection and community to build autonomy, recognising the individuals in the mix without replacing them.

Part of that recognition involves the power of emotion; although technology has no emotion of its own, it can provide a means for channelling memory, nostalgia, loss, and the desire for preservation. In Chapter 22, Nicholas Bowskill, Melody Harrogate, and David Hall identify as a form of altruism the drive of people to leave something of themselves in the digital record, a trace in the coding that they were there. The socially situated nature of knowledge allows us to apprehend and respond to the people we discover in the machine, not the machine itself.

And this idea leads us to the final chapter in the section, where Paul O'Kane looks at the crucial role that troubling plays in education, as long as we are the ones who trouble rather than simply reacting to the disruptions of technology. He celebrates the vitality that comes from questioning and critiquing, from taking risks and pursuing self-discovery, and from forging our own paths and not just following the worn tracks laid down by previous generations. Where technology can appear to be an unleashing of possibilities, it behoves us to ensure that we are not instead accepting other, more insidious constraints.

To be human is to be an active agent, engaged in connecting, questioning, and constructing knowledge in community with others. Yet the ongoing and accelerating melding of our agency, our essential humanness, with technology brings us firmly into the realm of the posthuman. Here, once again, we find Haraway's cyborgs, which represent 'the tensions and possibilities of technological mediation' (Bolter, 2016, p. 2), with technology playing a part in the performativity of our identity as humans. Although there is much that established and emergent technologies can add to the sum total of our experience, we should not allow that to happen at that experience's expense. We must create meaning out of our own stories and, through it, enter into relation with others. It is our responsibility to decide what those relationships should look like and how they should be formed, maintained, and strengthened. Skynet remains a story – for now – but the drivers for it are real. It's up to us to ensure that the machines remain our tools and that we remain human.

References

Anderson, J. (2022) Global innovations in education during the pandemic. *The Harvard EdCast Podcast*, 31 March 2022. Available at https://www.gse.harvard.edu/ideas/edcast/22/03/global-innovations-education-during-pandemic

Bolter, J. D. (2016) Posthumanism. In K. B. Jensen, E. W. Rothenbuhler, J. D. Pooley, and R. T. Craig (eds.), *The international encyclopedia of communication theory and philosophy*. https://doi.org/10.1002/9781118766804.wbiect220

JLDHE. (2021) Compendium of innovative practice: Learning Development in a time of disruption, *JLDHE Special Issue* (22). Available from: https://journal.aldinhe.ac.uk/index.php/jldhe/issue/view/36

Haraway, D. (2004) 'A manifesto for cyborgs: science, technology, and the socialist feminism in the 1980s'. In *The Haraway Reader* (pp. 7–46). Routledge.

OfS. (2023) *Blended learning and OfS regulation*. Available at https://www.officeforstudents.org.uk/publications/blended-learning-and-ofs-regulation/

Snelling, C. (2021) Lessons from the pandemic: making the most of technologies in teaching. Available at https://www.universitiesuk.ac.uk/what-we-do/policy-and-research/publications/lessons-pandemic-making-most

Xiang, C. (2022) AI isn't artificial or intelligent. Available at https://www.vice.com/en/article/wxnaqz/ai-isnt-artificial-or-intelligent

Chapter 19

What Digital Confidence Practice and Research Has Taught Us About Supporting Digital Change

Rachel Bancroft, Rachel Challen, Amanda Neylon, and Bethany Witham

Introduction

The authors support digital learning at Nottingham Trent University (NTU) at a school and institutional level, and this chapter explores the relevance of digital confidence to digital change.

Where We Started

During the rapid switch to remote teaching necessitated by the pandemic, we noticed that sometimes the barrier to adapting to urgent digital changes was not one of digital capability, though there were new skills to develop, but instead an issue of digital confidence. In response, we began locating and creating opportunities for the digital confidence growth needed to adapt and innovate during this period of rapid change and were able to identify some ways in which development of digital confidence could be nurtured (Bancroft et al., 2021). This growth in digital confidence accompanied further development and innovative practice, increasing the new digital learning opportunities for students.

Where We Are Now

We completed a scoping review to further explore the literature around digital confidence in tertiary education, and amongst the emerging themes was the suggestion that digital confidence may have a foundational role during times of change.

In our context, digital change has continued beyond the remote teaching of the pandemic as our colleagues continue to develop digital learning and teaching in innovative ways. In this chapter we share some examples of how opportunities to grow digital confidence are now embedded in the ways we support this innovation.

Alongside our research and the practice in our local context, our institution is journeying toward a 'digital sophistication' ambition, which represents digital change at scale. Digital confidence forms one of three strands of our transformation strategy, and we share how digital confidence is being considered as an important aspect of this digital transformation.

Digital Confidence Research

We sought to learn more about how others had understood digital confidence, and our scoping review aimed to answer the primary question: 'How is digital confidence in tertiary education currently represented in the literature?' (Bancroft *et al.*, 2024). Some of the emerging themes have particular pertinence to digital change.

Understanding Digital Confidence

Repeated use of the term in the literature indicated that digital confidence was valued, with increased usage over time suggesting a growth in importance. It seemed that consensus on the exact meaning of digital confidence was still being established, and its relationship to competence was a complex one (Bancroft *et al.*, 2024). Whilst the nature of digital confidence was almost always intertwined with digital competence or skills, there were occasions where it was mentioned and considered distinctly, and there were reports of digital confidence and competence being unaligned, where their levels differed. This suggests that there are potential implications for digital skills development provision.

Digital Confidence and Change

Emerging from the research, too, were insights into behaviours around digital confidence, including that digital confidence seems to be particularly significant during times of change. Digital confidence seems to support resilience during digital change, for example when facing new modes of digital teaching or learning to use new tools (e.g., Greener and Wakefield, 2015, Passey *et al.*, 2018, Armstrong, 2019, Maslin and Smith, 2017). This leads us to consider whether a digitally confident teacher may be more likely to explore a diverse range of digital learning options and feel more prepared to experiment with new tools and approaches.

Digital transformation represents just such a time of change, often at significant scale; therefore we consider that the growth of digital confidence is a key component that must be deliberately pursued.

Digital Confidence and Wellbeing

Further, digital confidence emerging as a potentially empowering element in times of change could have implications for wellbeing.

Digital change includes the potential for increased work stress, which can have an effect 'even among those employees who are highly competent in ICT' (Makowska-Tłomak et al., 2023, p. 5). Given that negative emotions (doubt, loneliness, fear of failure, etc.) seem associated in the literature with a lack of digital confidence, and positive emotions (enthusiasm, enjoyment, comfort, etc.) appear associated with having digital confidence (Bancroft et al., 2024), this could be a significant factor when considering the experience of those navigating digital change. This is an area with potential for further exploration.

Nurturing Digital Confidence

Finally, we noted that the literature also mentioned some actions that may relate to the growth of digital confidence. We grouped approaches that we recognised as similar and categorised these under the three interlocking headings in Table 19.1. We recognise many of these activities in our own practice, and we describe how we have embedded two of them below.

Growing Digital Confidence in Practice

Digital change is still underway in our local context – including the increased use of digital assessment and a digital focus within work to redesign modules – and this change is supported by digital confidence.

An Embedded, Research-Informed Approach

Rather than creating a series of training events, or offering workshops aiming to explicitly build digital confidence in our colleagues, we have embedded opportunities to grow digital confidence throughout our support for digital learning and teaching. One way we articulate this is that we act as springboard and safety net (Bancroft and Pearce, 2022), working with colleagues to launch ambitious digital projects and providing help throughout, and as spotlight

Table 19.1 Activities for digital confidence development

Social	Training/support	Doing
Modelling	Group workshops	Reflective practice
Mentoring	Pedagogical focus, not technical	Practice opportunities
Social support and influence	Self-directed learning materials	Embedded in curriculum
Engaging with online communities	One-to-one support	
Digital champions		
Peer feedback		

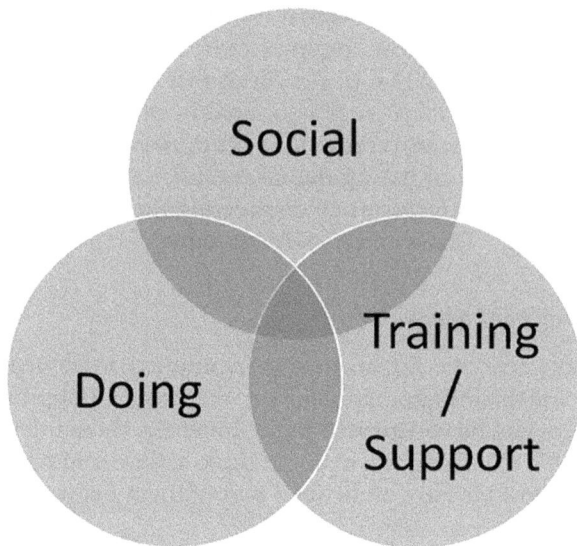

Figure 19.1 Categories of activities for digital confidence development.

(Witham, 2023), highlighting the innovative digital practice to both the colleagues involved and the larger institution.

We develop relationships with our colleagues over time that are rooted in trust and founded in collaborative ways of working. This has allowed us to see digital confidence grow over time, achievable due to the embedded nature of the team's support within our school and its curriculum.

Creating Opportunities for Digital Confidence Growth

We recognise most of the practices highlighted in Table 19.1 as present within our team's support to help build digital confidence. Two specific examples of this are outlined here.

Practice Opportunities

We intentionally create digital practice opportunities to support digital confidence development through the ways in which we offer support. For example, instead of taking over colleagues' screens or running through steps ourselves whilst they follow along, we always ask them 'to drive' and share their screens so *we* can follow along. This empowers them to practice using digital tools themselves as they demonstrate their digital approaches for us, reinforcing their ownership of the technology, with us there to offer support whilst they get started and in case things go wrong (springboard and safety net).

It's clear to see the impact of this approach, as colleagues now confidently volunteer to share their screens and ideas without prompting, trusting us with their developing practice and inviting us to give advice while they learn to use the tools that facilitate their digital teaching. The encouragement we provide in these moments, articulating their digital successes (spotlight), further builds digital confidence through recognition of their growing expertise.

Pedagogical, Not Technical

We also recognise the importance of a pedagogical focus in development and support, rather than purely technical, and work with our colleagues to explore possibilities with their specific learning outcomes and context in mind. Rather than tool-first, technically focused sessions, we provide the digital skills development they need to meet their articulated learning and teaching intentions whilst supporting their agency over their digital approaches. This often involves partnered collaboration, combining the expertise of those involved, and can lead to projects developed over time where personalised support for digital skills and confidence development is provided responsively depending on where that project leads. This approach allows for the pedagogy to remain 'entangled' with the technology (Fawns, 2022, p. 711).

Observing Digital Confidence

As a team we have started to develop a shared understanding of what digital confidence might look like in our context, recognising how it is demonstrated in knowledge, skills, and behaviours. The growth of digital confidence that we first noted during the pandemic has continued, and that is visible to us in many ways that are pertinent to the small- and large-scale digital change we find ourselves part of.

Curiosity and a Willingness to Try

We noted in the literature review a suggestion that digital confidence may impact a 'willingness to try', and the digital confidence growth we have observed has moved beyond this. Instead of a reactive willingness when presented with ready-made opportunities, colleagues are proactively demonstrating an appetite for developing ambitious digital learning approaches on which we collaborate.

There is a related growth in curiosity that is visible to us in the increasing complexity of the questions that colleagues raise. These thoughtful questions and follow-up queries that form the collaborative process suggest an investment in, and ownership of, digital approaches, and a confidence in their ability to understand and be part of finding an answer in the technological matters as well as the pedagogical ones.

Innovative Digital Teaching and the Student Experience

The growth of digital confidence in our colleagues, and the resulting thoughtful and innovative digital learning and teaching approaches used, has a clear impact on students. Arts and humanities as a discipline has traditionally included essays as a common means of assessment, but recent module redesigns in our school have moved further towards authentic assessments with creative digital formats, such as students creating podcasts and online exhibitions and receiving audio or visual feedback from colleagues. These authentic means of assessing and providing feedback for students have been shown to improve the metacognitive skills required for learning and enhance future employability (Villarroel *et al.*, 2018, p. 841).

The impact of staff digital confidence on the learning experience of students was also something we encountered in our literature review, for example, 'low levels of digital confidence in staff could impact not only what they teach, but also how they teach, potentially limiting the student experience of learning with digital tools' (Bristow and Smith, 2018). Instead, in our context, students have been able to experience varied digital tools and approaches that enrich their learning and may positively impact their employability.

Student Digital Confidence

We have also seen growing interest in fostering student digital confidence emerging from ongoing discussions with colleagues about the complexities of digital practice and confidence development. We worked with our colleague Dr Rebekah Pickering Wood to consider how to prepare students for an innovative digital assessment in which they would design an interactive digital game. Rebekah noted that whilst her students sometimes initially lacked confidence, past students had had a lot of success with the games they produced, suggesting a need for intentional digital confidence development alongside support for digital skills.

We chose to use White's digital visitors and residents mapping activity (White & Le Cornu, 2011) to initiate conversations with the students about their digital engagement and their confidence with the tools they already use. By using this model, which explicitly offers an alternative to the earlier digital natives and immigrants concept (Prensky, 2001), we also aimed to avoid any assumptions being made about digital capability based on age, a thread we noted in the literature review (Bancroft *et al.*, 2024).

Rebekah's students first mapped their online activities, then reflected on how confident they felt in different areas of their digital lives. Meaningful discussion emerged around the idea that there were no 'right or wrong' maps, with students sharing and displaying curiosity about their differences (cultural, digital, and individual), feeling connected through some previously undiscovered similarities, with Rebekah observing a more positive outlook regarding their digital confidence when approaching unfamiliar tools.

The Institutional Ambition and Digital Confidence

Our research and practice lead us to believe that digital confidence has particular relevance during times of change, making it important in the planning of digital strategy. At Nottingham Trent University (NTU), the acknowledgement of, and commitment to, digital confidence development is embedded within our ambition to be a 'digitally sophisticated' university by 2025. Through development of a menu of digital skills and pedagogy training for staff, our planned transformation aims to have the effect of bringing efficiency and innovation to the curriculum and university.

A growth in staff digital confidence, scaffolded by this programme of staff development, intends to create more opportunities for students to experience rich digital approaches through role modelling by teaching staff, and for these approaches to become an embedded part of their study and assessments. In our institutional plan, we aim to explore a range of events, resources, technical support, and access to relevant digital tools in order to support student digital skills and confidence development.

The literature review suggests a shared definition of digital confidence is still being formed. NTU is therefore also developing ways to describe some of the behaviours enabled by digital confidence for staff and students, and these provide the underpinning framework which articulates the relationship between digital confidence and digital sophistication.

Our institutional aspiration is that 'digital confidence will empower our students to harness the full potential of technology for learning, research, creative expression, and problem-solving, enhancing their academic journey and preparing them for success in employment' and one of our goals is that a digitally confident staff member is able to realise opportunities to 'streamline tasks, enhance productivity, and contribute innovatively to their work environment' (Nottingham Trent University, 2023). Both of these aspirations are rooted in change and represent a belief that having digital confidence is a key component for successfully navigating digital change.

Our Conclusions

Following reflection on our ongoing practice and results from our literature review, it seems no coincidence that our focus on digital confidence was born during a time of rapid and significant digital change.

In our practice and our literature review, we recognised the importance of digital confidence for getting started with new digital approaches and taking the first step to realising a digital ambition. We also recognised the role of digital confidence in times of digital change where innovating new digital practice is required. Digital confidence appears connected with a willingness to try new things and to build on existing abilities, which we see as potentially having a positive developmental effect on staff practice. We observe that staff digital confidence can affect opportunities for students to experience varied digital learning and teaching approaches, with potential impact beyond their studies.

We continue to explore the potential for digital confidence development to enable new digital practice throughout and beyond this time of change as new, more ambitious digital approaches are proposed by colleagues and developed in collaboration.

Digital transformation, both small- and large-scale, is ongoing throughout our sector, and the role that digital confidence could play in supporting staff in times of digital change has implications for practice at many levels. Whether change is small and local, such as in reimagining new creative digital assessments, or large and broad, such as institutional digital transformation, digital confidence could be an important enabler of digital change for innovation. Additionally, there may be opportunities to explore the effects of these digital confidence increases on the wellbeing of all involved in digital transformation or navigating a period of digital change.

Given that it has been observed that digital confidence and competencies do not always align, our work suggests a need to intentionally create opportunities for digital confidence development. As it seems that digital confidence may not necessarily be gained at a proportional rate as part of digital skills development, digital skills training alone may not automatically build sufficient digital confidence to support the practice development necessary for digital transformation.

Digital confidence is still an emerging area with opportunities for further exploration and definition; however, we believe that creating opportunities for digital confidence growth in addition to digital skills provision is fundamental if we are to realise our digital change ambitions.

Acknowledgements

With thanks to Rebekah Pickering-Wood for sharing her experience of fostering digital confidence with her students, Rosemary Pearce for proofreading, and Emily May for contributing grammatical corrections.

References

Armstrong, E. J. (2019) 'Maximising motivators for technology-enhanced learning for further education teachers: moving beyond the early adopters in a time of austerity', *Research in Learning Technology*, 27, pp. 1–23. https://doi.org/10.25304/rlt.v27.2032

Bancroft, R., Pearce, R., Challen, R., Jeckells, D. and Kenney, J. (2021) 'Locating opportunities for building digital confidence in staff', *Journal of Learning Development in Higher Education*, (22). https://doi.org/10.47408/jldhe.vi22.775

Bancroft, R. and Pearce, R. (2022) *Digital confidence: springboard and safety net*. Available at https://ntuhum-ltsu.com/digital-pedagogy/digital-confidence-springboard-and-safety-net/ (Accessed 12 February 2024).

Bancroft, R., Challen, R. and Pearce, R. (2024) 'Searching for a shared understanding of digital confidence in a tertiary context: a scoping review', *Journal of Learning Development in Higher Education*, https://doi.org/10.47408/jldhe.vi30.1061

Bristow, R. and Smith, R. (2018) Breaking through: stories of effective digital practice from UK further education (FE) and skills. Available at https://beta.jisc.ac.uk/reports/breaking-through-stories-of-effective-digital-practice-from-uk-fe-and-skills (Accessed 1 August 2023).

Fawns, T. (2022) An entangled pedagogy: looking beyond the pedagogy—technology dichotomy. *Postdigital Science and Education* 4, pp. 711–728. https://doi.org/10.1007/s42438-022-00302-7

Greener, S. and Wakefield, C. (2015) 'Developing confidence in the use of digital tools in teaching', *Electronic Journal of E-Learning*, 13(4), pp. 260–267.

Passey, D., Shonfeld, M., Appleby, L., Judge, M., Saito, T. and Smits, A. (2018) 'Digital agency: empowering equity in and through education', *Technology Knowledge and Learning*, 23(3), pp. 425–439. https://doi.org/10.1007/s10758-018-9384-x

Makowska-Tłomak, E., Bedyńska, S., Skorupska, K., Nielek, R., Kornacka, M. and Kopeć, W. (2023) Measuring digital transformation stress at the workplace:development and validation of the digital transformation stress scale. *PloS One*, 18(10), p. e0287223. https://doi.org/10.1371/journal.pone.0287223

Maslin, P. and Smith, N. (2017) 'Practicum as nexus: using student voice to improve digital pedagogy within ITE', *Waikato Journal of Education*, 22(3), pp. 47–61. https://doi.org/10.15663/wje.v22i3.376

Nottingham Trent University (2023) *Digital confidence action plan*. Unpublished.

Prensky, M. (2001, October). 'Digital natives, digital immigrants'. *On the Horizon*, 9(5). Lincoln: NCB University Press.

Villarroel, V., Bloxham, S., Bruna, D., Bruna, C. and Herrera-Seda, C. (2018) Authentic assessment: creating a blueprint for course design, *Assessment & Evaluation in Higher Education*, 43(5), pp. 840–854. https://doi.org/10.1080/02602938.2017.1412396

White, D. S. and Le Cornu, A. (2011) Visitors and residents: a new typology for online engagement. *First Monday*, 16(9). https://doi.org/10.5210/fm.v16i9.3171

Witham, B. (2023) Digital confidence: spotlight. Available at https://ntuhum-ltsu.com/digital-confidence/digital-confidence-spotlight/ (Accessed 12 February 2024).

Chapter 20

What a Person-Centred, Values-Based, and Blended Approach Taught Us About Transformative Online Pedagogies in Healthcare Disciplines

Debbie Holley, Anne Quinney, and John Moran

Introduction

Having experienced the pivot to online learning (Nordmann et al., 2020; Morley and Holley 2023), our challenge was to merge the valuable new knowledge and experience with our long-standing traditions underpinning curriculum design and delivery of in-person, practice-based, person-centred education informed by humanisation principles developed by scholars at our institution (Todres et al., 2006). Here we share how we embraced the inherent apparent paradoxes of social constructivist learning in an online, asynchronous, and distance-learning environment in a faculty of health and social care and beyond, using three inter-related examples.

These apparent paradoxes, in what could be seen as a disruptive scenario for teaching and learning, led to new approaches. Drawing on findings from an earlier body of research in the faculty exploring core aspects of this situation, including student experiences of technology-enhanced learning (Hutchings et al., 2013, Pulman et al., 2012) and the adoption of the 'flipped classroom' (Hutchings and Quinney, 2015), we tailored these building blocks to the 'pivot to online' and to embed them post COVID-19

Example 1: Designing and Delivering an Online PGCert

In designing and delivering a new distance-learning Postgraduate Certificate (PGCert) in academic practice, we utilised new tools and techniques for technology-enhanced and technology-transformed learning experiences. The humanisation aspect was expressed in the design of pedagogical interventions in a distance and online environment with a rich and varied curriculum, aligning with the move to *personalisation* in higher education by promoting social constructivist and situated learning theories (Lave and Wenger, 1991; Vygotsky, 1978; Wenger, 1998) within an aligned curriculum (Biggs and Tang, 2007). Embracing and emphasising the flexibility afforded by asynchronicity required

DOI: 10.4324/9781003503149-25

the need for *authentic* learning activities (Herrington *et al.*, 2004) which emphasise *the human* as well as *the technical*. Our strategies, informed by Nordmann *et al.*'s (2020) 'rules', included modelling online social presence in video materials and notice boards, building whole group and small group identity through peer interaction in creative asynchronous learning activities, and ensuring alignment through clear labelling and sequencing of materials. Individual synchronous video tutorials were key enablers for building trust, supporting assignment development, and providing an in-person dimension to the learning experience. Initially apprehensive and uncertain about the process of distance and online learning, in addition to the disciplinary and professional knowledge content being explored, learners were enabled to identify the transferable aspects of a range of online pedagogies for their own teaching and learning support roles through their engagement with the online spaces. An exploration of signature pedagogies (Shulman, 2005) in the participants' disciplines provided a platform for synergies of interdisciplinary learning.

The experience of staff members becoming students on this university-wide and externally facing programme provided unexpected insights into the realities of the student experience, such as managing deadlines, developing a deeper understanding of academic policies and protocols, navigating the virtual learning environment (VLE), and managing virtual group activities. These insights had the potential to lead to enhanced student-centred and technology-confident approaches in their own teaching. Learners developed alliances across disciplines and institutions, enriching their understanding of approaches to teaching and learning. They shared resources and skills and built a supportive network for future projects and mutual support. In the previous in-person version of the programme, learners gravitated to faculty colleagues or those from cognate subject areas, whereas in the online version these boundaries dissolved and new transformational opportunities for forging alliances across disciplines and institutions emerged. A focus on both process and content enabled subject knowledge to merge with the scholarship of teaching and learning in higher education and enabled learners from all disciplines to make connections with their area of expertise and across disciplines.

Whilst our approach was evidence-based and research-informed, we were fortunate to be able to draw on the knowledge, skills, and values gained over a career life-cycle that saw the shift to online as a natural development, employing disciplinary knowledge, including the scholarship of learning and teaching, interprofessional learning, and leadership skills to inspire learners and colleagues new to online pedagogies. A renewed understanding of factors that promote and inhibit learning in an online environment emerged from opportunities to share this knowledge with a new generation of staff who will embrace and promote the scholarship and artistry of teaching and learning in face-to-face, blended, simulated, or online environments.

Example 2: Embedding Digital Competencies into the Nursing Curricula

The digital confidence that emerged from the pivot to online brought unexpected benefits to the faculty. The *Topal Review* (2019) set out the expectations of how cultural and technological shifts in practice for the National Health Service (NHS) could benefit professional healthcare staff and their patients alike and prepare the healthcare workforce to deliver the digital future. The Humanising Framework (Todres *et al.*, 2006), embedded across the nursing sciences curricula, engendered an understanding of the practices of person-centred care. In addition, the 'Every Nurse Is an e-Nurse' report (Royal College of Nursing, 2018) emphasised the significance and urgency of embracing the digital. We were able to harness the positive experiences of staff who had participated in the online PGCert, newly confident in online and blended pedagogies for transformative learning, when responding sensitively to these key reports. Their increased awareness of the fundamental role of digital skills enabled the embedding of digital competencies in the nursing curriculum to be more easily achieved.

Early work on digital competency frameworks highlighted the significance of national standards (Evangelinos and Holley, 2014) in underpinning and enhancing digital skill development for learners. The UK nonprofit organisation Jisc was tasked with advising higher and further education institutions with building an evidence base for embedding digital competencies, key for workers entering the 21st-century workplace. Their digital competence framework (Beetham *et al.*, 2012) is acknowledged as sector best practice; and the revalidation of our nursing curricula offered the opportunity to embed this competency framework in a spiral, evidence-based model for underpinning the digital aspects of the programme.

The nursing curriculum was transformed through expanding the digital mapping, each digital competence located within the signature humanising framework whilst emphasising student digital wellbeing (Waight and Holley, 2020). The curriculum recognises the relationship between students, their identity and wellbeing, and the role of nurse academics in terms of the professional underpinning values, beliefs, and principles. These competencies, mapped across the preregistration nursing curricula, are:

- Digital proficiency and productivity (functional skills)
- Information, data, and media literacies (critical use)
- Digital creation, problem solving, and innovation (creative production)
- Digital communication, collaboration, and participation (participation)
- Digital learning and development (development)
- Digital identity and wellbeing (self-actualising)

With the fast pace of technological innovation, the evidence base demonstrates that nurse academics need specific and bespoke digital learning opportunities.

These opportunities feed forward in both their own and their students' technological capabilities and offer the potential to transform learning by designing opportunities to bridge the dimensions of time and place, negotiating different spaces between work and study, and moving seamlessly between formal and informal learning opportunities. These innovations can be applied in other disciplines where an embedded knowledge and application of the digital is crucial.

Example 3: Reconceptualising Simulation

Our work within the faculty post pandemic continues to harness technologies to develop student skills and integrate this work into the curricula. Grimwood and Snell (2020), in their survey of the use of technology in pre-pandemic healthcare, identified four key themes across the literature: the types of technologies used in healthcare education, the integration of technology into the healthcare curriculum, the skills and knowledge of the healthcare educators, and the benefits of using technology for the learners. The blurring of boundaries between learning and working creates unexpected experiences and hybrid scenarios offering different opportunities and challenges for learners (Cohen *et al.*, 2020). A revised conception of space is essential, as Stommel (2012) argues, which moves learning pedagogies beyond the technological, with hybridity offering the potential to reconceptualise the notion of place.

An in-person simulation exercise, the 'Martian Attack!', illustrates our simulation education strategy. Final year paramedic science students demonstrate their fundamental emergency care patient assessments in a simulated and authentic emergency environment in a university underground car park. In teams, they undertake patient assessment and treatment tasks under time pressures and complete an initiative exercise to immobilise a weighted mannequin for transportation using previously unseen equipment without instruction, using clinical teamwork principles. The finale of the simulated exercise tests the teams' communication skills. In pairs, and captured on a 360° camera, they present patient handovers for each of their simulated patients, then as a team complete a situational awareness report for the whole environment. This provided the mainstay of their digital feedback, allowing them to review their own and each other's handovers once they were uploaded into the VLE. The 360° capture enabled a unique perspective of the students' abilities to perform the fundamental communications skills essential when managing time-critical patients in an adverse prehospital environment (Bancroft *et al.*, 2022). Whole-cohort transformational learning was enabled by viewing their own and each others' handovers on the VLE.

This innovative simulation has developed into an annual interdisciplinary two-day event, with paramedic students participating on day one to focus on patient care in the immediate aftermath of the 'alien attack', then becoming the live simulated patients for student nurses in a 'field hospital' simulation on day two, where the casualties of the attack are treated. Faculty colleagues create bespoke scenarios to be filmed by the 360° camera, with other students as actors, including situations of child injury, mental health, domestic abuse, and hospital admission processes.

Interdisciplinary networks beyond the disciplines in the faculty had been nurtured during staff participation in the PGCert, enabling opportunities for Media School students to run a live newsroom event and providing on-the-spot journalism presence during the event. Students from the nearby Arts University practised their stage and make-up skills to create authentic-looking injuries for the 'patients' and casualties.

Each student team is required to hand over their patient(s) and debrief an expert facilitator. Feedback from the debriefing team of health experts who participate, including qualified paramedics, air ambulance staff, and nurses from the NHS, is overwhelmingly positive, particularly in relation to the technical and communication skills demonstrated by the students who debrief under pressure. The powerful blend of a live emergency event, simulation, and 360° filming can be seen in the range of innovative uses that staff and students make of the digital resources co-created from this transformational experience (Bancroft *et al.*, 2022). The dimensions of the humanisation person-centred framework are articulated in the design of the simulation cases, along with the professional values the students demonstrate to each other and to the 'patients' in their care.

Conclusions

In addition to our earlier recommendations relating to building a community of practice (Holley *et al.*, 2021) underpinning this work, these are the key points that can be adopted in other disciplines:

- Harnessing the power of optimum disruption can be transformative (Hutchings *et al.*, 2010) when thoughtfully applied with an awareness of the inherent challenges and managed well for both staff and learners.
- Technical affordances are an essential component of transformative change but must be combined with deeper level interpersonal and social connections to succeed.
- Forging interdisciplinary alliances can support the transferability of knowledge and skills.
- Creative use of the VLE is important, moving far beyond a one-dimensional storage facility, that is a digital cupboard, to becoming a magic wardrobe where transformative learning takes place (Quinney, 2008).

Acknowledgement

We would like to acknowledge the creativity and vision of our colleague, Adam Bancroft, who developed and led the 'Martian Attack' simulation.

References

Bancroft, A., Holley, D., Moran, J., Singleton, H. and Rolfe, U. (2022). *Martian Attack, the story so far*. Presented to the University of Kent Pedagogy and Practice when Teaching and Learning Online webinar series.16 February 2022.

Biggs, J. and Tang, C. (2007). *Teaching for quality learning at university*. Society for Research into Higher Education and Open University Press.

Beetham, H., Littlejohn, A. and McGill, L. (2012). *Beyond competence: digital literacies as knowledge practices, and implications for learner development*. Open University: Open University Scholarly Insights.

Cohen, A., Nørgård, R. T. and Mor, Y., (2020). Hybrid learning spaces—Design, data, didactics. *British Journal of Educational Technology*, 51(4), pp. 1039–1044.

Evangelinos, G. and Holley, D., (2014). *A qualitative exploration of the EU Digital Competence (DIGCOMP) Framework: a case study within healthcare Education*. In G. Vincenti, A. Bucciero and C. V. A. de Carvalho (eds.), E-Learning, E-Education, and Online-Training (ELEOT) First International Conference, Lecture Notes of the Institute for Computer Sciences, Social Informatics and Telecommunications Engineering. Cham: Springer International Publishing. doi: 10.1007/978-3-319-13293-8_11 http://www.springer.com/computer/book/978-3-319-13292-1

Grimwood, T. and Snell, L. (2020). The use of technology in healthcare education: a literature review. *MedEdPublish*, 9(1). Available from https://insight.cumbria.ac.uk/id/eprint/5615/

Herrington, J., Reeves, T. C., Oliver, R. and Woo, Y. (2004). Designing authentic activities in web-based courses. *Journal of Computing in Higher Education*, 16(1), pp. 3–29.

Hutchings, M., Quinney, A. and Scammel, J. (2010). The utility of disruptive technologies in interprofessional education: negotiating the substance and spaces of blended learning. In A. Bromage, L. Clouder, and J. Thistlethwaite (eds.), *Interprofessional e-learning and collaborative work: practices and technology*. IFS: New York.

Hutchings, M. and Quinney, A. (2015). The flipped classroom, disruptive pedagogies, enabling technologies and wicked problems: responding to 'the bomb in the basement'. *Electronic Journal of e-Learning*, 13(2), pp. 106–119.

Hutchings, M., Scammel, J. and Quinney, A. (2013). Praxis and reflexivity for interprofessional education: towards an inclusive theoretical framework for learning. *Journal of Interprofessional Care*, 27(5), pp. 358–366.

Holley, D., Quinney, A. and Moran, J. (2021). Building a values-based community of practice in nursing sciences during the pandemic. *Journal of Learning Development in Higher Education*, 22.

Lave, J. and Wenger, E. (1991). *Situated learning: legitimate peripheral participation*. Cambridge: Cambridge University Press.

Morley, D. and Holley, D. (2023). Interrogating the established knowledge and practice base of COVID-19 higher education learning. In G. Jamil and D. Morley (eds.), *Agile learning environments amid disruption: evaluating academic innovations in higher education during COVID-19*. London: Palgrave Macmillan.

Nordmann, E., Horlin, C., Hutchison, J., Murray, J-A., Robson, L. and Seery, M. K. (2020). Ten simple rules for supporting a temporary online pivot in higher education. *PLoS Computational Biology* 16(10). https://doi.org/10.1371/journal.pcbi.1008242

Pulman, A.J., Galvin, K., Hutchings, M., Todres, L., Quinney, A., Ellis-Hill, C. and Atkins, P. (2012). Empathy and dignity through technology: using lifeworld-led multi-media to enhance learning about the head, hand and heart. *Electronic Journal of e-Learning*, 10(3), pp. 320–330.

Quinney, A. (2008). *From the electronic cupboard to the magic wardrobe: exploring digital transformation.* Faculty Research Seminar Series. Bournemouth University.

Royal College of Nursing. (2018). *Every nurse an e-nurse: insights into a consultation on the future of nursing in digital competency.* Royal College of Nursing.

Shulman, L. S. (2005). Signature pedagogies in the professions. *Daedalus,* 134(3), pp. 52–59.

Stommel, J. (2012). Hybridity, pt. 2: What is hybrid pedagogy? *Hybrid Pedagogy.* https://hybridpedagogy.org/hybridity-pt-2-what-is-hybrid-pedagogy/ (accessed 8 February 2024).

Todres, L., Galvin, K. and Dahlberg, K. (2006). Lifeworld-led healthcare: revisiting a humanising philosophy that integrates emerging trends. *Medicine, Health Care and Philosophy,* 10(1), pp. 53–63.

Vygotsky, L. (1978). *Mind in society: the development of higher psychology processes.* Cambridge, Massachusetts; Harvard University Press.

Waight, S. and Holley, D. (2020). Digital competence frameworks: their role in enhancing digital wellbeing in nursing curricula. In S. Clarke and C. Devis-Rozental (eds.), *Humanising higher education: a positive approach to enhancing wellbeing.* London; Palgrave.

Wenger, E. (1998). *Communities of practice: learning, meaning and identity.* Cambridge; Cambridge University Press.

Chapter 21

What Blended Learning Taught Us About Supporting the Teaching of an Applied, Practical-Based Degree Course

Daniel James Tinnion, Thomas Ryan Simpson, and Mitchell James Finlay

Who? What? When? Where?

Many degrees currently offered in higher education (HE) could be described as applied courses. Sport and exercise science (SES) provides a popular example of this in the UK, wherein around 15,000 students each year (BASES, 2020) enroll in an undergraduate degree that requires the development of key competencies in practical environments such as applied seminars, laboratory practicals, and physical activity (Lane and Whyte, 2006). Accordingly, the challenge for educators training today's sport scientists is how to reliably develop theoretical knowledge and the key practical competencies necessary for students to practise beyond their initial degree (Keogh *et al.*, 2017).

Teaching and learning within practical environments broadly align with the reformation of HE approaches arguably ignited by Barr and Tagg (1995), particularly in terms of the educator (us) moving from an instructional teaching paradigm ('sage on the stage') to a learning paradigm ('guide on the side'). Example approaches utilised in emphasising active learner engagement may include problem-based learning (PBL), case-based learning, and team-based learning (Keogh *et al.*, 2017). Such approaches heavily utilise teamwork and communication (Dziuban *et al.*, 2004; Barr and Tagg, 1995), both independently valuable skills and as such widely adopted beyond SES.

The challenge originally posed to us as educators by the COVID-19 pandemic, from March 2020, was how to support the development of valuable practical competencies and retain a student-centred learning paradigm when such approaches could not be adopted normally. During the pandemic, students were unable to engage (or at least faced disruption) in hands-on learning and other important applied activity but were still expected to gain sufficient understanding without their own tangible experiences (Finlay *et al.*, 2022; Britt *et al.*, 2015). Novel approaches and consideration of practice across this time were therefore required. Collaboratively, we sought to make practical-supporting content accessible virtually and test broad ideas to bring technology deeper into each session, ultimately as part of a sustained blended learning

DOI: 10.4324/9781003503149-26

approach. The journey of transformative practice that emerged and, later, how this might be transferable to the practice of others can be distilled into three key points: First, the use of virtual tools – What was learned after the panic? Second, interactive online quiz-based learning – A little time has passed, now what? And finally, teacher-led demonstrations – Can we add to practice rather than just survive it?

Transformation of Our Practice

The immediate emergency response was dominated by asynchronous approaches (Clark and Mayer, 2023; Xie et al., 2018; Murphy et al., 2011; Bernard et al., 2004). For us, supplementing virtual material with improvised questionnaires represented the predominant method of testing student knowledge in the absence of opportunities to apply it practically. This had varied effectiveness, as covered by the interplay between media richness and media naturalness approaches (Blau et al., 2017; Lengel and Daft, 1984). The former describes the 'capability of a medium to (1) provide immediate feedback (*yes*), (2) transmit verbal and non-verbal communication cues (*little*), (3) provide a sense of personalisation (*some*), and (4) simulate a natural language (*little*)' (Blau et al., 2017). Medium naturalness is best achieved when communication can occur face to face, without which cognitive load may increase, communication may be ambiguous, and overall students may be less engaged. In Finlay, Tinnion, and Simpson (2022) we subsequently suggested that access to face-to-face teaching, even with social distancing measures, could explain the broader preference for blended versus virtual learning approaches in the same cohort. Before gaining this insight, how could we try to capture these missing characteristics in the virtual learning environment?

Interactivity in the virtual learning context denotes the possibility for learners to be socially and cognitively engaged in interaction with content through learning materials, interaction with peers, and interaction with teachers (Anderson, 2003). Underpinning this is the students' self-confidence in utilising relevant technologies, strongly linked to perceived learning and satisfaction (Malik et al., 2017; Alqurashi, 2016; Shen et al., 2013). Simultaneously, technology acceptance is predicated on the perceived ease of use and perceived usefulness of the tool (Šumak et al., 2011), an often-overlooked aspect in utilising virtual learning during the pandemic (Cicha et al., 2021). To keep the requirements simple and transition small, an important step for us was to synchronously deliver more interactive quizzes using Kahoot!, a game-based learning platform. While the gamification of education is nothing new (Belmas, 2021), such approaches are seldom used to replace practical classes, largely due to the time constraints placed on laboratory aspects. In line with our social constructivist approach, teams of students were able to confer during the practical elements of the quiz to build knowledge through interaction and ensure some degree of active learning (Woolfolk Hoy *et al.*, 2013; Prince, 2004). At the time we rapidly observed the continuing difficulty in managing students' learning motivation, now explained utilising self-determination theory (SDT).

Three fundamental psychological needs are covered by SDT; when these are addressed in a learning context, students are more likely to be intrinsically motivated, often demonstrating increased engagement and greater persistence (Schunk *et al.*, 2014). First, students should feel self-determining or autonomous in their decisions and thereafter feel a sense of control. Here, we considered our students may have felt a little limited in their options, particularly when confined to a virtual environment. Second, students should feel competent or capable to comply with task demands. We then realised that although we now had a forum for discussion and explanation, the practical applicability was still questionable. Third, students should feel social relatedness or inclusivity. In this area, clear progress had been made, given students appeared to enjoy the quizzes, but it was obvious that this was not perfect for all nor a permanent replacement for in-person, face-to-face delivery. Fabriz *et al.* (2021) substantiated this, noting that supporting motivation in SDT hinges on social context. Previous research has shown that lack of teacher input, lack of a genuine reason to communicate with peers online, low self-efficacy, and time and technology constraints can lower motivation (Hartnett *et al.*, 2011; Cheung *et al.*, 2008; Moos and Azevedo, 2008; Artino, 2007; Xie *et al.*, 2006). After adopting SDT in an online environment, Hartnett *et al.* (2011) observed that lack of activity relevance could undermine students' psychological needs.

Across the 2020/21 academic year, a large majority (88.5%) of UK universities eventually deployed an adapted blended learning approach (Student Crowd, 2021) once face-to-face delivery was made possible. A key discussion point for us was how to continue to use virtual components but also add greater relevance back to learning under social restrictions. Teacher-led demonstrations have been shown to positively impact learning of critical competencies like those in applied programmes such as SES (Gamage *et al.*, 2020; Ożadowicz, 2020). In our practice, we sought to pre-record the demonstration of key skills such as capillary blood sampling, which could then be replicated by students in a COVID-compliant manner. Such a transparent approach potentially allows for greater understanding and self-regulating abilities (Lillejord *et al.*, 2018; Prince, 2004) whilst retaining the (asynchronous–synchronous) link to the virtual environment. Indeed, the classroom was often 'flipped' (Moffett, 2015; Roehl *et al.*, 2013), encouraging students to prepare for face-to-face teaching by familiarising themselves with fundamental content in their own time. Aligning with SDT, students are given some degree of control, offered a means with which to feel competent to comply with task demands, and eventually find themselves in a social learning environment (Schunk *et al.*, 2014).

The development of virtual learning, in which students are provided with theoretically relevant information, bolstered by extension and applied work, has been discussed as a tool to develop practical competency in SES for at least 20 years (Lane, 2004; Haven and Botterill, 2003). Showing the relationship with other applied courses, Lane and Whyte (2006) proposed that SES educators 'borrow' ideas from nursing, where virtual resources have also been developed to support traditional teaching methods (McConville and Lane, 2006; Alinier *et al.*, 2004). Indeed, work to develop vocational skills in nursing used videos showing nurses in difficult or stressful situations, such as informing patients they are going to die. Students reported that the videos provided a meaningful experience and, usefully, gave a simple understanding of how to deal with such situations in real life (McConville and Lane, 2006). A more contemporary equivalent to this may be the use of computer-based laboratory simulations with varying results across disciplines (Antonelli *et al.*, 2023; Tsirulnikov *et al.*, 2023; Tuyizere and Yadav, 2023).

Transferability of Our Practice

In Tinnion, Simpson, and Finlay (2021), we discussed the power of collaboration to overcome shared challenges faced during COVID-19, using a general framework for engaging students until this scenario was better understood. In this chapter, we have documented some of that understanding, which we now summarise as the transformative journey to the more proactive, thoughtful use of virtual tools as part of a blended learning approach.

The use of educational technology ('virtual tools') was always predominantly a choice made by universities to differentiate themselves from other providers (Wong, Fink, and Bhati, 2021). That notwithstanding, many institutions still lean on information sharing such as lecture notes and occasionally lecture recordings (Nordmann *et al.*, 2019; O'Callaghan *et al.*, 2017). The new learning and teaching environment is one where synchronous and asynchronous practice coexist. As previously discussed, there are challenges involved in aligning these two types of delivery, but success may support lifelong learning (Beech and Anseel, 2020). Lifelong learning describes students taking control of their learning and engaging, communicating, and collaborating with others (Wong *et al.*, 2021). Our role as educators is to broker knowledge for students, facilitating discourse and reflection as well as interactions with the course material and other students. Proactive, thoughtful blended learning gives new opportunities to extend interactions across time, place, and space (Garrison and Vaughan, 2008). For this we return to a framework originally adapted by Scherman *et al.* (2023) as a guide for designing blended approaches in applied, scientific disciplines, and in explanation can demonstrate our continued journey.

Scherman *et al.* (2023) proposes the connection of certain facets of effective practice to give rise to three 'successful teaching actions', discussed in the following sections.

Identifying the Main Ideas and Planning Engagement with Science Information and Skills to Be Achieved

> *This requires educators to identify relevant ideas for students in constructing new knowledge or skills. The course must connect individual learning experiences and interconnected understandings.*

Gaining practical competency, that is, conducting exercise testing with participants, requires theoretical knowledge but also significantly leans on experiential knowledge (Borkman, 1976) – *doing*. One key tool that has transformed our approach to practical sessions is the use of follow-up learning journals (Langer, 2002). This describes a shift from entirely physical laboratory materials (i.e., worksheets) to encouraging students to negotiate time, space, and place in a manner that engages them in critical self-reflection, critical thinking, and hopefully better development of learned knowledge and competencies (Lew and Schmidt, 2011; Smith *et al.*, 2007). Following practical sessions, students are tasked with completing a short answer questionnaire to assess knowledge and reflect via their online platform. This process allows us to identify knowledge gaps and concerns students may have, and we have successfully applied it across the three separate institutions we now occupy. Whilst learning journals are not new (Langer, 2002), the transformative experience of the pandemic gave room to consider specific, more-informed ideas.

Eliciting Students' Ideas and Adapting Instruction

> *The educator figures out the resources students bring to the topic (possible flipped classroom approach). Sensemaking discourse of students is essential. The educator is scaffolding the dialogue by sharing the main ideas. Explicit thinking allows the students to learn through modelling.*

A common characteristic of those teaching applied, science-based courses, particularly sport (and others), in the UK is the freedom of Wednesdays during term-time from timetabled commitments. This has afforded all authors the opportunity to independently record 'pre-practical content' that covers their own relevant laboratories, for example, the human movement analysis laboratories delivered by Dr Finlay. Enhanced by other tools such as the learning journal, students are supported in this laboratory in a live, responsive manner. Content is both synchronous and asynchronous, where practical demonstrations (e.g., use of force plates) are supplemented with relevant journal articles (e.g., force plate data applied to an athletic population) to be discussed in class and/or with usable material such as a 'checklist'. Of this specific method, one student confirmed that 'tasks have been really useful and relevant to lab practical and assessment' while another recommended 'more time for hands-on practice with kit', which the authors understood as small confirmation of the essential nature of applied sessions, discussed elsewhere (Finlay *et al.*, 2022) and better aligned with a blended approach.

Supporting Ongoing Changes in Students' Thinking

> *This involves cycling between learning activities based on learning support materials and interactive, synchronous instruction. With group/pair activities, the group's ideas' presentation is recommended. Students learn to organise resources for solving problems and developing new knowledge. Peer group presentations also support the development of students' academic discourse.*

Grafstein (2002, p. 199) noted that

> [g]iven the seductively easy accessibility of masses of unregulated information, it is imperative that students, from the very beginning of their academic careers, adopt a critical approach to information and develop the ability to evaluate the information they encounter for authenticity, accuracy, credibility, authority, relevance, concealed bias, logistical inconsistency, and so on.

In maintaining the use of relevant journal articles discussed above, the authors have committed to a continuous journal club-type format. In this scenario, students work together to present the key findings or an overview of the article provided, which is then met by other presentations with slightly different findings. In this way, multiple perspectives are provided for which we (educators) can ask or field questions and create an environment for discourse. These ideas tally with Chappell's (2018) guidance on designing critical information processing activities – they should be taught, not caught. We go further and suggest that our proactive approach to blended learning makes it simpler to do so.

Conclusion

In this chapter, we have discussed the utility of blended learning approaches, stimulated by the response to the pandemic, aided by collaboration, and now maintained by a proactive approach. This approach (and the thoughts surrounding it) may feel like poking at the basics, and largely, it is. In Tinnion, Finlay, and Simpson (2021) we highlighted the words of Race (2003): 'amongst all the bells and whistles, teaching and learning can always be condensed into a handful of simple ideas', and we see that idea has once again proved to be true. What we have discovered through our experimentation in pandemic teaching is that – while indeed a simple solution – a proactive approach to blended learning can have a transformative impact on our teaching and positively enhance our students' learning.

References

Alinier, G., Hunt, W. B. and Gordon, R. (2004). Determining the value of simulation in nurse education: study design and initial results. *Nurse Education in Practice*, 4(3), 200–207.

Alqurashi, E. (2016). Self-efficacy in online learning environments: a literature review. *Contemporary Issues in Education Research (Online)*, 9(1), 45.

Anderson, T. (2003). Modes of interaction in distance education: Recent developments and research questions. *Handbook of Distance Education*, 129–144.

Antonelli, D., Christopoulos, A., Laakso, M. J., Dagienė, V., Juškevičienė, A., Masiulionytė-Dagienė, V. ... Stylios, C. (2023). A virtual reality laboratory for blended learning education: design implementation and evaluation. *Education Sciences*, 13(5), 528.

Artino Jr, A. R. (2007). Online military training: Using a social cognitive view of motivation and self-regulation to understand students' satisfaction, perceived learning, and choice. *Quarterly Review of Distance Education*, 8(3), 191.

Barr, R. B. and Tagg, J. (1995). From teaching to learning—a new paradigm for undergraduate education. *Change: The Magazine of Higher Learning*, 27(6), 12–26.

Beech, N. and Anseel, F. (2020). COVID-19 and its impact on management research and education: threats, opportunities and a manifesto. *British Journal of Management*, 31(3), 447.

Belmas, E. (2021). The origins of the gamification process: the case of pre-industrial societies. *The Gamification of Society*, 2, 47–65.

Bernard, R. M., Abrami, P. C., Lou, Y., Borokhovski, E., Wade, A., Wozney, L., ... Huang, B. (2004). How does distance education compare with classroom instruction? A meta-analysis of the empirical literature. *Review of Educational Research*, 74(3), 379–439.

Blau, I., Weiser, O. and Eshet-Alkalai, Y. (2017). How do medium naturalness and personality traits shape academic achievement and perceived learning? An experimental study of face-to-face and synchronous e-learning. *Research in Learning Technology*, 25.

Borkman, T. (1976). Experiential knowledge: a new concept for the analysis of self-help groups. *Social Service Review*, 50(3), 445–456.

Britt, M., Goon, D. and Timmerman, M. (2015). How to better engage online students with online strategies. *College Student Journal*, 49(3), 399–404.

Chappell, K. (2018). Helping students develop critical information processing skills. *Faculty Focus*. Available at https://www.facultyfocus.com/articles/course-design-ideas/helping-students-develop-information-processing-skills/ (Accessed 1 December 2020).

Cheung, W. S., Hew, K. F. and Ng, C. S. L. (2008). Toward an understanding of why students contribute in asynchronous online discussions. *Journal of Educational Computing Research*, 38(1), 29–50.

Cicha, K., Rizun, M., Rutecka, P. and Strzelecki, A. (2021). COVID-19 and higher education: first-year students' expectations toward distance learning. *Sustainability*, *13*(4), 1889.

Clark, R. C. and Mayer, R. E. (2023). *E-learning and the science of instruction: proven guidelines for consumers and designers of multimedia learning.* John Wiley and Sons.

Dziuban, C., Hartman, J., Moskal, P., Sorg, S. and Truman, B. (2004). Three ALN modalities: an institutional perspective. *Elements of Quality Online Education: Into the Mainstream*, *127*, 148.

Fabriz, S., Mendzheritskaya, J. and Stehle, S. (2021). Impact of synchronous and asynchronous settings of online teaching and learning in higher education on students' learning experience during COVID-19. *Frontiers in Psychology*, *12*, 733554.

Finlay, M. J., Tinnion, D. J. and Simpson, T. (2022). A virtual versus blended learning approach to higher education during the COVID-19 pandemic: the experiences of a sport and exercise science student cohort. *Journal of Hospitality, Leisure, Sport and Tourism Education*, *30*, 100363.

Gamage, K. A., Wijesuriya, D. I., Ekanayake, S. Y., Rennie, A. E., Lambert, C. G. and Gunawardhana, N. (2020). Online delivery of teaching and laboratory practices: continuity of university programmes during COVID-19 pandemic. *Education Sciences*, *10*(10), 291.

Garrison, D. R. and Vaughan, N. D. (2008). *Blended learning in higher education: Framework, principles, and guidelines.* John Wiley and Sons.

Grafstein, A. (2002). A discipline-based approach to information literacy. *The Journal of Academic Librarianship*, *28*(4), 197–204.

Hartnett, M., St. George, A. and Dron, J. (2011). Examining motivation in online distance learning environments: complex, multifaceted, and situation-dependent. *International Review of Research in Open and Distributed Learning*, *12*(6), 20–38.

Haven, C. and Botterill, D. (2003). Virtual learning environments in hospitality, leisure, tourism and sport: a review. *Journal of Hospitality, Leisure, Sport and Tourism Education*, *2*(1), 75–92.

Keogh, J. W., Gowthorp, L. and McLean, M. (2017). Perceptions of sport science students on the potential applications and limitations of blended learning in their education: a qualitative study. *Sports Biomechanics*, *16*(3), 297–312.

Langer, A. M. (2002). Reflecting on practice: using learning journals in higher and continuing education. *Teaching in Higher Education*, *7*(3), 337–351.

Lane, A. M. (2004). Exploring the relationship between Quality Assurance Agency grades and research assessment exercise scores for sport-related subjects. *Journal of Hospitality, Leisure, Sport and Tourism Education (Oxford Brookes University)*, *3*(2).

Lane, A. M. and Whyte, G. P. (2006). From education to application: Sport and exercise sciences courses in the preparation of applied sport scientists. *Journal of Hospitality, Leisure, Sport and Tourism Education*, *5*(2), 89–93.

Lengel, R. H. and Daft, R. L. (1984). Information richness: a new approach to managerial behavior and organization design. *Research in Organizational Behavior*, *6*, 191–233.

Lew, D. N. M. and Schmidt, H. G. (2011). Writing to learn: Can reflection journals be used to promote self-reflection and learning? *Higher Education Research and Development*, *30*(4), 519–532.

Lillejord, S., Børte, K., Nesje, K. and Ruud, E. (2018). Learning and teaching with technology in higher education: a systematic review. *Oslo: Knowledge Centre for Education*, *2*, 40–64.

Malik, M., Fatima, G. and Sarwar, A. (2017). E-learning: students' perspectives about asynchronous and synchronous resources at higher education level. *Bulletin of Education and Research*, *39*(2), 183–195.

McConville, S. A. and Lane, A. M. (2006). Using on-line video clips to enhance self-efficacy toward dealing with difficult situations among nursing students. *Nurse Education Today*, *26*(3), 200–208.

Moffett, J. (2015). Twelve tips for 'flipping' the classroom. *Medical Teacher*, *37*(4), 331–336.

Moos, D. C. and Azevedo, R. (2008). Exploring the fluctuation of motivation and use of self-regulatory processes during learning with hypermedia. *Instructional Science*, *36*, 203–231.

Murphy, E., Rodríguez-Manzanares, M. A. and Barbour, M. (2011). Asynchronous and synchronous online teaching: perspectives of Canadian high school distance education teachers. *British Journal of Educational Technology*, *42*(4), 583–591.

Nordmann, E., Calder, C., Bishop, P., Irwin, A. and Comber, D. (2019). Turn up, tune in, don't drop out: the relationship between lecture attendance, use of lecture recordings, and achievement at different levels of study. *Higher Education*, *77*, 1065–1084.

O'Callaghan, F. V., Neumann, D. L., Jones, L. and Creed, P. A. (2017). The use of lecture recordings in higher education: a review of institutional, student, and lecturer issues. *Education and Information Technologies*, *22*, 399–415.

Ożadowicz, A. (2020). Modified blended learning in engineering higher education during the COVID-19 lockdown—building automation courses case study. *Education Sciences*, *10*(10), 292.

Prince, M. (2004). Does active learning work? A review of the research. *Journal of Engineering Education*, *93*(3), 223–231.

Roehl, A., Reddy, S. L. and Shannon, G. J. (2013). The flipped classroom: an opportunity to engage millennial students through active learning strategies. *Journal of Family and Consumer Sciences*, *105*(2), 44.

Scherman, R., Islam, M. S., Dikaya, L. A., Dumulescu, D., Pop-Păcurar, I. and Necula, C. V. (2023). Learning design for future higher education–insights from the time of COVID-19. *COVID-19 and Beyond: From (Forced) Remote Teaching and Learning to 'the New Normal' in Higher Education*, 16648714.

Schunk, D. H., Pintrich, P. R. and Meece, J. L. (2014). *Motivation in education: Theory, research, and applications* (4th ed.). Boston: Pearson.

Shen, D., Cho, M. H., Tsai, C. L. and Marra, R. (2013). Unpacking online learning experiences: online learning self-efficacy and learning satisfaction. *The Internet and Higher Education*, *19*, 10–17.

Smith, K., Clegg, S., Lawrence, E. and Todd, M. J. (2007). The challenges of reflection: students learning from work placements. *Innovations in Education and Teaching International*, *44*(2), 131–141.

StudentCrowd. (2021). *University responses to Covid-19*. Available at: https://www.studentcrowd.com/article/university-responses-to-covid-19

Šumak, B., Heričko, M. and Pušnik, M. (2011). A meta-analysis of e-learning technology acceptance: the role of user types and e-learning technology types. *Computers in Human Behavior*, *27*(6), 2067–2077.

The British Association of Sport and Exercise Sciences (BASES). (2020). *A guide to careers in Sport and Exercise Science*. BASES.

Tinnion, D., Simpson, T. and Finlay, M. (2021). Face-to-face teaching changed too! Perspectives on the transition from large to small group teaching and learning from graduate teaching assistants. *Journal of Learning Development in Higher Education*, *22*, 1–6.

Tsirulnikov, D., Suart, C., Abdullah, R., Vulcu, F. and Mullarkey, C. E. (2023). Game on: immersive virtual laboratory simulation improves student learning outcomes and motivation. *FEBS Open Bio*, *13*(3), 396–407.

Tuyizere, G. and Yadav, L. L. (2023). Effect of interactive computer simulations on academic performance and learning motivation of Rwandan students in atomic physics. *International Journal of Evaluation and Research in Education, 2252* (8822), 8822.

Wong, C., Fink, E. and Bhati, A. (2021). Future of learning and teaching in higher education post-COVID-19. In *Digital Transformation in a Post-COVID World* (pp. 221–244). CRC Press.

Woolfolk Hoy, A., Davis, H. A. and Anderman, E. M. (2013). Theories of learning and teaching in TIP. *Theory into Practice, 52*(supp. 1), 9–21.

Xie, H., Liu, W. and Bhairma, J. (2018). Analysis of synchronous and asynchronous e-learning environments. In *2018 3rd Joint International Information Technology, Mechanical and Electronic Engineering Conference (JIMEC 2018)* (pp. 270–274). Atlantis Press.

Xie, K. U. I., Debacker, T. K. and Ferguson, C. (2006). Extending the traditional classroom through online discussion: the role of student motivation. *Journal of Educational Computing Research, 34*(1), 67–89.

Chapter 22

What Educational Participatory Archiving Taught Us About Online Altruism and Collective Knowledge

Nicholas Bowskill, Melody Harrogate, and David Hall

Introduction

We have previously explored the experience of teachers during the COVID-19 pandemic (Bowskill *et al.*, 2022). Specifically, we examined the early period of Spring 2020 at the start of the pandemic, investigating how teachers coped with the closure of schools and the sudden shift to working remotely online. We focused on two case studies from our wider set of research interviews, selected because those respondents cited nostalgic feelings arising from their collaborative experiences during the pandemic. In both cases, teachers at their respective institutions, one in China and the other in England, had created digital resources for their students and shared them online with colleagues. This was done as colleagues worked to support each other whilst under intense pressure. Our research sought to better understand these positive emotional reactions partly for their novelty within the wider set of interviews and partly because they initially appeared to be a counterintuitive response to an educational emergency.

Our analysis of interview transcripts showed how teachers' experience of remote collaboration generated a shared sense of mutual care amongst colleagues. Educators felt they *mattered* to students, parents, and each other as they worked to deliver effective support during the pandemic. Sharing these self-authored digital materials evidenced and visualised the collaboration amongst colleagues, leading to a greater sense of *belonging* amongst these teachers. Consequently, as teachers reflected upon this collegial and digital experience of collaboration, it generated a sense of *nostalgia* from that sense of achievement and togetherness under extreme pressure.

Figure 22.1 shows our emergent model of digital collegiality which maps these emotional responses onto functions of the technology during online collaboration. While acknowledging the need for further research to validate this view, we argue that this model has potential to be generalised beyond educational emergencies, with consequent implications for learning design, wellbeing, and implementation of collaborative learning.

DOI: 10.4324/9781003503149-27

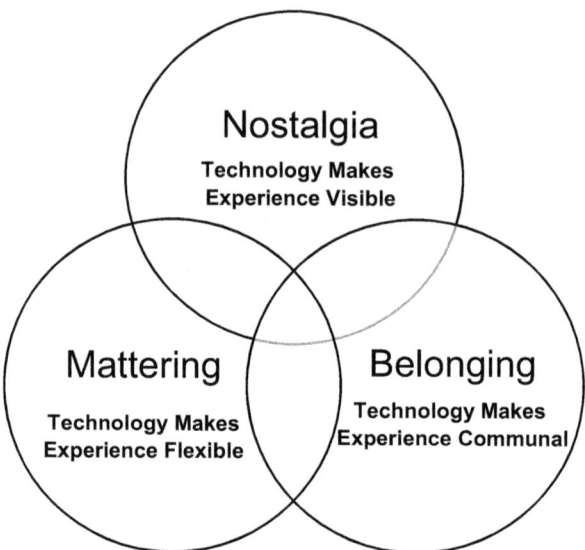

Figure 22.1 Model of Digital Collegiality (Bowskill et al., 2022).

In this chapter, we conceptualise this mutual support amongst teachers as a form of altruism. Specifically, we theorise our digital collegiality model as an outcome of online collaboration motivated by desire to help others. In what follows, we first discuss the relevance of altruism to our analysis and then follow that with a discussion of digital archiving. We then consider the wider implications for theory, practice, and research.

Altruism

Altruism refers to the desire to act primarily for the benefit of others in ways that do not seek recognition or reward for oneself (Dovidio and Penner, 2003). Despite this lack of personal reward, being altruistic can have various health benefits for the help-giver including the possibility of improved wellbeing and greater happiness (Post, 2005), sometimes referred to as 'helper's high' (Luks, 1988, cited in Bowskill, 2024). Altruism may result in greater empathy and resilience (Bushey, 2023). Strong positive reciprocity, related to altruism, is where observers of altruism may behave in a similarly altruistic manner, which may generate greater social connectedness through a knock-on altruistic effect (Lehmann, 2007, cited in Bowskill, 2024). However, these benefits may not accrue if the help-giver is overwhelmed by the task (Post, 2005).

We argue that our home-based educators were engaged in altruistic acts when they created and shared their digital teaching materials. These documents were pooled online and shared across the school, helping each other to address the sudden shift to online learning. Witnessing this sharing of digital materials online made this collegiality visible. We argue this is strong positive reciprocity which strengthened social connectedness, as evidenced by the reported nostalgia.

This analysis is consistent with work done elsewhere that suggested a range of emotional and practice-related benefits from teacher collaboration (Prenger *et al.*, 2019). For example, teachers in professional learning networks experienced a subsequent improvement in their sense of belonging, leading to improved teacher retention (De Lay, 2009). In the context of the COVID-19 pandemic, stronger teacher relationships were positively associated with improved wellbeing (Blair *et al.*, 2023), and therefore teacher collaboration and collegiality offer many benefits providing a goal worthy of further development.

As already mentioned, witnessing altruism can exert a prosocial influence (Rushton and Littlefield, 1979) and induce altruistic behaviour in others (Schnall *et al.*, 2010). Therefore, we argue that by using technology to capture and make altruism more visible, we may support widespread altruistic behaviours across an organisation. Similarly, if witnessing altruism has these prosocial benefits, then archiving such actions may further enhance digital collegiality. In the next section, we therefore turn to consider archiving before applying it to education.

Archiving

Archival theory is the analysis of how archivists think about the archive and the nature of that which is recorded (Duranti, 1993). Archives can be seen as a collective memory of what mattered and may still matter to a given community (Tai *et al.*, 2019). This becomes known as 'the past' (Ernst, 2013). Archives can thereby create a shared identity and act as a 'public good' (Cox and Wallace, 2002, p. 1) and be a source of healing (Redwood, 2018). Although archives can exclude, marginalise, and mute certain voices while foregrounding others (Carter, 2006), equally they can bear witness to the experiences of teachers and teaching (Hansen, 2017).

The conventional model of archives is sometimes understood as a form of 'warehousing' for object collections. In this model, archives 'contain' the artefacts in collections that are assumed to be largely complete. These objects are deemed to be representative of phenomena and thereby understood as largely inclusive. However, archives are never innocent due to the gaps they contain (Derrida, 1996) and the way they preshape conversational possibilities (Foucault, 2002). As such, archivists and archives 'produce' the memory of phenomena (Bosch, 2016), and this can often lead to gaps in representation.

This 'archive-as-storage' model is epistemologically problematic for the way it portrays a view of archival knowledge as being collective and representative while simultaneously existing apart from society (Eveleigh, 2015). Based on this, knowledge is implicitly conceptualised as 'over there' and as something to be visited. It exists outside the user and is communicated outwardly from the archive to the public. Consequently, knowledge is accessed rather than created by users, and in the pre-digital era, this exclusion and alienation was compounded where archives preserved knowledge of the privileged few (Giannachi, 2023).

An alternative participatory model of the archive (Huvila, 2008), specifically when enabled by technology, enables us to move beyond the warehouse model, inviting us to rebalance the public record with the addition of other voices (Benoit and Eveleigh, 2019). The internet itself can be understood as an archiving technology for the way it automatically captures all online interaction (Giannachi, 2023); networked technology as a whole enables a participatory model in allowing other contributions to inform and shape the archive (Eveleigh, 2015). This supports a more inclusive approach with a wider range of participants able to 'inscribe' the digital archive through acts of engagement (Giannachi, 2023).

This participatory model has epistemological consequences. These acts of inscribing function as contributions to knowledge in a fluid digital archive (Eveleigh, 2015). In a sense, they add to the knowledge store and help rebalance the public record, resolving some of the tensions between representation, knowledge, and archival collections (Giannachi, 2023).

What does participatory archiving mean for education? There are related ideas that have already been applied to student classroom learning. For example, 'pedagogical documentation' is at least implicitly a form of archiving in early years education (Wien, 2011), and it has been applied to recording the lives and thinking of teachers (Kocher, 2008; Lim, 2016). This approach stands in contrast to administrative documentation; the pedagogical variant is valued for the way it captures learning and makes thinking visible, creating a 'listening pedagogy' (Rinaldi, 2005).

How does this relate to the teachers in our cases? We argue that online teachers creating and sharing digital content with colleagues, and motivated by strong positive reciprocity (Lehmann, 2007, cited in Bowskill, 2024), are engaged in a form of pedagogical documentation. They effectively 'inscribed' the digital archive of their institution and their shared documents to form an emergent collection (Giannachi, 2023). We argue this is an educational form of participatory archiving.

The significance of educational participatory archiving in an academic context is that such document sharing activities help redefine contributions to pedagogical knowledge as part of a shared witnessing project (Eveleigh, 2015). This collective action adds to our knowledge of educational emergencies in different settings. Through educational participatory archiving, we agree with Scheinfeldt that original contributions to knowledge can thereby be recognised as relational and collective rather than solely the work of 'heroic' academic individualism (Scheinfeldt, 2010, cited in Eveleigh, 2015). The resulting digital archive serves to bear witness to the work of educators during the pandemic, both to themselves and others.

We therefore recognise the contributions made by the teachers in our cases not only as acts of altruism but as epistemologically significant. Their self-authored documents evidence their role, their service, and their active engagement with an educational emergency. This goes far beyond any official records produced externally and distinct from those automatically generated within any learning management system. We argue that their bravery and collective heroism during the COVID-19 pandemic is memorialised through their creation and sharing of digital objects as an act of educational participatory archiving, thereby extending our knowledge beyond official records.

Impact on Practice

In response to the above, we are beginning to consider the implications of student engagement in online learning courses not only as the fulfilment of learning responsibilities but as acts of educational participatory archiving. We regard students' engagement as inscribing the digital module and the way it might otherwise be automatically archived within the institutional learning management system. These inscriptions happen within the pre-shaped digital learning environment. We are therefore exploring the idea of student contributions as 're-archiving the archive' (Giannachi, 2023).

What does this look like in practice? As an initial response, we have made several changes to an online module on '21st-Century Teaching', to give three outcomes:

1 The module explores and further memorialises the interviewees in our research, which is documented in the reading list. This list also extends to incorporate archival theory and education.
2 The online actions made by the students over the length of the module are conceptualised as participatory contributions to the emerging module archive. This transforms a traditional view of engagement, typically seen as individual students posting messages. In its place, this becomes the enactment of a social and participatory archival process.
3 To reflect this change in thinking, the final unit invites students to review the module as a social memory. This new closing unit, called Digital Archives and Education, includes learning activities that invite students to evaluate the module as a witness to their presence. Students are invited to consider and reflect upon the resulting knowledge co-inscribed within the module archive.

In line with this perspective, students are also invited to reconceptualise their online teaching practice in their own local contexts within the frame of the digital educational archive. Student-teachers on this module quite reasonably and routinely view online learning in terms of design choices to create different activities for their learners. Such conceptions focus engagement on structural decisions about whether to use synchronous or asynchronous strategies with their learners. Decisions often include whether to use hybrid, flexible, or online learning. Instead, we invite our teacher-students to reimagine online education within archival theory, both in the module and in their local practice, and to then reflect on the consequences of such a transformation. In doing so, we hope they might then reconsider online learning not just as comprising learning activities and the acquisition of ready-made knowledge but as the co-construction of social memory.

Relatedly, through exploration of educational participatory archiving and archival theory, we encourage students to reflect on the digital legacy of their schools and the digital materials they previously co-constructed with colleagues during the pandemic. Although some of the objects in that archive are being reused and revisited in the post-pandemic era, much of it has been left behind. Perhaps understandably, much is being forgotten in the rush to restore classroom-based learning. There are opportunities to revisit these archives to bear witness to the commitment of professional educators in the COVID-19 pandemic and to achieve some of the prosocial benefits already identified. These institutional archives likewise serve as original and collective contributions to knowledge in isolation and in relation to others.

With this archival perspective on education, there are many new questions and considerations arising from this epistemological and theoretical reframing of the pandemic. An educational participatory framework allows us to explore the gaps that exist in the archive. Which voices are underrepresented? What additions might be made and by whom? What are the pedagogical and research possibilities of understanding digital education as participatory archiving? Educational participatory archiving goes far beyond: 'what have you learned from the course?' Participants are bearing witness to their presence in the online module and in doing so they are evaluating the representation of their engagement whilst co-creating original and relational contributions to academic knowledge.

Conclusions

We began our research with a set of interviews exploring the experiences of educators around the world in fulfilling their role during the early stages of the COVID-19 pandemic. Arising from those interviews, we identified two interesting cases in which interviewees had experienced nostalgic emotions as a reaction to coping during an educational emergency. Our initial analysis showed that these were affective outcomes from creating and sharing digital learning materials with colleagues online whilst working largely from home. This resulted in our digital collegiality framework, which showed the relationship between mattering, belonging, and nostalgia as inter-related consequences of online collaboration.

In this chapter, we further conceptualised our digital collegiality model as being the result of altruistic behaviour. As such, the creation and sharing of digital content by these educators is not merely a fulfilment of their professional responsibilities. They should be understood as prosocial responses arising from our teachers being altruistic or witnessing altruism. We have argued that the creation and sharing of digital objects can be understood as a form of pedagogical documentation within a conscious framework of educational participatory archiving. These digital objects then document and witness the professional work of educators in an educational emergency. This witnessing is made visible within the emergent digital archive of the institution. Some of this institutional archive is automatically generated by systems, and some is inscribed by the participation of stakeholders. Finally, we put forward the idea that these actions are simultaneously contributions to the institutional archive and collective contributions to original and socially situated knowledge. In making this case, we have transformed the initial actions of a few teachers into a different way of understanding and witnessing online collaboration within the digital archive. This epistemological shift thereby recognises these activities as the coauthoring of original knowledge in the field of digital education.

The professional work of educators is hereby memorialised, affirming the presence and inclusion of teachers and the fluidity of the digital archive. Seen as educational participatory archiving, these teachers have a voice in the production and review of the archive. The otherwise pre-shaped institutional archive, which is automatically generated by various digital learning systems, becomes reauthored and reinscribed to form an online collection of digital educational artefacts that individually and collectively bear witness to the archived heroism of educators in the COVID-19 pandemic.

References

Benoit, E. & Eveleigh, A. (eds.) (2019) *Participatory archives: theory and practice*. London: Facet.

Bosch, T. E. (2016) 'Memory studies, a brief concept paper', MeCoDEM Working Papers Series, University of Leeds. ISSN 2057-4002

Blair, E. E., Sandilos, L. E., Ellis, E. and Neugebauer, S. R. (2023) 'Teachers survive together: teacher collegial relationships and well-being during the COVID-19 pandemic'. *School Psychology*, 39(5), pp. 499–509. https://doi.org/10.1037/spq0000596

Bowskill, H. (2024) *The role of attachment style in the relationship between childhood adversity and altruism*, BSc Dissertation, University of Lincoln, UK (unpublished).

Bowskill, N., Hall, D., Harrogate, M., and Hutchinson, L. (2022) 'Nostalgia, belonging and mattering: an affective institutional framework for digital collegiality drawn from teachers' experiences of online delivery during the first wave of the Covid pandemic', *Journal of University Teaching & Learning Practice* 19(4). https://ro.uow.edu.au/jutlp/vol19/iss4/17/

Bushey, J. (2023) 'A participatory archives approach to fostering connectivity, increasing empathy, and building resilience during the COVID-19 pandemic', *Heritage*, 6(3), pp. 2379–2393.

Carter, R. G. (2006) 'Of things said and unsaid: power, archival silences, and power in silence' *Archivaria*, 61(September), pp. 215–233. https://archivaria.ca/index.php/archivaria/article/view/12541

Cox, R. J. and Wallace, D. A. (2002) 'Introduction', in R. J. Cox and D. A. Wallace (eds.), *Archives and the public good: accountability and records in modern society*. Westport, CT: Quorum Books.

De Lay, A. M. (2009) 'Behold! The power of teacher collaboration'. *Agricultural Education Magazine*, 82(1), 7–8.

Derrida J. (1996) *Archive fever: A Freudian impression*. University of Chicago Press.

Dovidio, J. F. and Penner, L. A. (2003) 'Helping and altruism,' in *Blackwell handbook of social psychology: interpersonal processes* (pp. 162–195). Malden, MA: Blackwell Publishers.

Duranti, L. (1993) 'The archival body of knowledge: archival theory, method, and practice, and graduate and continuing education', *Journal of Education for Library and Information Science*, 34(1), pp. 8–24. https://doi.org/10.2307/40323707

Ernst, W. (2013) *Digital memory and the archive* (J. Parikka, Ed.). University of Minnesota Press. USA http://www.jstor.org/stable/10.5749/j.ctt32bcwb

Eveleigh, A. M. M. (2015) *Crowding out the archivist? Implications of online user participation for archival theory and practice*, Doctoral dissertation, University College London.

Foucault, M. (2002) *The archaeology of knowledge*. Translated by A. M. Sheridan Smith. London: Routledge.

Giannachi, G. (2023) *Archive everything: mapping the everyday*. MIT Press.

Hansen, D. T. (2017) Among school teachers: bearing witness as an orientation in educational inquiry. *Educational Theory*, 67, pp. 9–30.

Huvila, I. (2008) 'Participatory archive: towards decentralised curation, radical user orientation, and broader contextualisation of records management', *Archival Science* 8, pp. 15–36.

Kocher, L. (2008) *The disposition to document: the lived experience of teachers who practice pedagogical documentation-a case of study*, Doctoral dissertation, University of Southern Queensland.

Lim, S. M. (2016) *Documenting the process of documentation: Making teachers' thinking visible*, Doctoral dissertation, Kent State University.

Post, S. G. (2005) 'Altruism, happiness, and health: it's good to be good', *International Journal of Behavioral Medicine*, 12, pp. 66–77.

Prenger, R. Poortman, C. L. and Handelzalts, A. (2019) 'The effects of networked professional learning communities', *Journal of Teacher Education*, 70(5), pp. 441–452.

Redwood, H. A. (2018) *Accounting for violence: The production, power and ownership of the International Criminal Tribunal for Rwanda's archive*. Doctoral thesis, Kings College London.

Rinaldi, C. (2005) 'Documentation and assessment: what is the relationship?' In *Beyond listening* (pp. 17–28). Policy Press.

Rushton, J. and Littlefield, C. H. (1979) 'The effects of age, amount of modelling, and a success experience on seven- to eleven-year-old children's generosity', *Journal of Moral Education*, 9, 55–56.

Schnall, S., Roper, J. and Fessler, D. M. (2010) 'Elevation leads to altruistic behavior'. *Psychological Science*, 21(3), pp. 315–320.

Tai, J., Zavala, J., Gabiola, J., Brilmyer, G. and Caswell, M. (2019) 'Summoning the ghosts: records as agents in community archives', *Journal of Contemporary Archival Studies* 6(1), 18.

Wien, C. A. (2011) 'Learning to document in Reggio-inspired education', *Early Childhood Research & Practice*, 13(2), n2.

Chapter 23

Painting by Numbers?
What My Lockdown Teaching Experiments, Followed by Encounters with a New Kind of Unit Design, Taught Me About Fine Art and Its Special Approach to Higher Education Teaching and Learning

Paul O'Kane

Introduction

In two short pieces on lockdown teaching and learning experiences (O'Kane, 2021a, 2021b), I strived to wriggle out of the pandemic dilemma. I felt proud of the way in which both those pieces, and the practices they describe, helped me to find creative 'wiggle-room' in which to reach across a divide between lecturer and students, opened by suddenly imposed screen-based, online teaching and learning (Wolff, 2013). Since then, however, I and some of my colleagues have encountered a new kind of unit design that seems to have been influenced, in its own way, by lockdown. Colleagues from colleges other than my own have recognised my description and experience of these unit designs and expressed similar concerns to those voiced in what follows. It is not yet possible to name this kind or type, and so I have evolved an acronym based on one colleague's summarisation of 'the rapid emergence and dominance after the pandemic of a *new* type of *teaching and learning* [NTL], one that can be *counted, measured* and *controlled* [CMC]' – hence NTLCMC. In this Chapter, I critique and share ideas emerging in response to my experience of these NTLCMCs. I hope to thereby help peers and colleagues to prepare for encounters with NTLCMCs while taking the opportunity to clarify, defend, and promote the highest values of fine art teaching and learning.

Vending Machine or Farmers' Market?

My recent, highly varied, lockdown and post-lockdown experiences have taught me that we should not allow the experience of a pandemic – or comparable crises – to allow lower bars of creative and pedagogical aspiration to take hold of fine art units or courses (Gunderman, 2013). Rather, we should continue to aim high, higher, and highest; fine, finer, and finest, as our students, our forebears, and future generations would surely want and expect us to do,

DOI: 10.4324/9781003503149-28

always pursuing the special excellence that resides at the heart of fine art's ever shifting and slightly mysterious goal (Brack and Cowling, 2015).

While it is clearly a managerial issue as to how to contend with a pandemic or other significant disruption, it is nevertheless fine art's role and duty not only to innovate and excel, but to disrupt and 'trouble' – as Judith Butler (1999) would put it – the given and prescribed structures, methods, and values. Fine art teaching is always a creative and speculative discussion between generations of artists, and this dialogue might be diminished by NTLCMCs.

The constant, dynamic, and difficult exchange that associates fine art with progressive and ethical issues dates back to an era when modern art first defined itself in part by overthrowing academicism. However, NTLCMCs, with their relatively generic, design-oriented aims and prescriptive means, could mislead us into a new academicism, anathema to fine art's famously progressive legacy (Harrison *et al.*, 1998; Barlow, 2000).

NTLCMCs seem designed in such a way that, should a pandemic once again seal us within our cells with the result that 'in real life' teaching and purpose-built college rooms become inaccessible, or should a lecturer's strike or similar disruption mean that live lecturers are unavailable, then an adequate modicum of higher education might still be provided. Admittedly, it is worthwhile having such facilities available for emergencies, but it would be a mistake to allow them to become unquestioningly deployed in ways that diminish or suppress the unique tradition of our best fine art teaching and learning (Wolff, 2013). The fear arises that qualities and standards of teaching and learning in NTLCMCs might be reduced to that of a pedagogical 'vending machine' with its limited array of fast food choices, compared with (to extend the metaphor) the *dégustation* or 'farmers market' represented by the best fine art teaching and learning.

Driverless Cars

NTLCMCs, which involve students from many courses and disciplines all following the same tracks, seem to have been encouraged by the pandemic. While following these more prescriptive, more technologised units, students are invited to regularly respond at given points, usually in the form of a brief textual or visual input, such as a file uploaded to a conveniently designed piece of software. This may have already become a familiar model in secondary education and crept into higher education where fine art has had to adapt and work around it. However, NTLCMCs seem to take this tendency to a new limit. We might even say they are designed with the potential to run like driverless cars. After all, while working on one such NTLCMC I noted that a single graduate teaching assistant (GTA; recently graduated student helper) would be sufficient to guide a group of about 30 students through the unit. However, this meant that the unit was anathema and even disabling to my own seasoned fine art teaching skills, for which I was unable to find any place or use. This was a painful personal experience, but it is noteworthy for a wider audience that a teaching unit can be designed in such a way as to make a seasoned, highly skilled and qualified lecturer feel superfluous (Wolff, 2013; Crook, 2015). Nevertheless, this may, in turn, encourage us to think carefully about some critical questions: How are we teaching future generations of not just fine art students but fine art *lecturers*? What kind of teaching environment will future lecturers grow into and inherit? What skills will they need, or perhaps no longer need?

Ultimately, for NTLCMCs, the lecturers or GTAs, as well as the students themselves (assuming courses of this kind might go ahead without a lecturer present) do not really require specialist fine art experience, qualifications, and skills; students and staff simply need to be briefed, and repetitively if necessary, on how to follow, complete, and assess an NTLCMS unit's relatively limited, linear, and prescriptive format. But note that a repetitive briefing, which might take up one or two mornings, here becomes comparable with or equivalent to years or decades of rich, hard-won experience, research, qualifications, and skills. Again, these developments should be noted, critiqued, and monitored (Brack and Cowling, 2015).

Progressive Pedagogy?

The NTLCMC unit that I experienced at first hand (I cannot say I 'taught' on it) appeared to encourage students to explore, experiment, and research, and yet this seemed to me, as a fine art lecturer, to mean sticking too closely to a prescribed journey and working towards too prescribed a goal while keeping within certain guidelines and using specific (and again prescriptive) software. All of this might add up to a version of teaching and learning that, while attractively cost-saving, time-saving, and space-saving, is not so much a form of progressive pedagogy as it is a prescribed and linear *image* of progressive pedagogy. The special idiosyncrasies, unique perspectives, and emerging agendas of fine art staff and students are thereby compromised or set aside for the sake of satisfying a sense of effective completion. Interestingly, however, this has taught me to keep in question any presumption that fine art education should be as concerned with 'completion' as it currently is. Perhaps, after all, too much attention and energy is currently given to 'completion', for example in the ritualistic finality of the awarding of degrees; in spectacular graduation events and degree shows; as well as in the regular 'completion' of units that have – we might say falsely – dissected, quantified, and geometrised a far more mercurial and heterogenous experience of teaching and learning that HE fine art students may actually experience.

Fine Art Versus Design

While writing this chapter I received reports from colleagues that both anecdotal evidence and official surveys showed that, on these NTLCMC units, fine art students in particular are often dissatisfied and confused, while design students, whose training involves more prescriptive brief-setting exercises, are more satisfied and less puzzled (O'Kane, 2021a; O'Kane, 2021b). This discovery then led me to question anew the traditionally assumed association of 'art' with 'design', and to wonder if these quite different disciplines could or should be converging or diverging today. That is, should 'art' and 'design' perhaps be treated as more different and more distinct than in recent decades they have habitually been perceived to be? Furthermore, should we unquestioningly combine students of different disciplines and professions into homogenising and generic teaching units on the assumption that this is always a positive and progressive notion? After all, the process might suppress or disguise just how radically different these disciplines are, and, correspondingly, how special and bespoke the skills of their lecturers and the requirements of their respective students might be.

Collaboration and Playpens

If NTLCMCs reveal a tendency towards a more prescriptive, generic, homogenising, and high-technologised form of teaching and learning, the unit I witnessed also came clearly wrapped in an advocacy of 'collaboration'. However, from a fine artist's perspective this seemed to presume too harmonious a compliance between student and student, as well as between student and lecturer; and one that might suppress more real and productive difference and difficulty. Collaboration, in the sense that I know it from fine art teaching and practice, acknowledges that creative work, and any accompanying political and ethical debate, often emerges from real tension and difficulty, from honestly working with difference and even encountering alterity. Collaboration then, in fine art, is not presumed or prescribed as a successful achievement, neither is it seen as primarily pragmatic and utilitarian – as it might tend to be with design subjects.

Another fear arises here that an enthusiasm for collaboration could be misused on an NTLCMC as a convenient way to leave students in charge of their own and each other's education, effectively play-penned by a sequence of prescribed and scheduled tasks (James and Nerantzi, 2019). Students thereby become self-supervising, without the need for a lecturer present. But is this 'higher' education? Does it truly challenge, encourage, and allow students to raise their standards, increase their knowledge, and develop their skills? One second year fine art student described their NTLCMC (in a one-to-one tutorial) as 'A-Level-ish' – hinting at an infantilising effect. But this criticism has allowed me to begin to identify and articulate a special kind of maturity and responsibility, perhaps peculiar to fine art, that rubs along with its more playful and anarchic attributes (Haraway, 2016).

New Technologies and Painting by Numbers

During the process of writing this chapter I have also learned, or been reminded of, the fact that the central and crucial value of fine art education involves giving students of a new generation opportunities to expand their own ideas, confidence, and powers, and in such a way as to enable them to question everything and anything. This includes questioning the ethics, aesthetics, forms, processes, and contents of any pedagogical exercise proposed to them by representatives of another generation and culture. But as well as the widest range of permissible ethical agendas, fine art students should also and always be encouraged to experiment with *all* the tools and possibilities available to them, whether these be lucratively acquired high-tech teaching-and-learning software, or relatively 'lo-fi', cheap, anachronistic, or traditional resources (Brack and Cowling, 2015). It is therefore notable that, in NTLCMCs, new technologies seem to play an even more significant part than is already common in the daily lives of fine art students – and this despite the fact that we know that both students and lecturers are already suffering from high-technology overload, and despite the fact that fine artists and fine art students are unusually open to exploring the widest range and the longest histories of both 'high' and 'low' technologies (Brack and Cowling, 2015).

We only have to check who the richest organisations in the world are today to note that educational technology is highly profitable, and so it is perhaps inevitable that we begin to see the technological 'tail' wagging the pedagogical 'dog', as teaching and learning software comes to shape, determine, and predict the development of teaching and learning, lecturer and student (Vega, 2013; Witte, 2008). We seem to be rapidly reaching a point where, rather than teaching and learning technologies providing us with helpful tools to enable the delivery of our materials, we find that teaching and learning is being increasingly designed *for* a particular software.

Two currently popular softwares (many seem fly-by-night), Miro and Padlet, might be salient examples, recently building, as they do, upon the transformative millennial eruption of PowerPoint and Google into our classrooms. I have heard Miro and Padlet championed by lecturers as being 'less linear' than some other technologies. However, I would argue that both significantly reduce and tie down the potential for fine art students and lecturers to think and work outside the high-technology 'box'. They therefore diminish opportunities to think and work in more diverse, heterogenous, multidimensional, unexpected, even culturally traditional or 'old fashioned' ways (Vega, 2013; Witte, 2008). Indeed, several of my fine art students are currently showing a renewed interest in their unique and personal handwriting, perhaps as a riposte to inhuman, intimidating, homogenising, and alienating software, and now AI also appearing on their horizon.

The fundamentally *quantitative* basis of computer logic seems not adequate or appropriate to the exceptionally *qualitative*, multisensual, affective, and often disorganised realm of fine art thinking and making that Deleuze and Guattari's (2013) concept of a 'body without organs' captures as perhaps a useful model for accommodating twenty-first-century complexities via acknowledgment of formless becomings, intensive behaviours, and refusal of a paradigmatic modern tendency to organ-isation. Thus NTLCMCs, and their tendency to prescriptive, high-technologised teaching and learning (according to which the student progresses towards a pre-desired outcome via a pre-established route within a particular software) may be fairly compared with the childhood game of 'painting by numbers'.

It may be that, technically speaking, whenever we wield new technologies, we are dealing with zeros and ones and therefore *literally* painting by numbers, echoing the key theme of Sadie Plant's book *Zeros and Ones* (1998). But we can pursue this idea metaphorically too; a child, when recreationally painting by numbers, is encouraged to keep within prescribed lines and to adhere to a pre-established code that determines which colour equates with which number. This achieves the fleeting satisfaction of revealing a desired outcome latent within the exercise, but this approach is antithetical to fine art students' critical and creative pursuit of open-ended speculation, genuine risk, and discovery. It also contradicts a perennial invitation for each new cohort of fine art students to trouble, question, and disrupt given and established norms – to question and even break the rules of any game with which they are presented (Butler, 1999; Haraway, 2016).

Where Do We Go from Here?

Fine art, and its current generation of lecturers, enthusiastically accommodates the rich array of twenty-first-century difference that annually comes to UK colleges from all over the world, made up of students who aim to explore and question themselves and the wider world, just as much as they aim to explore and question fine art (Butler, 1999; Haraway, 2016). Those fine art students are chosen as ready and able to disrupt and deconstruct, trouble, and transgress established values. Thus, we should always be asking our fine art students to engage with, exchange, and challenge the incumbent generation's ideas, ethics, politics, skills, and experience and not provide them with generic and prescriptive exercises based on currently established beliefs, positions, and opinions.

The best fine art teaching and learning in which I have been privileged to participate during 25 years of lecturing involves a particular lecturer candidly sharing, trying out, and creating – more or less 'live' – their own idiosyncratically accumulated knowledge and hard-won research, the result of – in many cases – decades of genuine risk and speculation often precariously founded on the gamble of a life and career nervously built upon the speculative adventure that is fine art (Brack and Cowling, 2015; Wolff, 2013). By contrast, the NTLCMCs discussed above seem designed to be delivered not by any particular person, artist, and lecturer, but remotely, as if from on high by an anonymous author, the distanced designer of a generic unit that, once created, can be delivered by any lecturer or GTA anywhere in the world, and even played out and worked through by students without need of external assistance (French and Kennedy, 2017).

However, as we have spent recent decades conscientiously inviting, encouraging, and cultivating the increasingly diverse student intake who now boost and transform our colleges with a newly vibrant multi- and global-cultural profile, surely we should not confront these students with an unprecedentedly generic, highly prescribed, software-defined, and homogenising form of teaching and learning? If so, we risk squandering our proud legacy and might become incapable of building and growing the future of our institution upon our celebrated local idiosyncrasies and unique forms of excellence (Vega, 2013; Witte, 2008).

NTLCMCs may be convenient, cost-effective, and profitable, and they may be useful in an emergency like a pandemic or strike, but if they are allowed to become a rule rather than an exception they could deprive us of the rich, varied, and challenging qualities of fine art teaching and learning for which our courses and colleges won their formidable renown as now world-famous 'brands'. And it is worth noting here that these reputations have been won not by the rapid deployment of the latest technologies in a defensive moment of managerial anxiety but through decades of dedicated, experimental, and creative teaching and learning, perennially provided by generations of passionately devoted fine art lecturers, always creatively and inventively working through a more or less constant state of crisis in art and education.

The recent encounters that have motivated this text have also suggested to me that measurements of progress and achievement of fine art students' work should be regularly renegotiated by and with students and staff, as appropriate to each particular project, exhibition, event, or workshop; as appropriate to fine art as a particular discipline; as appropriate to a particular year group; and as appropriate to a particular time and place in a rapidly changing world. In this way, we might eschew the imposition of inappropriate, unwieldy, overly quantitative, geometric, generic, and homogenising methods of fine art teaching and assessment.

Therefore, when it comes to innovative and progressive unit and course design, rather than placing our trust in prescriptive units, quantified progress, and lucrative software to nurture and cultivate our fine art students' potential, we should use to their best advantage the rich 'grass roots' resource of our subject in the form of our new and experienced lecturers and GTAs, working sceptically, critically, creatively, and radically with students at the 'coalface' of our dynamically evolving discipline.

Finally, through my own encounter with lockdown and then soon after working on an NTLCMC, I have been reminded that fine art should always be *anything but* convenient, generic, and prescriptive. Unwieldy difficulty and difference are crucial parts of the identity and history of our famously progressive and speculative fine art teaching and learning, for which 'trouble', particularly in the wake of Judith Butler's use and dissemination of the term and its subsequent promotion by Donna Haraway, is a desirable value, a tool – even a destination (Butler, 1999; Haraway, 2016). Therefore, we should not respond defensively to difficulty, passively accepting the imposition of flat-packed, top-down models of fine art teaching and learning. Doing so will always be contra the hard-won, long-standing, noble, and progressive profession of fine art teaching and learning in HE, whose standards today's fine art lecturers, GTAs, and students have a duty, a right, and a responsibility to uphold.

References

Barlow, P. (2000) Fear and loathing of the academic, or just what is it that makes the avant-garde so different, so appealing? in R. C. Denis and C. Trodd, *Art and the academy in the nineteenth century*. Manchester University Press.

Brack, C. and Cowling, M. (2015) How digital natives are killing the sage on stage, *The Conversation*, 6 May. Available at https://theconversation.com/how-digital-natives-are-killing-the-sage-on-the-stage-39923 (Accessed 13 August 2021).

Butler, J. (1999) *Gender trouble: feminism and the subversion of identity*. London: Routledge.

Crook, C. (2015) Should all university lectures be automatically recorded? *The Conversation*, 8 April. Available at https://theconversation.com/should-all-university-lectures-be-automatically-recorded-39158 (Accessed 14 August 2021).

Deleuze, G. and Guattari F. (2013) *Anti-Oedipus: capitalism and schizophrenia*. Trans. R. Hurley, M. Seem, and H. R. Lane. London: Bloomsbury Academic.

French, S. and Kennedy, G. (2017) Reassessing the value of university lectures. *Teaching in Higher Education*, 22(6), pp. 639–654. https://doi.org/10.1080/13562517.2016.1273213

Gunderman, R. (2013) Is the lecture dead? *The Atlantic*, January 29. Available at http://www.theatlantic.com/health/archive/2013/01/is-the-lecture-dead/272578/ (Accessed 26 November 2015).

Haraway, D. J. (2016). *Staying with the trouble: making kin in the Chthulucene*. Durham, NC: Duke University Press.

Harrison, C., Wood, P. and Gaiger, J. (1998) *Art in theory 1815–1900: an anthology of changing ideas*. Oxford, Blackwell.

James, A. and Nerantzi, C. (eds.). (2019) *The power of play in higher education: creativity in tertiary learning*. Cham, Switzerland: Springer.

O'Kane, P. (2021a) Lectures in lockdown: trying to rescue the lecture as event. *Journal of Learning Development in Higher Education*, Special Issue 22: Compendium of Innovative Practice.

O'Kane, P. (2021b) Small worlds and short stories: play, pleasure and imagination deployed as a salve to isolated learning. *Journal of Learning Development in Higher Education*, Special Issue 22: Compendium of Innovative Practice.

Plant, S. (1998) *Zeros + ones: digital women + the new technoculture*. London, England: Fourth Estate.

Vega, G. (2013) *Technology and case pedagogy: the tail wagging the dog?* https://www.academia.edu/11172114/Technology_and_Case_Pedagogy_The_Tail_Wagging_the_Dog

Witte, J. P. (2008) Why the tail wags the dog: the pernicious influence of product-oriented discourse on the provision of educational technology support. *Annual Review of Applied Linguistics*, 27, pp. 203–215. https://doi.org/10.1017/S0267190508070104

Wolff, J. (2013) 'It's too early to write off the lecture', *The Guardian*, 24 June. Available at: https://www.theguardian.com/education/2013/jun/24/university-lecture-still-best-learning

Afterword

The stories collected in this book capture a moment in time – a time of profound disruption, uncertainty, and unexpected potential. But rather than simply refracting it towards the 'new normal', they show that for universities, the COVID-19 pandemic was more than just a phase through which we passed from one static 'pre-pandemic' state to a different, 'post-pandemic', one. Indeed, the transformative practices shared by our contributors reveal the changes catalysed by the disruption to be part of an ongoing and dynamic space of 'becoming' in academia. Deleuze and Guattari's (1987) radical concept offers us a powerful framework for understanding change and transformation in higher education. Their rhizomatic model critiques the idea of a linear pathway or journey through an experience or towards a specific goal, since 'a line of becoming has neither beginning nor end, departure nor arrival, origin nor destination' (pp. 341–342). In rejecting a fixed starting point or final objective, the rhizome is instead 'the conjunction, "and … and … and …"' (p. 26), allowing space for multiplicities, fluid connections, and porous boundaries (Gravett, 2021). Paired with their image of the assemblage, defined as 'active, always emergent and changing confederations of bodies, objects, spaces, affects, forces and desires' (Taylor and Harris-Evans, 2018, p. 1258), transformation becomes a continuous, dynamic process of becoming: always in flux, never finished.

The four themes explored in this collection – reimagining time and space, building connections, crossing boundaries, and navigating digital environments – can be seen as different territories within this space of becoming. They are not separate areas of change but interconnecting, interacting, reconfiguring spaces within a rhizomatic network that is continuously unfolding. In the stories shared by our contributors, we can see those fluid, mutually linked, and ongoing processes of experimentation, reflection, and evolution occurring within the broader territory of HE. Each chapter illustrates the constant negotiation and redefining of boundaries between traditional and innovative approaches, between digital and physical spaces, and between educator and learner roles, capturing not just what was done then but how educators and institutions continue to adapt and evolve now. These different pedagogical approaches, technologies, and human experiences interact and transform each other through an evolving and open dialogue and serve as an invitation to explore new territories and forge new connections without the need for a fixed endpoint.

The contributors to this book have embraced this ethos of restless change and development, only too aware that returning to some pre-pandemic state is neither desired nor possible. Transformative practices are those that challenge assumptions and reshape worldviews (Wolff *et al.*, 2022). We cannot undo the experiences we have had, forget the innovations, or rebuild boundaries, but we can use them to build the future, seeing ourselves as also transformed. Partly, this is a practical development. Where once online course development was the purview of specialised teams, it became the responsibility of all educators, regardless of their experience or confidence (Hodges *et al.*, 2020). Many more educators now have these options at their disposal, having brought tools, techniques, and mindsets into their own assemblages; the shift to online teaching and learning expanded the territory in which teaching could take place (Littlejohn, 2022). For our students, too, their expectations and understanding of what higher education could be have been irrevocably transformed, with many now demanding more opportunities to learn online (Coffey, 2024). Documenting the innovations in this book is an attempt not to waste the crisis or the learning that resulted from it. As we continue to evolve as practitioners, these examples offer opportunities to adapt, sculpt, or be inspired to devise our own transformative practices.

We began this book by comparing it to a photograph album, albeit one which carries as much discomfiture as delight. In this new light of becoming, we can see this album as being unmade and incomplete, and that it always will be so. We may have mapped out these chapters and the examples of practice that they contain, but they sit in relation to each other, contextually contingent, an assemblage that can be remade and reconsidered in endless combinations across these pages and those yet to be filled. In this sense, each 'photograph' in this album represents a space that fosters and encourages continuous adaptation and innovation. The creativity, resilience, and adaptability demonstrated by our contributors during the pandemic are not temporary responses to a crisis but essential qualities for navigating this ever-changing landscape. We offer them as an invitation to never stop exploring new territories, forging new connections, and continuing to innovate in service of more inclusive, responsive, and transformative learning experiences. In doing so, we can all participate in reimagining higher education as a vibrant and ever-evolving space of possibility.

References

Coffey, L. (2024) Demand for online courses surges, creating cultural tensions. *Inside Higher Ed*. Available at https://www.insidehighered.com/news/tech-innovation/teaching-learning/2024/08/13/report-most-institutions-see-tension-over-online

Deleuze, G. and Guattari, F. (1987) *A thousand plateaus: capitalism and schizophrenia.* London: Continuum.

Gravett, K. (2021) Troubling transitions and celebrating becomings: from pathway to rhizome, *Studies in Higher Education*, 46(8), pp. 1506–1517. https://doi.org/10.1080/03075079.2019.1691162

Hodges, C. B., Moore, S., Lockee, B. B., Trust, T. and Bond, M. A. (2020) The difference between emergency remote teaching and online learning. *Educase Review*, 27. https://er.educause.edu/articles/2020/3/the-difference-between-emer.ency-remote-teaching-and-online-learning

Littlejohn, A. (2022) Transforming educators' practice: how university educators learned to teach online from home during the COVID-19 pandemic. *Higher Education Research & Development*, 42(2), pp. 366–381. https://doi.org/10.1080/07294360.2022.2073982

Taylor, C. A. and Harris-Evans, J. (2018) Reconceptualising transition to higher education with Deleuze and Guattari, *Studies in Higher Education*, 43(7), pp. 1254–1267. https://doi.org/10.1080/03075079.2016.1242567

Wolff, L-A., Shephard, K., Belluigi, D. Z., Vega-Marcote, P., Rieckmann, M., Skarstein, F., and Cheah, S. L. (2022) Editorial: transformative learning, teaching, and action in the most challenging times. *Frontiers in Education* 7, 1041914. https://doi.org/10.3389/feduc.2022.1041914

Index

Pages in *italics* refer to figures and pages in **bold** refer to tables.

Academic development 8, 10, 47–52, 55–56, 58, 61, 104, 121, 129–130, 150, 155–157, 161, 170
Academic skills 16, 29–30, 32–33, 35–37, 150–153
Active learning 59, 104, 156, 158
Advocacy 58, 61, 66, 68, 80, 125–127, 129–132
Artificial intelligence (AI and genAI) 2, 4–5, 9–10, 39, 41–45, 47–48, 52, 54–55, 60–61, 92, 155, 173–174
Assessment xvii, 3, 15–16, 26, 32, 41–42, 44–45, 47, 51–52, 61, 66–67, 79–80, 89–90, 92, 99, 106–107, 121, 129, 134–135, 142, 150, 156–161, 164, 166–169, 179, 182–184, 189, 198, 210, 217
Asynchronous 33, 51–52, 59, 126, 151, 158, 174, 186–187, 194–197
Attainment 21, 106
Attendance 26, 74, 95, 99, **157**
Audience 15, 36, 57, 107–108, 114–116, 131, 212
Authentic 4, 9–10, 24, 37, 44, 66–68, 71–72, 74, 76, 95, 113, 119, 125–127, 129, 131, 156, 158, 168, 174, 182, 187, 189–190

Belonging 1–3, 9, 20–28, 31–32, 50, 66, 69, 82, 87–89, 91–94, 96–98, 134, 167, 173, 203, *204*, 205, 208, 209
Blended learning 32, 51, 120, 139, 142, 144, 147–153, 173, 186–188, 193–199

Capacity building 121, 159, 161
Change management 39, 120, 139
Co-creation xvii, 97, 121, 127, 147, 151–152, 164–165, 168–169
Collaboration 1, 4–5, 13, 16, 35–36, 66–67, 71, 73, 75, 77, 79–80, 119–121, 134, 142, 150, 158, 161, 165, 169, 181, 184, 188, 196, 198, 203–205, 208–209, 214
Community xvii, 7, 9, 20–21, 27, 35–36, **40**, 41, 43–44, 48, 66–67, 73, 81–84, 94–95, 103, 106, 119, 125–128, 130, 133, 135–136, 141, 143, 168, 175, 190, 205
Community of practice 34–35, **40**, 42, 51, 68, 72–73, 75–76, 80–81, 136, 190
Compassionate pedagogy 3, 10, 49, 53
Confidence 4, 5, 9, 18, 35–36, 75, 81–82, 91, 96, 98, 107, 114, 127, 135, 168–169, 174–175, 177–184, 188, 194, 215
Creative xvi–xvii, 1–5, 25–26, 42, 61, 65, 71, 95, 114, 116, 120, 133–137, 175, 182–184, 187–188, 190, 211–212, 214, 216–218, 220
Curriculum development 41, 51, 142, 156, 167, 169, 186
Customisable resources 121, 157, 159–161

Data informed teaching 90–92, 126
Democracy in education 103, 121, 164
Digital skills 31, 36, *140*, 174, 178, 180–184, 188, 207–209

Index

Digital transformation 120, 139–141, 143, 145, 178, 184
Diversity xvii, 33, 52, 61, 114, 129, 131, 158

Engagement 29, **40**, 44, 56, 61, 73, 79–84, 96, 121, 141, 147–149, 152–153, 158, 160, 175, 182, 187, 197, 207
Equality 22, 33, 52, 126, 131
Equity 41, 44, 51, 57, 119, 125–126, 129, 131
Evaluation 29, 34, 36–37, 56, 80, 157
Evidence 36–37, 51, 58, 145, 166, 187–188, 203, 207, 213
Expectations 14, 22, 33, 37, **40**, 59, 68, 74, 96, 99, 134, 144, 188, 220

Feedback 30, 36, **40**, 44, 66, 87, 90, 98, 126, 128, 142, 156, 167, 179, 189
Framework 26, 39–43, 45, 55–58, 72, 75, 106, 129, 139–140, 188, 196, 208
Future 2, 8, 29, 32, 100, 111, 136, 149, 152, 159, 161, 211, 213, 217, 220

Hybrid 48, 52–53, 128, 130, 133, 175, 189, 208
HyFlex 10, 32, 55, 60–62

Identity 9, 35, 72, 74, 89, 119, 175, 187–188, 205
Inclusion 8, 10, 33, *34*, 52, 56–57, 129, 131, 141, 209
Institutional change 3, 8–9, 55, 61–62
Interdisciplinary xvii–xviii, 4, 119, 120–121, 133, 147–152, 155, 187, 189–190
Iterative approaches 37, 125–127, 158–159

Leadership 4, 9, 50, 56, 119–120, 125–131, 156, 187
Learning and teaching (L&T)/Teaching and learning (T&L) xvii, 1–5, 7, 13, 29, 32, 39, 45, 47–48, 50, 53, 56, 60, 65–66, 68, 72–74, 86, 92–94, 97, 100, 102, 104, 106, 120, 133, 135–137, 139, 141–142, 145, 151, 155–156, 159–161, 164, 173, 177, 179, 181–182, 184, 186–187, 193–194, 196, 199, 211–218, 220

Learning Development 9, 15, 29, 35, 80, 82–84, 95, 99, 104, 128, 134–135, 148
Learning management system (LMS) 67, 74, 87, 89–91, 95, 120, 134, 139–146, 156, 159, 207
Learning spaces 10, 60, 67, 94–97, 121

Mattering 9, 20–21, 26, 94, 96, *204*, 208
Mentoring 49, 51, 72, 125, 127–128, 130, 179

Networks 20, 23, 25, 36, 50–51, 53, 65–68, 71–74, 76, 81, 83–84, 106, 119–120, 127, 133, 135–136, 175, 187, 190, 205–206, 219

Online learning 8, 17, 36, 51, 59, 75, 87–89, 95, 98, 120, 137, 147, 155, 160, 186–187, 205, 207–208
Online pivot 2, 4, 9, 29–32, 34–37, 47–48, 52, 61, 65, 81, 94, 133, 135, 164, 186, 188
Openness 9, 44, 59, 81, 131
Organisational change 74, 120, 139–140, 146

Participation 23, 26, 60, 76, 81–84, 149, 156–158, 166–167, 188, 190, 209
Partnership 22, 25, 65, 83, 105, 121, 127, 129, 131, 137, *140*, 143, 174
Pedagogy xvi, 2–3, 5, 9–10, 14, 20, 22–23, 26, 29–30, 32–33, 39, 42–45, 49–50, 53, 59–62, 68, 80, 100, 102, 104–108, 120, 126, 133–134, 136, 147–148, 150–151, 158, 179, 181, 183, 186–189, 206, 208–209, 211–213, 215, 219
Peer review 36, **40**, 82, 145
Peer support 8, 20, 23, 25, 36, **40**, 50–51, 53, 76
Personalised learning xvii, 67, 89–91, 181
PGCert 133–135, 137, 186, 188, 190
Policy 9, 41–43, 47, 53, 56–57, 79–80
Professional development/CPD 3, 8, 10, 49–53, 84, 119, 157

Reflection 7–9, 29, *30*, 33, 37–38, 56, 59–60, 80, 100, 135, 137, 153, **179**

Scholarship 4, *30*, 67–68, 79–84, 102, 116, 128, 187
Skills development 62, 147, 150–153, 178, 181, 184
Student engagement 3–4, 29–30, *34*, **40**, 96, 149, 160, 207
Student experience 9, 26, 31, 37, 147, 157, 182, 187
Student voice *30*, 31, 36, 136
Synchronous 31, 33, 51–52, 57, 59–60, 88–89, 126–127, 151, 158, 174, 186–187, 194–198, 208

Teaching writing 15–16, 35, 42–45, 90, 102, 110–116, 134–135
Third space 3–4, 66–67, 71–72, 84, 119, 125, 128, 130
Transition 16, 33, *34*, 43, 47, 56, 60–61, 87, 141, 147–148, 152, 194

Transparency 35, 59, 129, 131
Trust 18, 35, 59, 76, 103, 121, 127, 129–131, 164, 169, 180, 187, 217

Values xvii, 2, 4, 10, 55–56, 58, 66–67, 76, 130, 186–190, 211–212, 216

Wellbeing 3, 8–10, 20–22, 26, 32, 41, 47–53, 57, 61, 92, 96, 110, 178, 184, 188, 203–205
Widening participation *34*, 57, 134, 148
Workshops 23–26, *34*, 36, 51–52, 58–61, 75–76, 99, 142, 144, 147, 156, **157**, 160, 167, 169, **179**, 179, 217
Writing 68, 81–83, 110–116, 125, 128, 131, 133, 174

For Product Safety Concerns and Information please contact our EU representative GPSR@taylorandfrancis.com
Taylor & Francis Verlag GmbH, Kaufingerstraße 24, 80331 München, Germany

www.ingramcontent.com/pod-product-compliance
Ingram Content Group UK Ltd.
Pitfield, Milton Keynes, MK11 3LW, UK
UKHW020055160325
456294UK00017B/217